HOW TO ORGANIZE
YOUR WORK
AND YOUR LIFE

Robert Moskowitz

HOW TO ORGANIZE YOUR WORK AND YOUR LIFE

DOUBLEDAY
NEW YORK LONDON TORONTO SYDNEY AUCKLAND

PUBLISHED BY DOUBLEDAY
a division of Bantam Doubleday Dell Publishing Group, Inc.
666 Fifth Avenue, New York, New York 10103

DOUBLEDAY and the portrayal of an anchor with a dolphin
are trademarks of Doubleday, a division of Bantam Doubleday
Dell Publishing Group, Inc.

Library of Congress Cataloging in Publication Data
Moskowitz, Robert.
How to Organize Your Work and Your Life.
 ISBN 0-385-17012-2 (pbk.)
 1. Executives—Time management. 2. Businessmen
—Time management. I. Title.
HF5500.2.M654   658.4′093   80-1815

CONTENTS

HOW TO ORGANIZE
YOUR WORK
AND YOUR LIFE

1

THE BASICS OF GETTING RESULTS

How much time do you have left? And how many more goals and achievements do you want to attain? When you strip away all the camouflage and get right to the heart of the matter, you're a serious, capable person who has more than enough ambition. You take your commitments and responsibilities to heart. In your own way, you honestly try your best to achieve what you want, what you promise, and what's expected of you.

But the time goes so fast! And sometimes it seems as though Murphy's Law: "Anything that can go wrong, will go wrong," is the dominant law of the universe. Even when your private life and your job are going smoothly, you find it takes too long to reach your goals, to attain what you want. And that's not the end of it because you always want to do, see, and accomplish even more.

This book can change all that for you. It gives you a method of organizing everything you do, everything you want to do, and everything you must and must not do. It gives you a system of principles, ideas, and specific actions that will speed up every project and every effort and help you get what you want much quicker, easier, sooner.

What holds you back right now is the tremendous amount of

wasted time, misdirected energy, and subtle "friction" in so much of what you do. Whether you admit it or not, a good portion of every day goes down the drain, and you use too much of what's left without thinking, without direction, without A Master Plan. With this book to guide you, though, you can change all that. You will accomplish more every hour, every day of your life. First, you will see dozens of better ways to direct and control your efforts, push yourself toward the rewards you want and hold back from trivial or worthless projects. Second, you will find many ways to obtain more results from every effort, to increase the response and rewards you get from every purposeful minute of your life.

These are the benefits you'll find in this book. And they extend to anyone: Everyone who embraces the principles, actions, and ideas you'll find here. Whether you are a tan-worshipping lawyer in the Sun Belt or a radio producer in Cincinnati, an aspiring painter in New York, or a parent home all day with demanding children, even if you are someone else or somewhere in between, the material in this book can open a whole new world of satisfaction and achievement no matter what you set out to achieve.

But general talk like this will not improve your effectiveness or change your method for handling opportunities. You need more motivation to make the needed changes. And nothing is more motivating than a specific look at the details of what you can hope to gain. Use Work Sheet 1 to give yourself that look right now.

WORK SHEET 1

Self-evaluation:
Benefits You Can Expect
from Boosting Your Effectiveness

In the spaces below, list eight of the most important projects and activities in your life and/or your career which you feel you have been neglecting recently. Stick with your own evaluations, judgments, and standards of importance in this self-evaluation. For example, you may feel you are neglecting your professional education or your physical fitness, but other people may not recognize these problems or may think there are more important ones.

Once you have identified your neglected projects and activities, list for each one the benefits you feel you will obtain when you complete the project or undertake the activity.

Item 1:   Neglected Project_____

          Anticipated Benefit_____

_____

_____

_____

_____

_____

Item 2:   Neglected Project_____

          Anticipated Benefit_____

_____

_____

_____

_____

_____

Item 3:   Neglected Project_____

Anticipated Benefit_____

_____

_____

_____

_____

Item 4:   Neglected Project_____

Anticipated Benefit_____

_____

_____

_____

_____

_____

Item 5:   Neglected Project_____

          Anticipated Benefit_____

          _____

          _____

          _____

          _____

Item 6:   Neglected Project_____

          Anticipated Benefit_____

          _____

          _____

          _____

Item 7:   Neglected Project_____

          Anticipated Benefit_____

          _____

          _____

          _____

Item 8:   Neglected Project_____

          Anticipated Benefit_____

_____

_____

_____

_____

This work sheet helps you specify some of the most immediate and concrete results you can obtain. Focus your thinking on them as you go through the ideas, principles, and techniques in the rest of this book. Test your new knowledge and your new skills on them at every opportunity. The more directly you tie the material in this book to these important items, the more you will benefit.

———————

Work Sheet 1 helps you focus on the rewards you can and will accumulate as a result of being more effective. You can have them if you will change your habits and procedures. If you don't believe you can get satisfying and desirable benefits from better methods, if you don't try these ideas and techniques in your own situation, you are doing yourself a terrible disservice.

The most frequent reason for holding onto less-effective procedures is uncertainty. You may feel uncertain about the value of these methods. You may feel you can't change or that any changes you can make won't be worthwhile. You are wrong.

Achievement, success, and high levels of effectiveness are not determined by your genes, you know. You learn how to get what you want from the world around you, and sometimes you learn how not to. You ape your achievement level from the people and the situations around you. It's a haphazard process, at best, and it stops most people well short of their highest potential achievements. If you are not happy with your results, you're in luck! You are now holding the very instrument to help you change, improve, and attain more of what you want! You can have what you want starting now. All you have to do is read. I will do the rest.

KNOW WHERE YOU ARE HEADED

Do you know what accomplishments would make today satisfying for you? If you do, then in a sense you know where you are headed. You may or may not achieve the accomplishments you have in mind, which means you may or may not gain the satisfaction you want from your efforts. But at least you are in position to try. Other people, and you perhaps on other days, have no idea what accomplishments would make the day satisfying. This means they have no basis inside them for choosing what to do first. And if they also have no structure outside of them to give them directions, their accomplishments and feelings of satisfaction will be determined by chance or by other factors beyond their personal control.

One good way to think of this all too common situation is to visualize yourself alone, adrift, afloat in the Caribbean. It's warm, it's sunny. There's no particular danger: We've banished all sharks and jellyfish. But you have the natural urge to get back on dry land. Yet alone and adrift, you don't know either where you are or which direction to go. Now imagine that you spot an island. Suddenly, you have a direction! Your pulse quickens, you feel a burst of motivation. You look for a way to reach the island, exert yourself, and make it! Your sighting of a goal brought everything else into focus, including the wind, the tide, the current, your own strength and fitness. While a great many factors help determine whether or not you reach the island, the process begins only when you *sight* a goal.

What if you had never looked around you? What if you had merely been drifting, preoccupied only with your immediate surroundings. You might have passed, unknowingly, within two hundred yards of a bountiful island paradise. And if no rescuer had come out to get you, you would never even have seen the paradise as you drifted past! The point is this: You must not only be concerned with your immediate surroundings, you must constantly scan the horizon for new and better opportunities for attainment.

Many people have the mistaken idea that mastering time and shaping your results to suit your desires are fanciful notions, not rooted in reality. If they happen to believe in magic, they may think these techniques are a cure-all for every problem. If they disbelieve in magic, they may think the skills are at best a foolish fancy, at worst a charlatan's hustle. But all these people ignore the basic practicality and realism of conscious efforts to be more effective. There is nothing fanciful about them. You start by establishing goals and achievements that will satisfy you. Nobody else, only you! No one dictates any particular goals to you, nor does anyone tell you how much effort to put in. The procedure works for everyone because it is so basic: First determine what in the world will satisfy you, and only then concern yourself with making specific progress in those directions.

The method is so powerful that people who practice the ideas and techniques you are about to learn are a long step ahead of others who do not. Regardless of any other factors, people who organize their work and their life know where they are headed. And like the ocean drifter, they are in position to make whatever progress they can toward the satisfying goals they have in sight.

And you are not limited to one goal at a time, either. You can use the satisfaction of one accomplishment to fuel a separate effort toward another goal. You can have, and work toward as many goals as you like. The next goal may lie two hundred miles to the west, or it may be attainable right on your island. No matter. The methods and techniques work just as well no matter what your ambitions; no matter what you want to accomplish.

However, while I am not concerned with your particular goals, you most certainly must be. In fact, the specifics of the goals you set for yourself determine in great measure what you accomplish, what you achieve, and ultimately your happiness. You need explicit goals in mind as you go through this book or you'll miss the chance to put what you learn into practice immediately. In order for me to make this book more effective, I have to help you make your life and career goals more explicit. You will work on this more throughout the book. But get started right now with Work Sheet 2: Your Life and Career Goals. Go through the work sheet and answer the questions as well as you can for now. Even if you cannot give a final answer to each question, be thinking about your answers as you read the rest of this book.

WORK SHEET 2

Self-evaluation:
Your Life and Career Goals

This is a Self-evaluation Work Sheet. Only your own feelings, beliefs, ideas, and judgments are relevant to how you will work through it.

1. Make a list of ten "goals" you would like to achieve in your personal life during the next ten years. Each goal should describe an achievement, or an honor or reward recognizing an achievement, you would be proud to accomplish. Each goal should be expressed in specifics so you or anyone else can determine whether or not you achieve it. Examples: a) establish five close friendships with people who truly like you; b) travel around the world; c) go camping in Brazil; or d) learn to play five songs on a guitar.

a. _____

b. _____

c. _____

d. _____

e. _____

f. _____

g. _____

h. _____

i. _____

j. _____

2. Make a list of ten "goals" you would like to achieve in your career during the next ten years. Each goal should describe an achievement, or an honor or reward recognizing an achievement, you would be proud to accomplish. Each goal should be expressed in specifics so you or anyone else can determine whether or not you achieve it. Examples: a) win an Academy Award; b) earn a promotion or a salary increase to a specific level; c) accomplish a specific project or specific amount of work by a certain deadline.

a. _____

b. _____

c. _____

d. _____

e. _____

f. _____

g. _____

h. _____

i. _____

j. _____

3. Name two other activities, accomplishments, rewards, or recognitions that would bring you the highest level of satisfaction.

a. _____

b. _____

4. What would you have to give up to have a chance to obtain each of the items you answered for question 3?

for a. _____

for b. _____

5. What will you have to give up to obtain each of the personal and career goals you specified in questions 1 and 2?

6. What preparation would you need to have a chance to obtain each of the items you answered for question 3?

7. What preparation will you need to obtain each of the personal and career goals you specified in questions 1 and 2?

THERE'S ONLY SO MUCH TIME

Unfortunately, in a given day you just do not have enough time to take all the significant actions you dream of. Even with single-minded determination, you can reasonably complete as few as one or as many as three or four significant actions, the kind you anticipate for several days ahead. These might include: reading or writing vital reports, attending crucial meetings, visiting close friends or lovers, making life-changing or career-changing choices, watching historic sporting events, or any other memorable experiences.

Theoretically, you can make dozens of giant decisions in a single day: decisions on whether or not to purchase Arco Oil Company, fly to the moon, embark on an around-the-world cruise, or marry the person of your dreams. You *can* make such decisions because a decision takes only two seconds to make. But practically speaking, a significant action represents much more preparation time, thought, and action than the few seconds you need for the decision. Considering the required preparation, contemplation of your options, work with others, and so on, you usually cannot manage more than one or two significant actions a day.

The Self-evaluation Work Sheet 3 is a good way to visualize the difficulty of operating without strict control. It gives you a structured method for comparing your stated goals with the *de facto* goals you actually work to achieve. You will probably find major discrepancies between what you want to achieve and what you strive to achieve. In the course of this book, you will learn to erase most or all of these discrepancies.

WORK SHEET 3

Self-evaluation:
Priorities/Activities
Comparison Sheet

This is a device to help you compare the projects and activities to which you *say* you give a high priority with the projects and activities to which you actually give time.

1. List the 10 projects, activities, or goals that are your "highest priorities" for today and/or for the next few weeks. If you like, use some of the same goals you listed in Work Sheet 2:

a. _____

b. _____

c. _____

d. _____

e. _____

f. _____

g. _____

h. _____

i. _____

j. _____

2. List the 10 "most important" and/or "most time-consuming" projects, activities, or goals to which you gave time today:

a. _____

b. _____

c. _____

d. _____

e. _____

f. _____

g. _____

h. _____

i. _____

j. _____

3. Compare your two lists: How many serious goals received no effort or attention from you today? How many "no priority" items received a good portion of your effort today?

WORK SHEET 4

Complete List of Desirable Goals

INSTRUCTIONS:

1. List everything you would like to do during your lifetime.

_____

_____

_____

_____

_____

_____

_____

_____

_____

_____

2. Count them. How many lifetimes would you need to do them all?

Sample items:

People to See	Places to Go	Things to Do
Paul McCartney	To live in Paris	Play in an All-Star Game

| Francis Ford Coppola | To the moon | Star in a feature film |
| Stash Karczewski | To Surinam | Earn $1,000,000 |

You add your own items below:

Limited opportunities to act still permit you to control and aim your efforts. In fact, a minute's clear thought will show you the *necessity* of organizing and controlling your actions and efforts to make your limited opportunities count the most and yield as much as possible of what you want. To drive this necessity home, you may want to ponder the full range of your virtually insatiable desires. Work Sheet 4 is a tool to help you.

When you compare your desires with your realistic potential for accomplishment, the picture becomes painfully clear: There's no way you can accomplish all the goals that are most important to you, especially pestered as you are by the little details of the business of living. The only way to cope with this overload—*the only hope*—is to focus on key goals and strive toward them.

KNOW WHAT TO SPEND TIME ON NEXT

Mastering your time has a second benefit, equally as powerful as establishing goals and equally rooted in practicality and realism. Merely having goals means you are ahead of others who do not. Once ahead, you get the second benefit: the opportunity to direct your efforts toward your goals. This gives you more results for every "unit" of effort you put in. In effect, once you know what accomplishments would satisfy you, you can see and take the proper steps to help you achieve what you want.

In practice, this comes down to a series of choices concerning "What to do next." I have labeled this your Basic Choice, and in Chapter 3, you will learn how to ask and answer this question automatically. The Basic Question always leads you to the *one* opportunity for action that gives you the *best* chance for the *most* satisfaction. Once you get the hang of setting up and making your Basic Choices, you can apply the idea very quickly in any situation. The choice you make sets a definite direction to investigate and a definite goal to pursue.

LEARN TO DO THE MOST
IN THE LEAST TIME

In this book, time-saving techniques are only one part—although a vital part—of the entire organizing and achieving process.

Once you establish goals, once you choose your next step, you enter the arena of real-time/real-life action. Here is where you put theory and principle into action. Here is where you convert all your plans, hopes, and dreams into put-up or shut-up performance. And here, if your actions are not fast, smooth, and directly to the point, you are in very, very big trouble.

We all have to enter this arena on a regular basis. And the results of how well we do here impact heavily on our lives. For example, betting at the race track puts you smack in the middle of this arena. If you win, you're a hero. If you lose, you're a bum. And no amount of talk or action can ever undo what you did.

The ability to perform superbly in this real-time/real-life arena is one central benefit you will get from this book. The general skills and specific techniques you will learn here will work in an assortment of situations. And not only will you save time, you will get the job done quickly, smoothly, and directly.

Knowing how to perform well in the real-time/real-life arena has three related parts to it: 1) knowing the principles behind controlled accomplishment, 2) knowing appropriate techniques for working faster, better, and smoother, and 3) knowing yourself and your personal patterns. You can get the first two right out of this book. But to learn the third, you have to look in a mirror.

The best sort of mirror to learn how you operate would be a realtime, twenty-four-hour-a-day videotape, with the camera following you everywhere. Since the chances of your arranging for that service are practically nil, count on getting the same knowledge of yourself a bit differently.

The primary tool for learning your personal patterns and what they reveal about you is the Time Log. This is a detailed record you keep over a period of several weeks. Here's how it works: Every few minutes, you record (in one second or less) how you have spent the time since you last marked your Log. At the end of each day, you have used only a minute or two to make a complete record of where you put all your time. At the end of several weeks, you have a complete record that reveals: 1) details of how you spend your time, 2) your overall patterns of behavior, 3) opportunities for concentrating on your more important goals, 4) possibilities for holding back from unimportant projects or activities, and 5) habits you can learn to make you more effective automatically and effortlessly. You can find directions for using a very effective Time Log method in Appendix A.

And as you'll experience, a thorough examination of yourself via your Time Log is doubly important because it gives you: 1) the motivation to change your ways, as well as 2) the information you need to know specifically what changes you should make.

KNOW WHEN TO WORK
ON EACH ITEM

Now we get into the realm of scheduling; the fine art of packing every day just full enough of the most useful activities. Too full, and you lose time and energy to unavoidable distractions, interruptions, and emergencies. Too loose, and you're wasting yourself like the proverbial race horse pulling the milk wagon. The idea is to have every day—and every project—under control, and thus be able to make the best choices regarding when to work on each and every item.

Most people find it hard to recognize the "right time" to turn to a particular project or activity. As a result, most people don't bother thinking about it. They simply work on whatever catches their interest, until either: a) something else catches their interest, or b) something or someone else grabs them and pushes them, face first, into a new project or activity.

For example, one young woman I know of has a career, a family, and an itch to go back to school. Between all three, she has dozens of "important" projects and activities all clamoring for her attention and interest. Before she can even finish one item, several more are insisting on immediate attention. In fact, she is so "busy" that she cannot allow herself to become fully immersed even in her favorite projects. If she did, she might pay "too much" attention to one and have to shortchange another. Her days are madhouse encounters, a constant stream of commitments and activities all requiring action, like trying to fit twenty-five square pegs into fifteen round holes. She pays absolutely no attention to her Basic Choice because she feels herself to be at the mercy of her tasks. At every hesitation, invariably two or three items rear their heads and demand attention.

An accountant I know is in the same fix. His clients and their papers call the shots regarding when he works on an account. He doesn't find a chance to make a thoughtful selection, or even a thoughtless one, for weeks on end. As a direct result, he is not very good at achieving what he wants.

A pattern like this makes it hard for anyone to achieve what he or she wants. When outside factors have too much control over your days, your own desires go out the window. Your effectiveness will suffer and so will your hopes and dreams, until you take back control of your efforts and your energy.

To take that control, you need to know and act on four sets of information:

1) The relative importance of each item facing you

2) The amount of time each item will require from you for "optimum" results

3) The amount of time between this minute and the deadline for each item

4) Your current capacities, strengths, and weaknesses.

This may seem like a great deal of unrelated information. But it is right to the point, and you can keep track of it all quite easily. In fact, that's the simplest part. With practice and experience, you can sniff out this information as easily as you can now see the color of every item of paper work that's facing you.

It is much harder to act on the basis of this information: to pick and choose, from all the items you could work on, the *one item* that takes you most directly toward your desired goals and objectives right now.

KNOW THE PEOPLE TO TURN TO

Achieving what you want doesn't happen in a vacuum. As much as 90 percent of your effectiveness comes from people—people like you and me who take action to create results, or who use human resources skillfully to accomplish their desired purposes.

Very few of us can accomplish our goals individually. Most jobs, most private lives, and most personal dreams are intimately caught up with the work, the lives, and the personalities of people around us. The techniques in this book are not sterile quantities suitable only for machines and machinelike people. These are available if you want them, but they don't work. The ideas, principles, and techniques in this book make full allowance for human frailties, and at the same time capitalize on human strengths.

In a real sense, everything comes down to people: good or bad, effective or ineffective, cheap or expensive. We judge what we see in terms of its impact on people. You can ignore the people factor if you wish. You can mechanically try to achieve what you want by forcing through changes and treating people like units. But you can get much better results if you use all your skill and talent to work with people as smoothly as you work with forms, figures, and equipment. And if you must emphasize one side of your skills more than another, your people-oriented skills are probably more useful.

Sometimes, you can achieve more of what you want simply by taking advantage of your personal contacts and affiliations. For example, an unemployed hod carrier was desperate for both work and a feeling of purpose. In desperation, he turned to his union officers for help. Because they knew him and his capacities, the union people gave the man both responsibility and income. For him, turning for help to people he knew was the most effective and fruitful way to attain his goal.

This is probably nothing new to you. People have been turning to friends, relatives, and acquaintances since cave men first cooperated in a dinosaur hunt. And the technique has lasted this long because it is useful. Work Sheet 5 gives you a starter sheet to begin organizing and keeping track of the people you know. The idea is to use this list of your human resources as a tool in your effort to accomplish your purposes. Whatever you want to accomplish, whatever help you need, you can look at Your Human Resources Checklist to see if you know someone to turn to. As you expand your contacts and experience, you will soon find that you can get much of the help you want and need from the people on your list.

WORK SHEET 5

Your Human Resources Checklist

Fill in one copy of this Checklist with information on each of the people you might conceivably ask for help. Keep the Checklists handy and update them when you make new contacts or learn new information about people you already know. Then, whenever you feel a need for help, advice, or special treatment, go over your Checklist to see if you know anyone who can help you.

Name

Special Knowledge

_____

_____

_____

Special Skills

_____

_____

_____

Special Access

_____

_____

_____

Special Contacts

_____

_____

_____

In many situations, the simple act of coordinating the actions of a group of people can instantly accelerate their effectiveness, and yours, by 20–50 percent. For example, a group of professionals working individually were each spending about ten hours a month planning a complex part of a chemical plant. Once they began coordinating their efforts, they found they could each complete the required work in just six hours a month.

People are often effective information sources, too. You can find the answers to questions, get advice and ideas from people three to five times faster than you can get comparable information from machines or from books. And sometimes there is no comparable information. For example, a research assistant once spent dozens of hours poring over science texts looking for information on gravity, light waves, and other electromagnetic radiation. Finally, he gave up on textbooks and began looking for someone to give him the information. In a few days, he had located someone qualified in his own town, and in just a four-hour interview he had learned the answers to all of his original questions, plus a few extras that occurred to him as he listened to the expert.

WHAT YOU CAN DO

In this book, you can learn a whole new way to operate in this world, a method that is careful, thoughtful, and above all, effective.

Some day techniques for achieving what you want will be taught in public schools. They will be recognized as a basic part of a modern education, as basic as driver or sex education. While the idea may seem bizarre, after you have been through this book, you will agree that what you learned is:

1. Results oriented

2. Useful in almost any situation

3. Practical and easy to apply

4. Flexible enough to suit anyone

5. An effectiveness-booster that really works.

For these reasons, the study of effective achievement techniques is for everyone and anyone who has something in his or her mind or heart he or she would seriously like to accomplish.

Good luck!

2

YOUR LIFE AND CAREER GOALS WILL SHAPE YOUR DIRECTION

Goals are the first step in any serious effort to improve your effectiveness and accomplish what you want in your life and work. First of all, you need them just to measure your progress. Until you have a goal or a set of goals in front of you, there is no way to measure whether you are achieving any more or less, or getting any better or worse results, than you were before.

Even more important, goals are the basic direction arrows of your life. In Paris, whenever you get on the underground Métro, you choose your direction by heading toward a *Destination*, the last station on a particular line: Porte de la Villette, for example, or Porte d'Orléans. If you want to go in a different direction, you simply follow the signs to a different *Destination*, such as Porte Dauphine or Charenton-Écoles. You may transfer from one train line to another, from one direction to another, many times in your journey. But you always keep track of where you are headed by noting the ultimate destination of the train you are riding.

Goals serve the same function in your work and your life. (They serve other functions as well, but let's concentrate on this one for now.) You don't have to arrive at your goal for it to have provided a worthwhile direction. In fact, most goals are not reached. As in the Paris Métro, most times we don't travel all the way to the end of the line. Most times we simply exchange one goal for another and keep on moving.

And there's nothing wrong with exchanging goals quite often. In general, you should feel perfectly free to adopt a goal for as long as it suits you, then exchange it for some other objective when the time seems right.

Face it: There's little or no virtue in sticking to a goal that no longer feels right to you. A century ago, for example, it was fashionable to think that a serious young gentleman should totally dedicate himself from youth to a lifetime goal, often a financial one. People who did not persevere in one major effort were said to be frivolous.

And this attitude was nothing new. The Bible even tells the story of Jacob, who worked seven years for the hand of Rachel, the woman he wanted to marry. But Rachel's father, Laban, forced Jacob to marry, instead, the girl's oldest sister, Leah, saying: "How can my younger daughter marry before her elder sister?" Jacob, apparently a man who knew his goals and stuck by them, toiled for another seven years, and eventually earned the hand of Rachel in marriage.

That was fine for Jacob. Such unswerving perseverance may have been the best way for him to accomplish what he wanted. But today, we are a little more understanding of people who want to be flexible.

Today, Jacob would probably elope with his true love. Or, having learned that he would have to marry Leah before Rachel, he might have changed his mind about the entire family. He would realize that a more reasonable goal he could still believe in would be more likely to lead him to the satisfaction and success he undoubtedly deserved.

And changing your goals is one good way—a perfectly fair way—to be sure you accomplish what you want. The paradox is this: You can achieve more of what you want if you quickly abandon your unreasonable goals. You see, with the time and effort you would expend struggling toward but not reaching one unreasonably difficult goal, you can reach and accomplish several smaller but still desirable ones. Goals you cannot achieve with a reasonable effort are not rewarding, and they are not motivating at all. Instead, they sap your strength, demoralize you, and make you more likely to settle for limited success on other, easier goals, when you shouldn't. When the goal is too much to hope for with reasonable effort, as Jacob's goal of marrying Rachel turned out to be, you can usually make more progress in a different direction.

The best goals lie in a middle ground between dearly sought-after goals that may be impossible to achieve, and meaningless goals you can reach without effort. I take it for granted that all of us need some sort of goals to provide direction to our lives and our efforts. Now the problem becomes: what kind of goals, how difficult, how long-range, how flexible?

TYPES OF GOALS

Goals break down into two basic categories: externally imposed and self-imposed goals. Each category has a representative "motivational profile": A pattern of rewards, threats, and sources of satisfaction that help determine how, when, and even whether you will exert yourself to achieve them. It's useful to recognize the various categories and types of goals so you can better control your responses to each one.

Externally Imposed Goals

My father used to suffer from too many externally imposed goals. For example, he had to learn to dance when he and my mother planned a vacation or an ocean cruise. He didn't care much for dancing. He didn't set this goal for himself. But nevertheless he had to meet the goal.

Externally imposed goals tend to be inflexible, often absolute, dictated by outside forces that leave little or no room for compromise or negotiation. There seems to be a relationship that makes the strongest external forces impose the most obnoxious, demanding goals. Externally imposed goals can be further categorized into personally, impersonally, and organizationally imposed goals, according to the source of the imposition. For example, a child who couldn't care less has the goal of "making" the school orchestra imposed by eager parents. This is an externally imposed goal of the personal type. An executive who dislikes detail work is given the assignment of sifting stacks of financial records to find a few financial ratios or a history of past performance. This is an externally imposed goal; organizational type. When you are driven to look for shelter by a sudden rain squall, you are responding to an externally imposed goal; impersonal type.

We never accept externally imposed goals freely, but are forced to accept them in most cases as the lesser evil of a choice we never wanted.

Organizational-type, externally imposed goals are all the job assignments, performance specifications, and behavioral demands employers make on employees. A classic example is the employer who asks his management people to accomplish 10 percent more this year than last with the same budget and resource allocations. Or consider the organization that shifts to data processing equipment. Suddenly, everyone concerned with timely information must learn to work with the new routines, regulations, and demands.

There is nothing intrinsically wrong with a goal imposed on you by your organization. It may or may not be interesting, challenging, or exciting. It may offer you some personal satisfaction. But most often, the organization benefits more from your accomplishments than you do.

This is too bad. In many situations, the people who set up the organizational goals could and should set goals that will benefit both workers and the organization when achieved. This adjustment would tune the motivational profile of the organizationally imposed goal to fit the people who will be asked to accomplish it. The impact would be to produce much higher levels of motivation, achievement, and success.

In the absence of such direction at your work, you will have to take your own steps to make your work-related goals more satisfying and rewarding. The techniques you will learn as you go through this book will enable you to "hang" many goals on your special motivational "hooks." The effect is to supercharge your motivation level and make you more eager and more likely to reach the goal.

In my experience, this is not the common practice in most organizations. Most goals that organizations impose on their people are poorly or not at all tuned to their wavelengths. Sometimes it seems the very opposite is true. In my view, part of the reason for declining productivity, poor use of time, and the disenchantment with certain businesses is the wide gulf between the satisfactions available from organizationally imposed goals and the satisfaction and achievement needs of the people hired to accomplish them.

Self-imposed Goals

There is no such gulf when we look at self-imposed goals. You almost always get some direct satisfaction from every goal you impose on yourself. If you didn't, you probably wouldn't set the goal to begin with.

Self-imposed goals are the ones we hear about in storybooks or made-for-TV movies. For example, the story of the poor boy who becomes a millionaire is a story of a self-imposed goal. The athlete who overcomes incredible obstacles to win the Gold Medal is also responding to a self-imposed goal. Achievements aimed at self-imposed goals demand your finest efforts and bring you tremendous feelings of satisfaction and self-worth along with whatever tangible rewards they may earn.

And it is probably no surprise to you, once you think about it, that your self-imposed goals are usually the most motivating goals in your life. They start out linked to huge pools of emotional energy, so you can easily stick with a single goal long enough to achieve it. And the target you pick is mostly one that will feel good when you attain it. What's more, your self-imposed goals tend to reflect your deep-seated desires, interests, and abilities. Even if your head doesn't know what it wants, some part of you is alert enough to self-impose goals that point to the projects and activities that definitely turn you on.

A self-imposed goal is also likely to contain an attractive package of secondary motivators, like the prestige you want, the influence you crave, or the good feelings of doing something useful that you miss on routine, externally imposed assignments. These secondary motivators are not related as much to the final aim as to the process you must employ to reach that aim. They make the job of reaching your goal itself a motivating activity. And your self-imposed goals hold out whatever promises of ultimate rewards you fabricate for yourself from your own imagination. Who can resist such a one-two combination?

Self-imposed goals are so powerful you can "turn up the throttle" on your own achievements simply by adjusting your goals. There is a simple and direct relationship between your goals and your achievements. Set them effectively, and you will become more effective. Allow them to be set for you, and you place the direction of your career and your life in other people's hands. Of course, just setting a goal does not guarantee you will achieve it. But it does guarantee you are moving in the right direction to satisfy yourself and accomplish what you want in life. Later on, we'll work on the techniques to boost your performance toward maximum. These techniques are the best guarantee of achievement you can get. But before you can achieve, you must first understand the importance of goals you set for yourself, and must start the process of goal setting in your own life.

SETTING YOUR OWN GOALS

This is one of the most difficult questions for anyone to answer—not because it's so hard to figure out, but because so few of us take the time or trouble to ask ourselves about where we are headed and what changes in direction we might like to make. No one can give you any better answers than you can give yourself, and most times the answers other people give you, like the goals imposed on you by others, don't fit you very well. All it takes to begin to set your own goals is to sit down with your thoughts and feelings and work them out: out into the open and out to their logical implications. Start with a simple question: "If I had more time, what would I do with it?"

Try to list all the uses to which you could put your time as they occur to you. Don't hold anything back. After all, no one has to see this list except you. You can't get hurt, no matter what you write down. In fact, you can burn the list when you're through with it. Do anything—promise yourself anything—to feel comfortable putting every thought down in writing. You will get a great deal of extra benefit from an honest, a wild, even a slightly "crazy" list. Such a list contains ideas that tend to express your more hidden desires and secret urges. I advise you to cross off the list everything that is the least bit illegal, immoral, or fattening! But almost all the rest is fair game for our program to help you organize your work and your life to accomplish more of what you want.

WORK SHEET 6

If You Had More Time,
What Would You Do With It?

a. What would you do with one hour extra per week?

_____

_____

_____

_____

_____

b. What would you do with one day extra per week?

_____

_____

_____

_____

_____

c. What would you do with five extra hours per week?

_____

_____

_____

_____

_____

d. What would you do with one extra week per year?

_____

_____

_____

_____

_____

BE SPECIFIC!

Looking for Continuity in Your Goals

The basic method of establishing goals is to look over the list you put together in answer to Work Sheet 6. Try to group similar ideas, and then to boil down your wild ideas and impractical dreams into concrete, desirable, positive goals you can reasonably expect to achieve. This takes practice, but it gets much easier as you go along. The biggest difficulty—you might be surprised to discover—is simply to sit down and do it.

As you begin to spot some viable goals for yourself, you'll probably notice they have a certain familiarity. For example, one man I know set himself the personal goal of learning to play chess at a comfortably high level of excellence. Later he remembered having been in the chess club in high school, and having an early affection for the game. His feelings for the game and the satisfaction he received from playing it well had been buried for more than twenty years. But once revived, they were as strong as ever.

In another situation, a lawyer used this goal-setting exercise to trigger a decision to emphasize a certain part of his current practice (specifically, defending doctors in malpractice cases). This was an area of law he had always enjoyed, but which he had neglected under the pressures of building a new practice. Now reminded of his interest, he made the decision to commit time and energy to acquiring skill and experience in this area. He hoped to maintain or expand his practice—and his income—while actually increasing his satisfaction from his everyday work.

What Is Your Mission?

I find the best way to visualize, organize, and decide on my goals is to think in terms of my "mission." A military word, "mission" connotes a degree of seriousness and dedication that has been washed out of the word "goals" through overuse. "Mission" also implies importance, and your goals should be important—important to you.

What is your mission? You may have the goal of graduating from college, earning a salary increase or promotion, accomplishing a particularly challenging assignment, or getting far enough ahead of your obligations to take a vacation in your particular paradise. But your mission goes beyond this! Your mission is something inspiring, something you long for, the crowning achievement of ten years or more of your life. Set up your mission so it will be enough of an accomplishment to satisfy you for the rest of your life.

It's not difficult to find your mission; the hardest part is to think about it seriously and then carry it out.

Work Sheet 6 gives you an easy first step toward finding your current mission. Go through this exercise every day for a week. Answer seriously, putting down not what you think you should, such as: "Spend more time with Mother," but what you truly feel, like: "Retire at age 40," or "Prove to everyone the value of my idea." Your answers are valid only if they come from your deepest feelings.

Use this exercise to get into yourself. Reach down into that snake pit of feelings you never, never open during the workday and see what you really want to do with your life. Didn't you have an idea a while back? Something super that you thought of, that you wanted to pursue, that you were sure would be great, if only you could iron out one or two little difficulties or get some backing or find time to work on it? Sure you did. Or if you didn't, then you probably would, except you won't let yourself think about one or remember it if you do. "Too impractical," you probably say to yourself. Well, maybe. But those "impractical" ideas and aspirations are the clues you can follow until you reach a practical, satisfying, truly great idea you can and should and will pursue to a successful conclusion.

That idea is part or all of your mission, your goal, the "rainbow" you will not only reach, but climb with the ideas and information in this book. What will it be? Just for fun, put the book down and spend ten minutes daydreaming or thinking about your mission. Include in your thoughts the rewards you will receive for completing it. Reflect on your list from Work Sheet 4. When you have some ideas you like, come back and read on.

Translate Desires into Goals

Your first list is not the be-all and end-all of organizing your life and work, you understand. For most of you this is but the first—tentative—stage in the process of building your effectiveness. You have begun, and you will soon learn to control and shape your efforts and through them your results. But first you must know the results you want the most. These will be your goals.

Your goals will reflect what you want from life. And this you can learn only from your list of hopes and dreams, the list you began in answer to Work Sheet 4.

By now you've thought about what you would do with some extra time, and you've begun to connect this initial list with past interests that you may have buried or put away under the pressures of your everyday life.

Now refine the initial set of Life and Career Goals you put together in Chapter 1. Take a good look at that list once again. Does it talk to you? How many of the items make your skin tingle with excitement? How many of them fire your imagination and make your blood run fast? How many of them leave you cold; your eye skipping right over the line in your hurry to look at better targets for your accomplishment? Sure, it's idealistic, but I'd like you to get to the point where every one of these goals fires you up, fires your imagination, and fills your motivational cup to overflowing. You can do it.

Start by working on the list you prepared for Work Sheet 2 in Chapter 1. Give each of those goals a score from 0 to 100. Make it an overall, cosmic, what-it-is-worth-for-your-whole-life score. The more it is worth, the higher the number. Sure, you'd like to double your income. Who wouldn't? But is that a goal that will really make you happy, make you satisfied? Once you've doubled your income, won't you want to double it again? If so, take points away from that goal. You can always double your income by becoming more effective and achieving more of the lucrative results you want. It's too early to zero in on such narrow targets.

Now try to shoot for the individual, unique, global goals that you feel will absolutely and for sure make you happy, satisfied, or successful. Be careful, you may have lesser targets in sight by mistake or by neglect. For example, I know one business executive who is absolutely tops at financial management. He plays with large sums of money in ways I can't even fathom. When I asked him to show me his objectives, his mission as he saw it, he responded with a clear, concise set of targets for improved performance of himself and his company. So I asked him, "Tom, suppose you reach all these goals. Suppose six months or a year from now you look at this list and consider that you've accomplished every single item you've put down here. Will you be happy?"

"Sure," he told me. "You asked me for my goals, and here they are."

"Right. I understand that. But will you be happy? I mean, will you be able to stop right there and count yourself lucky to have come so far and accomplished so much?"

"No way," he answered. "These are just my goals for the next year or so. I don't expect to be able to reach all of them. But even if I did, I'd be setting other goals farther out, more demanding. I'd want to do even better the next year."

This was a fine set of goals, but it failed to meet the basic criteria for a "mission." Tom lacks a clear picture of what he really wants to accomplish. If I pressed him, he'd tell me that his direct road to business success lies in a series of personal and company performance goals. But there's no end to that series and, consequently, no point at which he'd be content to stop. He's lacking the perspective that comes from knowing your mission, and so he's handicapping himself in his efforts toward lifelong achievement, satisfaction, and success.

No matter what your efforts, to get the most from them you have to know your mission in detail. Then you can aim directly for what you want. Start thinking about your mission, and start defining it in more detail.

In all probability, your "hopes and dreams" list from Work Sheet 6 is a more accurate guide to your mission than your goals list from Work Sheet 2. That's not a criticism, just an observation based on what I've seen most people write down in response to these kinds of probing questions.

It takes practice and personal honesty to begin nurturing what you really want to do amid all the underbrush with which you fill up your days.

You can do it, though, by asking some pointed questions and listening hard for the answers from deep inside yourself. Go slow with this question-and-answer session. Consider the questions often. Don't expect to find the full answers for at least a few hours, perhaps several days or a week. That's one reason to live closely with Work Sheet 6 for a while.

Actually, your search for life and career goals is an ongoing process that should be part of you—although mostly on the back burner. Very few of us are lucky enough, as Vincent Van Gogh was, to determine what we want to do, who we want to be, and what we want to accomplish with so much fervor we never have to think about those questions again. And even that great painter went through several other "careers" before settling on painting as his final choice of "mission."

So use the exercise labeled Work Sheet 7 to help refine and define your serious goals. Remember, at this point you do not have to inscribe your goals in stone. You merely have to find ones you believe in, goals that—if achieved today—would strike you as a life's worth of effort and accomplishment. Tomorrow you'll be perfectly free to change them all around or exchange your goals for different goals. But in practice, you won't change so often, and the mission you determine for yourself will be a guiding light long enough to be useful.

WORK SHEET 7

Defining Your Mission

1. For what accomplishments would you like to be known after your death?

_____

_____

_____

_____

2. Who are the people whose respect for your accomplishments (past and future) means the most to you? What accomplishing would they most appreciate from you?

_____

_____

_____

_____

_____

3. Imagine yourself 10, 20, 30 years from now. You will be relaxing and evaluating what you will have accomplished. Which of

your achievements will make you the happiest? Which ones will
you regret?

_____

_____

_____

_____

_____

4. Think about where you were, what you were doing 5, 10, 15
    years ago. Compare those days to your present situation. Have
    you made progress? In what direction(s)? Do you want to con-
    tinue on? Might you receive more satisfaction, pleasure, or per-
    sonal reward from some other direction(s)? Which one(s)?

_____

_____

_____

_____

_____

WHAT TO DO WITH YOUR GOALS

Your personal goals are an important part of your new program to
boost your effectiveness and accomplish more of what you want.
While the goals you are selecting today don't have to be permanent
choices, they are more helpful the more you want to reach them. In
most cases, a goal is valuable if you can keep after it for six months
or a year. In special circumstances, though, shorter term goals can
work just as well. For example, I know an artist who experimented

with pottery instead of his usual oil paints and acrylics. He gave himself three months to become acquainted with the new form. If he liked it, he would stick with it. If not, he would go back to oils. But he made no long-term commitment. His goal was to work steadily for three months in order to give himself a fair chance, and then to re-evaluate.

A goal is valuable, but not if you keep pursuing one long after you have lost interest in it. Your goals will mainly help you insofar as they: 1) reflect your deep desires for accomplishments and direction, and 2) keep you focused and moving ahead on a relatively steady course over a useful period. Goals you care about and hold onto can be very powerful. They can guide your efforts and help you expand your results. Goals make it much easier for you to fine tune your efforts so they do the most good. They also help you discard relatively worthless activities in favor of more valuable ones, activities whose value you may not even recognize right now.

You see, you cannot see which activities are worth more than others unless you have some form of yardstick to help you measure them. And the most effective yardsticks you can have are the goals you impose on yourself.

A Preliminary Yardstick Test

Just to give you some experience with the value of goals and the process of measuring results, let's measure today's activities against today's goals to see how effective you are at this point in your life.

Work Sheet 8 gives you a quick method of comparing what you "planned" on doing with what you "actually" did during a given day. There are some inaccuracies in this quick look, just as there are if you look into the shiny bottom of a frying pan or a clear pool of water to see your reflection. But if this is the only mirror you have, it can still be a revelation!

WORK SHEET 8

Planning vs. Working
A Comparison Sheet

This is a quick inventory of what you "plan" to do versus what you "actually" do during a given day. In reality, your "plans" are probably a good part "hope," and your "work" is probably a good part "dreams." But the comparison can nevertheless tell you a great deal about your current achievement problems and your potential for improvement.

Date:

ANSWER THIS QUESTION AT THE BEGINNING
OF THE DAY

1. List everything you plan to accomplish today:

_____

_____

_____

_____

_____

_____   _____

_____

_____

_____

_____

_____

ANSWER THIS QUESTION AT THE END OF THE DAY

2. List everything you actually did today:

_____

_____

_____

_____

_____

_____

_____

_____

3. Compare: How many items of your plans did you actually work on? How many items did you actually work on that were not in your plans?

_____

_____

_____

_____

_____

_____

_____

_____

_____

_____

4. How would you rate your "effectiveness" today, in terms of: a) progress toward your goals, and separately b) results you achieved in relation to time and effort you expended.

_____   _____

_____   _____

a) Little Progress or Results   Great Progress or Results
    1   2   3   4   5   6   7   8   9   10

b) Little Progress or Results   Great Progress or Results
    1   2   3   4   5   6   7   8   9   10

Later on, of course, you'll have a more detailed log of your activities and a highly refined set of goals, a combination of which gives you far more accurate measurements. But you can get a rough measure even without this.

HOW TO TELL WHAT'S USEFUL

Most people recognize only the tangible utility of an action—the immediate results you get directly from what you do. But true effectiveness can often result from actions you take with long-term instead of immediate results. In general, there are four guidelines against which you can measure the utility of your actions.

Guideline 1:
Active Progress Toward a Goal

This is usually the most direct form of utility, another reason goals are so important. If you have a single or a set of well-defined goals you find desirable, you can measure the usefulness of what you do quite directly. The more progress you realize toward a goal from each step you take, the more useful that step was or will be.

For example, if your goal right now is to trim excess spending from your budget, which would be more useful: a) going out and buying something you have been itching to acquire, or b) reviewing past and contemplated purchases with an eye for unnecessary or wasteful spending? I hope you answered "b." That is the more useful action because it leads more directly to your current goal.

If your current goal is to improve your results, which action would be more useful: a) celebrating the occasion by taking the afternoon off from your responsibilities to watch TV in a local bar, or b) sitting quietly and trying to decide what you would like to accomplish during the coming year? If you agree with me that "b" is the better answer, I advise you to let your actions suit your words. Do it!

Guideline 2:
The Rule of Readiness

This rule states that any action that helps you get ready to meet a future goal is as useful as direct action toward that goal. With this rule in mind, you can make your Basic Choice of what to work on next a little more flexibly. The idea is to maximize progress toward your goals, and sometimes this means choosing not to take direct action toward a lesser goal in order to get ready for direct action toward a more important goal.

For example, if you have the chance to take a dead-end job at a high rate of pay or a lower paying job leading to opportunities you want very much, the Rule of Readiness will justify taking the low-pay job. In the long run, such tactics will earn you more money, satisfaction, and results than you will get from always grabbing for immediate benefits.

Remember, effectiveness and the ability to achieve what you want lie not in the specific actions you take, but in how accurately what you do leads you toward what you want to accomplish. And this measure of accuracy is not a shallow glance favoring what appears to be useful right now, but an in-depth, enlightened evaluation favoring what will bring maximum goal-oriented results over the long haul. There can be quite a difference.

Guideline 3:
Preparation for Action

Visualize a World War II movie. It is just before the Nazis come storming over the hill, or just before the big landing on the enemy-held beach. The tension is tremendous, but there's little to do except wait. What are the characters doing? There is always that one guy worrying, crying, and complaining about the spot he's in. He's unhappy. He's concentrating on his own thoughts and fears. He's not alert to the world around him. He probably doesn't make it to the end of the film.

But look around. There's always another character who is quieter, calmer. He's sharpening his bayonet or oiling his machine gun. He's preparing for action. You somehow know he has already done the best he could in target practice, physical conditioning, and hand-to-hand combat. You can bet he has mastered the recognition signals so he won't be shot by his own troops in case he gets separated from his buddies. And now that there is nothing to do but wait, he's honing that edge, fine tuning his preparedness. And his thorough mental and physical preparation will make a big difference in his effectiveness. We know he makes it to the end of the film, and you can bet he gets a medal along the way.

Adequate preparation is vital to your effectiveness. Without it, you probably won't accomplish what you want. For example, in business, I have known managers to pore over studies and sweat their way through detailed information only to postpone any action because a crucial bit of information is missing. Unless it arrives very quickly the tired executive will have to restudy the very same material at some future date. The work so far yielded zero results, and thus had no utility.

However, the work could have some utility according to our Guidelines if, for example, the preliminary perusal helped him get ready to make his decision or prepare some action. The effort could also have been useful in another way.

Guideline 4:
Learning

Learning experiences can often provide "utility" to gray-area efforts which aren't clearly justified for other reasons. For example, a meeting you attend may seem useless. But not if you learned to avoid such meetings in the future. In fact, if you learned anything useful, gained any good experience, or met one helpful or stimulating person, the meeting had learning value and utility.

Of course, if you are too generous with yourself here, you can begin valuing the learning experiences of watching four hours of TV soap operas or playing fifty hands of gin rummy when you have better things to do. Don't fall into this trap. Follow your Basic Choice and work toward your most valuable goal before all others.

Now here's a method of measuring the direct utility of your daily actions.

First, make a list of what you are trying to accomplish today. If today is a workday, be sure to include the three or four main work items you tried (or are trying) to get done. In any case, list what you're trying to do, such as:

a. loaf around watching TV_____

b. get the car washed_____

c. straighten the house_____

d. cook a good meal_____

e. make a date with a friend_____

plus whatever else you want to do:

f. _____

g. _____

and

h. _____

_____

_____

_____

_____

_____

Keep this list confidential, so you can be honest about what you put down.

Now make a rough list of what you have accomplished today so far. (If it is now too early in the day to have accomplished much, run this entire test for yesterday's goals and accomplishments.) Include the small tasks and short items you attempted, as well as the prominent items. Despite your lofty and noble accomplishments, it is in the details of your day's activities that you see your true level of effectiveness. If you ignore the details and look only at the big picture, you lose too much accuracy.

Take your rough list of what you actually did, and hold it alongside your list of what you were trying to do. Compare. Try to match up each activity with one or more of your aims. How much of what you did had little or no relation to what you were trying to accomplish? How much of what you were trying to accomplish found little or no expression in what you did?

Compare your unmatched aims and activities with those that match up. The more matches you have—and the higher the proportion of matches to non-matches—the more effective you probably are. How big are the gaps between what you did and what you want to accomplish? The gaps are probably this big for you most of the time. Score your results on Work Sheet 9 and use the same form to record the results of your future comparisons as well.

As you become more effective—better able to attain the goals and achieve the results you want—the gaps between your aims and activities will narrow. You'll find yourself able to accomplish what you set yourself to do with much greater precision and reliability.

WORK SHEET 9

How Useful Are Your Activities?

Date	# of Actions	# of Goals	# of Matches	# of Unmatched Activities	# of Unmatched Aims (Goals)

GOALS YOU CAN WORK TOWARD TODAY

Now that you've examined some of the values and uses of goals, you can better continue the process of setting some of your own. The primary reason most people go through life without a set of serious goals is lack of motivation to stop and set them. We don't "believe" the goals will be worth the trouble it takes to have them. And why should we? For most of us, our parents were not conscious goal-setting people. Our friends and social peers don't usually interrupt the flow of talk about money, sports, and relationships to discuss their goals. We have rarely seen concrete proof that goals exist, or that having them has any tangible value. It's no wonder so few people are aware of their value in everyday life and work.

But I can't just order you to set goals. You won't. Instead, I have to motivate you to set them. Properly motivated, you'll set yourself goals, and once you have them, you'll learn first hand their terrific and tangible values. Once I get you started, I know you won't stop. The difficulty is getting you started.

So far we've had a chance to explore goals in general, and your long-term goals in particular. But the rewards from such discussions are general and long-term in coming. To give you more immediate motivational energy, we'll turn now to more immediate goals—objectives and attainments you can reach right away. But to maintain a serious and useful purpose to these goals, we'll tie them as closely as we can to some larger objective that's important to you.

The exercise labeled Work Sheet 10 gives you a set of guidelines for translating a long-range goal into a series of relatively short-term and immediate steps you can start and finish in a single day. This one-day activity is an important standard for you to maintain. Projects that take longer often become subject to procrastination, declining priorities, and lack of immediate rewards. The more you stick with simple steps you can start and finish in a single day, the more steadily you will progress toward your larger goals.

WORK SHEET 10

Self-evaluation:
Goals You Can Work Toward Today

PART A

(Complete this part for one important goal)

Life or Career Goal:

_____

_____

My deadline for completion or achievement:

_____

What I will have to accomplish during the first 20 percent of this deadline period:

A. _____

B. _____

C. _____

What I will have to accomplish during the second 20 percent of this deadline period:

A. _____

B. _____

C. _____

What I will have to accomplish during the third 20 percent of this deadline period:

A. _____

B. _____

C. _____

What I will have to accomplish during the fourth 20 percent of this deadline period:

A. _____

B. _____

C. _____

What I will have to accomplish during the final 20 percent of this deadline period:

A. _____

B. _____

C. _____

PART B

(Complete this part for each 20 percent period in Part A)

Number of days in this period:_____

Interim steps required to complete desired accomplishments:

Step	Number of days required

1. _____

2. _____

3. _____

4. _____

5. _____

6. _____

7. _____

8. _____

9. _____

Total number of days required:

PART C

(Complete this part for each interim step in Part B)

Interim step to be completed:

_____

One-day tasks leading toward completion of this interim step:

Monday _____

Tuesday _____

Wednesday _____

Thursday _____

Friday _____

These one-day steps represent the building blocks with which you can construct a "body of work" to represent you. Put these together in any reasonable order and you're bound to accomplish a great deal. And not just any "great deal," but a specific type and style of accomplishment that springs from your own inner desires and reflects your unique interests, talents, and gifts.

Almost certainly, no one else in the world could conceive of the projects you set for yourself or organize them the way you will. For sure, no one else would undertake any of them just your way! The same holds true of goals others set for you, but which you organize and divide into one-day steps. Try to interest other people in doing some of the one-day tasks you've outlined, and you'll see how unique your contribution will be.

The one-day tasks you've just discovered lie within you—no one else. They are uniquely your own. And no one but you has a prayer of traveling this road or completing the journey. If you do, satisfaction and happiness await you, not only from the end results but from the very process of achieving them. For you, reaching this goal, and in fact doing anything that in any useful way brings you closer to reaching it, is the organized direction you can follow to boost your effectiveness and obtain the results you want from your life.

3

WHAT TO DO NEXT: HOW TO DECIDE ON PRIORITIES

Organizing your life and work, and maximizing your results and
accomplishments require the scientific approach: You must consci-
entiously and assiduously apply the general methods in this book to
specific situations around you. You don't have to be a true scientist,
of course. Where scientists design experiments, you design strategies
and tactics of accomplishment. And where scientists accumulate
knowledge, you accumulate results.

Accumulation is the key word here. There are few opportunities
for you to suddenly achieve tremendous results in a single day, week,
or month. Oh, these opportunities arise, and you'll soon be in a good
position to create a few such opportunities and to take advantage of
them when they occur. But they are relatively rare.

Much more common are the opportunities to accomplish a little
extra here and there throughout the days, weeks, months, and years
of your work and your life. They occur at certain key points of the
day and at certain Choice points that you pass as you move from one
activity to another. Each of these opportunities is of relatively little

importance. You can always afford to miss one and not look back because another will be along very shortly. Yet without going crazy or becoming a perfectionist, the more of these opportunities you convert into extra-result realities the better because they accumulate very quickly.

But converting these opportunities is only part of the trick. The other part is converting them without extra effort. If you exert yourself tremendously to achieve tremendous results, you are certainly doing well. But when you develop the habits and carefully cultivated patterns of action to convert these opportunities automatically, you can accumulate a huge amount of extra achievements with virtually no additional effort. And that is the best way to do it.

You can think of it as a process of collecting wild daisies. Imagine you're walking in the woods with a friend where wild flowers grow along the path. If you concentrate all your energies on watching for the flowers, then picking them, looking them over, arranging them, and counting them every few steps, you won't pay enough attention to your friend or the rest of your surroundings. The flowers—and the process of collecting them—will dominate your thoughts and block out your ability to do much else.

On the other hand, you could take the same walk through the same woods with the same friend, but this time leave the flower collecting to "take care of itself." You could probably collect the flowers "absent-mindedly": stooping, picking, and holding them without special thought, while you concentrate on your friend, your conversation, and the sights, smells, sounds, and textures of the forest. At the end of this walk, you would have the same handful of flowers. But you wouldn't remember picking them, nor would they have taken much attention away from your friend.

That's the way to convert your daily opportunities for extra results. Convert them automatically, without thought, and each little bit extra you accomplish will add to the tremendous "free bonus" you'll accumulate over the long term.

The basic method for accumulating these opportunities is to identify your most valuable goals, and to keep your efforts directed toward them as much as possible. The "opportunities" we are talking about are the opportunities to work toward these goals rather than any lesser ones. As we have seen, sometimes the road to such achievements can be fairly direct—as when you decide to cut your budget, and immediately spend an hour deciding where to make the required cuts. But the four Guidelines in Chapter 2 showed you how to make valuable progress toward goals in less direct ways, too. With the four Guidelines in mind, you will see many, many ways to work toward your primary goals rather than other, more immediate but less valuable objectives.

This process of concentrating your efforts toward your most important goals has two sides:

On the positive side, it requires that you:

a.   Identify your most important goals,

b.   map out plans to achieve them, and

c.   put these plans ahead of all the other items that seem to demand your time and energy.

On the negative side, the process requires that you:

d.   Identify your less important goals,

e.   link them to the actions and efforts that would move you toward these goals, and

f.   consciously and deliberately refrain from these actions in favor of those in "c" above.

On one hand, you devote your time to your important goals. On the other, you withhold your time from less important ones. The net result is a focused beam of your personal effort that moves you rapidly toward the goals and objectives you want to attain.

In practice, concentrating your efforts on your most important goals comes down to a matter of choice. And the most common—most important—choice you can ever make with regard to organizing your work and your life and obtaining the results you want from your efforts is: "What am I going to do next?" This is the Basic Choice in your life.

You make this Basic Choice dozens of times a day. And your ability to achieve that extra bit, to accomplish what you want, depends largely on how well you make your Basic Choices—even under adverse conditions, when you're not feeling well, under pressure, in the midst of chaos, or when you're groping blindly in the dark. If this were an easy Choice, everyone would make it perfectly all the time.

But comfort yourself with this thought: You don't have to build a perfect record. You are allowed ample lapses. The fact of having to

WHAT TO DO NEXT: HOW TO DECIDE ON PRIORITIES 59

make a Basic Choice is nothing you can avoid by ignoring the ideas and techniques in this book. You make the Choice just by continuing to live, to work, to hope, and to dream. You make the Choice of "What to do next?" whenever you finish a project, hang up the telephone, start or stop a chain of thought—or even pause between activities.

Now look back at your comparison of goal and activities in Work Sheet 8. You probably didn't do very well at first. But that measure of your effectiveness will now begin to improve. Make a note on your calendar to make the same comparison between current goals and actions in exactly two weeks, and again two weeks after that. Remember to count both the matched and the unmatched items. Your score will improve two ways: You will find your actions staying closer to your goals, and you will find you have more goals to stay close to. Both are basic measures of effectiveness.

THE ONE BEST ITEM

Once you begin to see your level of accomplishment as the sum result of your many Basic Choices—"What will I do next?"—a lot of abstract principles and high-sounding philosophy suddenly melts into concrete form.

To organize your work and your life, to achieve what you want faster and more accurately, make your Basic Choices in favor of your goals. Begin noticing how often that Basic Choice presents itself. And get into the habit of scrutinizing your options to find the best Choice possible, as often as you can.

You can begin by paying attention to how often the Basic Choice occurs in your life. For example, think back on today. Use the exercise labeled Work Sheet 11 to help you recall some crucial Choice points and how well you converted them to extra results and accomplishments.

WORK SHEET 11

Finding Basic Choice Points

Use this form to structure your thinking about today (or any given day):

1. When you woke up this morning, what did you do the very first thing?:_____

List five other options you had for your first action of the day?

a) _____

b) _____

c) _____

d) _____

e) _____

2. Between breakfast and lunch today, name three goals you worked toward:

a) _____

b) _____

c) _____

List five other goals you could have worked toward this morning, and indicate by a "+" or a "−" whether each one is more or less important to you than the goal you actually pursued.

a) _____

b) _____

c) _____

d) _____

e) _____

3. Between lunch and dinner today, name three goals you worked toward:

a) _____

b) _____

c) _____

List five other goals you could have worked toward this afternoon, and indicate by a "+" or a "−" whether each one is more or less important to you than the goal you actually pursued.

a) _____

b) _____

c) _____

d) _____

e) _____

4. Between dinner and bedtime today, name three goals you worked toward:

a) _____

b) _____

c) _____

List five other goals you could have worked toward this evening, and indicate by a "+" or a "−" whether each one is more or less important to you than the goal you actually pursued.

a) _____

b) _____

c) _____

d) _____

e) _____

5. Go back over each period, and write down (merely explaining to yourself in your head won't benefit you) why you chose to do what you did.

First thing:

_____

_____

_____

_____

_____

_____

_____

_____

Morning:

_____

_____

_____

_____

_____

_____

_____

Afternoon:

_____

_____

_____

_____

_____

_____

_____

_____

Evening:

_____

_____

_____

_____

_____

_____

_____

The questions in Work Sheet 11 are designed to elicit from you a random sample of the reasons you work toward whatever goals and objectives you choose. I suspect that most of these reasons have not been entirely conscious before this. In other words, you may have to sit and think a spell before you can write down a solid reason for whatever Basic Choices you analyze.

That's all to the good because unconscious—and untrained—Choices are probably poor ones. Later on, your unconscious will be superbly trained to handle your Choices accurately and effectively with no conscious thought. You'll be choosing "automatically," picking up those daisies without taking any attention away from the people and the situations around you. For now, you'll be more effective if you pay strict attention to where you direct your efforts. By watching what you do, and later by trying to direct your efforts in carefully planned out patterns, you'll almost instantly increase your level of results and the amount of satisfaction you can generate in a day.

Of course, it's tedious to pay attention to your Basic Choices, just as it would be tedious to pay much attention to the simple act of walking. Most of us just walk. But think of this as something more than walking. It is more like running a long-distance event—every day for the rest of your life. Suddenly, your every movement becomes extremely important. The slightest flaw in your running style can hamper your efforts, waste precious energy, and ultimately slow you down. Similarly, slight flaws in your Basic Choices will ultimately reduce your effectiveness and hamper your efforts to achieve what you want. For now, pay attention to detail.

Eventually you will get the knack for making the best Choice almost without thinking. For example, I'm working and the telephone rings. It is someone calling to discuss one aspect of another project I'm involved in. Instinctively, I ask questions to determine if I have to talk about this right now. As in most situations, there is some flexibility. Next, I use my own criteria and guidelines to measure the importance of this new item in relation to the one on my desk. Even before my associate can get the conversation going, I hear my voice saying:

"Listen, I'm right in the middle of something else right now. Can we talk about this later?"

It's easy to make an appointment to discuss the matter two days from now, far enough away that I can factor it into my schedule. Even a one-hour delay would enable me to reach a natural breakpoint in this project, and thus avoid an interruption that interferes with my thinking and lowers my overall effectiveness.

It's easy to keep forging your schedule ahead of you. But in the beginning you can benefit from having some of the rules and criteria carefully laid out. As you assimilate them and incorporate them into your pattern of life and work, you'll spend less and less brainpower keeping on the right side of what they tell you. Eventually you will use them automatically. I guarantee it.

Before we get to specific criteria, let's examine the concept of the one "best" item for you to work on. Again, it's not a narrow, mathematical construction that dictates all your actions or that raises concrete results above other values and benefits. Too many people use "effectiveness" and the quest for maximum results as excuses for neglecting people or ignoring their emotional and social aspects. They wind up acting more like machines than people. This is not the "best" course for you to follow.

The idea of there being one "best" item to absorb your efforts at any given moment seems almost to demand some kind of objective accounting procedures to keep track of your options and to put them in rank order. But while this seems like a good idea, in practice it would be absurd to begin trying to compare and to rank such disparate demands as:

your kids

your current love affair

a consuming interest in a new topic

a long-term marriage

a broken car

an impending deadline at work

They all demand your attention, and it's never easy to put numbers on these items and rank them.

Think about these teasers:

Which is the more valuable effort?

a. listening to your child tell you excitedly about something inconsequential that went on at school today, or

b. hearing what the garage mechanic on the telephone has to say about your broken starter?

Should you tackle that amazingly difficult report your boss threw at you yesterday and demanded back completed by 5 P.M. today? Or dare you even work on it, with the vision of that "special someone" you met last night dancing before your eyes?

Your options for directing your efforts at any given moment form a dazzling array of the practical and the fantastic, the must-do and the should-do, the interesting and the deadly dull, and much more.

So how, then, to know which of all your options is the "best" for you?

BEST DEPENDS PARTLY ON "WHEN"

To make life practical, limit your Basic Choice to a few juicy options. Divide your life and work into several Periods of Priority. Instead of considering every possibility at every opportunity, limit your Choice to the most relevant options that fit with your priority at the moment.

During working hours, for example, you tend to limit your consideration of "What to do next?" to work-related objectives and goals. Your "one best" option during working hours is, quite naturally, different from your "one best" option in the library. Your best option for lunch is much different from your best option just a few minutes before or after. Use the same idea to make your Basic Choices simpler after hours. Ignore (or give less consideration to) work-related options in favor of other specialized goals and activities. For example, at the football game, your Basic Choice can be narrower than when you are at home on a Sunday afternoon. By focusing on a small, appropriate list of options, you greatly simplify your Basic Choice of "What to do next?"

You can get more practical benefits from this concept by clearly blocking out whatever Periods of Priority you can think of. Define what hours of the day, what days of the week you will be primarily concerned with your work. For most of us, that's from 9 A.M. through 5 P.M. five days a week. Others will have other hours when work takes top priority.

Then map out other Periods of Priority: for family and friends; for sports, exercise, or hobbies; for socializing and entertainment; for home-maintenance jobs like shopping, repairs, cooking, cleaning, and laundry; for mental exercises, meditation, reading, or study; even for self-improvement through whatever means appeal to you.

The main purpose of defining your Periods of Priority is to simplify your Basic Choices during each Period by ruling out vast portions of all the items you could possibly tackle next.

BEST DEPENDS PARTLY ON YOUR MOOD

In addition to Periods of Priority, there is plain and simple saturation. Say, for example, you love to work in your garden. Your Choice of "What to do next?" leads you to spend half a dozen hours there during the first two or three days of the week. Fine. But now you begin to feel you have gardened enough. For the moment, you don't want to do it any more. You are saturated with gardening. And so you temporarily block off gardening from consideration when you wonder "What to do next?" Saturation makes your Basic Choices simpler. It works almost like a negative priority, in effect, because you say something like: "No matter what, I'm not gardening for a while."

Just as you have negative urges to avoid certain saturated activities, such as the gardening example, you have positive urges you want to pursue. For example, no matter what, you want to watch TV. No matter what, you want to eat some pizza. Most of the time, positive urges lead to saturation, which leads to negative urges until you're balanced once again.

BEST DEPENDS PARTLY ON EXTERNALS

Your environment also helps limit your Basic Choice, in both favorable and unfavorable ways. For example, at social gatherings you don't generally work out mathematical models or practice your hobby of duck calls. Instead, you respond to your environment and converse with the people around you. You don't read heavy philosophy at amusement parks; you go on simple-minded rides. In the country, you admire the trees, the sky, and the smell of good clean air. Whatever you do, you probably don't go looking for a nightclub or a stock exchange. The act of sticking with the environment helps you limit your Basic Choice to more manageable proportions.

A COMPREHENSIVE CHOICE

Your Basic Choice of "What to do next?" should select an option that best suits all your emotional, spiritual, physical, financial, and other needs, along with needs for Utility and Goal Orientation. In this comprehensive view, we are not automatons blindly throwing our available energies into the most practical project available.

Rather, we are wholistic human beings who cultivate both short-term and long-term values with a balanced program of activities that serve all our needs. We want to develop new goals as well as attain our current ones. In all that follows, stay aware of your total human self. You are not merely a producer, not merely a consumer, not merely an achiever or a worker. You must learn to achieve what you want not only to accumulate wealth and power, but to earn greater satisfaction and leave a better world for those who follow.

It takes practice to learn to make these Choices and to reach all your goals most effectively. Starting now, and continuing well after your experience with this book, I want you to practice, evaluate, and attempt to control your efforts, your achievements, and your results. Work Sheet 12 is designed to make you think about the range of Choices available in your current situations.

WORK SHEET 12

Self-evaluation:
Choosing Tomorrow's Achievements

Think about tomorrow. What have you planned? What are you going to work toward and accomplish?

1. List the projects, hobbies, or "general agenda" items you expect to pursue tomorrow.

_____

_____

_____

_____

_____

_____

_____

_____

_____

_____

_____

_____

_____

_____

   a. How many are there? Rank the items in two sets: first the items you consider to be of "major" importance, and separately the items you consider to be of "minor" importance.

2. List twice as many alternatives as you have numbered items of relatively little importance. (For example, if you numbered seven items in this category, think of seven more minor items you could choose to do tomorrow.)

_____

_____

_____

_____

_____

_____

3. List twice as many alternatives as you have numbered items of major importance. Try to relate the new items to your stated important goals.

_____

_____

_____

_____

_____

_____

_____

4. Go through each list separately. Pick the ones you want to work on tomorrow. Make sure you can do them all in one day! Write down your reasons for choosing the ones you did.

_____

_____

_____

_____

_____

_____

_____

5. Tomorrow, follow your Choices from this exercise.

URGENCY IN A BASIC CHOICE

Another element to consider in your Basic Choice is an item's urgency. Urgency is a dangerous factor. People like to put urgent tasks ahead of more important ones, despite their knowledge that urgency is no clue to important goals or desirable results.

For example, say your goal is to write an opera by age thirty-five. This is not urgent until well after your thirty-fourth birthday. But by then it's too late! You missed it, but the goal was important to you.

Focusing on urgency will cause you to ignore consistently the long-range projects that require training, momentum, confidence, and experience. Yet these are the ones that can bring you the most satisfying results. If you focus on urgency, you'll emphasize rapid-fire details over slower, more meaningful achievements. You won't get what you want, whether that is to write operas, run a small business, find a better job, or complete any project that requires initiative and good planning.

Urgency is a factor, though, particularly as a tie breaker when the rest is well balanced. For example, you would normally choose a less urgent task that is clearly the more valuable of your options. But if three tasks have about the same value, you would be right to pick the most urgent, provided that urgency is real.

For example, imagine you have just finished work on an item and you are at your Basic Choice point. Say you have a choice of:

a) reading a current journal

b) returning a phone call from a stranger

c) thinking about your day and what you would like to accomplish, or

d) handling an urgent problem before your bank closes.

The problem may be a valid one, but the urgency may be a mirage. If you can call the bank after closing time, or handle the problem in a letter, you have no real reason to put that item ahead of others more important. It requires steady nerves and good judgment to discriminate true urgency from all the apparent urgency with which trivial problems cloak themselves. Yet the nerves and judgment are important to cultivate if you are going to improve your effectiveness and achieve more of what you want.

Basic Choices, you are learning, are fundamental but not easy. The idea is to make your Basic Choice in favor of the one activity that moves you farthest toward an important goal. If the right task does not leap out at you, you can help it along by creating plans and breaking them into one-day tasks. Soon you'll be in position to initiate your own goal-oriented tasks instead of blindly obeying the summons of a less important alternative.

But talking about them won't help you. Basic Choices are best learned by making them and making them and making more of them until you have the habit of putting your shoulder not just to the next available wheel, but to the one wheel in the area best suited to your larger goals and purposes.

Use Work Sheet 13 as a guideline for some of your thinking as you try to decide how to answer each of your Basic Choices for improving your results and accomplishing more of what you want.

WORK SHEET 13

Self-evaluation:
Making the Basic Choice

Use this exercise to help you choose between the alternatives that seem to have equal claims upon your effort and attention. On closer inspection, you will probably find that one alternative has a stronger claim, based on what you want to accomplish and how you plan to accomplish it. Use these questions to start probing for that one most important opportunity to improve your results.

Step 1: Write down everything you might possibly *do* next.

a. _____

b. _____

c. _____

d. _____

e. _____

f. _____

g. _____

h. _____

Step 2:   For each one, list the potential results you might achieve, and the *probability* you can achieve them.

	Results	**Probability**
a.		
b.		
c.		
d.		
e.		
f.		
g.		
h.		

Step 3:   For each one, rank from 1 (least) to 5 (most) how directly it leads you to one of your major goals.

1. _____

2. _____

3. _____

4. _____

5. _____

6. _____

7. _____

8. _____

Step 4: For each one, rank its degree of urgency from 1 (hardly urgent) to 5 (very urgent). Also note the likely results if you do not pursue it at this time.

	Urgency	Likely Outcome if Neglected
1.		
2.		
3.		
4.		
5.		
6.		
7.		
8.		

Step 5: Which alternative seems to be the best answer to your Basic Choice right now?_____

_____

Don't forget to factor into your Basic Choices some of your own qualifications, as well. As you'll see in forthcoming chapters, you can be much more effective if you work on what you do best. So the best answer to your Basic Choice will depend on your current strengths and weaknesses. The more accurately you recognize them, the more effort you can direct yourself toward achieving your best objectives.

For example, you may be better off having a tax professional do your tax-related paper work. Unless you have special training, you probably are not qualified to muddle through the regulations, recent changes, and interpretations of the law in search of compliance and your lowest tax. Similarly, 75 percent of your paper work is probably suitable for others to handle. Admit this, and let them do the work! Subordinates, colleagues, outside consultants, and professionals can take a huge burden of this and other types of work from your shoulders. Let them. And then direct the energy and effort you have set free toward projects and objectives only you can achieve.

ACQUIRING THE INTUITIVE KNACK

By now you are probably feeling overburdened by all the factors you must consider every time you make a Basic Choice. If you're like most people on their first exposure to these ideas, you can't even keep it all straight. You certainly have trouble balancing every factor that bears on your Basic Choice. And to do this quickly is impossible.

There is a trick you can use here, though, to "program" all this material into your subconscious mind. Once you program it, the right half of your brain worries about "What to do next?" Your conscious, achieving, work-a-day half is free to concentrate on the task itself, and to do so with maximum energy and minimum fuss. Putting your Basic Choices under control of your "other half" is by far the best way to handle them. Otherwise, you work harder pondering what to do than doing it.

Here is a simple three-step process for turning your Basic Choices over to the quiet side of your brain:

1. Read page 56 to page 78 of this book in one sitting. Read it straight through from beginning to end. While you're reading, make notes in the margins. If any questions pop up about how to handle specific situations, formulate answers that satisfy you. Try to understand the material in a cohesive unit. You may not succeed at one sitting, but try. Go over the material again every three days until you feel you understand how all the factors fit and work together in your own special situation.

2. After each reading, put down the book and for a few minutes try to imagine yourself using this material to make your Basic Choices instantly and accurately. Absorb the feelings, the benefits, the accomplishments your new mastery will result in. Will it reduce tension?

Smooth the flow of work? Help you achieve lifelong goals? Be specific about the benefits you expect. From then on, try to be more conscious of your Basic Choices as you make them. Notice each Choice point. Identify your options. Rate your quality of Choice. Don't fret or spend long minutes on each Basic Choice. Simply note it, make it, and follow what you chose.

3. Look back at your Basic Choice once or twice a day. Even once or twice a week can help program the Choices in your mind. During your informal evaluations, consider the goals and objectives you have and have not pursued most recently. Notice any improvements and continue with the program.

Over a period of several weeks and months, you'll begin integrating more of the important factors smoothly into your Basic Choices. And you'll make each Choice a little faster, a little better, a little more confidently than before. Soon the entire process will be so automatic and intuitive you will almost feel as though the one "best" alternative for action leaps at you of its own free will.

"What Choice?" you'll soon be saying. "I had no Choice. There was only one 'best' thing to do, and I did it!"

4

GETTING DOWN TO SPECIFICS: HOW TO ACCOMPLISH MORE IN LESS TIME

Effectiveness, satisfaction, and accomplishing what you want all depend on results. And given that you know what you want, the more results you obtain, the better. In this chapter, you'll find hundreds of specific techniques for obtaining more results faster, smoother, and more effortlessly than you ever thought possible. The techniques from this compendium that apply to your situation are an integral part of your effort to shape your results and to make the best possible use of your time, your energy, and your resources.

In effect, this is the practical side of effectiveness. The philosophical side came up when you began zeroing in on your life and career goals: among all things possible, picking those few you wanted to attain or achieve. The managerial or executive side came up when you faced your Basic Choice: "What am I going to do next?" Here the object was to stimulate your leadership qualities—even if you lead only yourself.

Now we're at the technical side of effectiveness, concerned solely with how we can move quickly along the road that our "executive" sides have chosen as the best way toward the objectives our "philosopher" sides have designated.

HANDLING ALL YOUR PAPER

Forms, letters, memos, reports, items to be filled in, read, analyzed, written, and talked about. Paper work is a well recognized problem. But very few of us are doing anything to solve this particular problem.

Unless you have a clerical job sorting, filing, retrieving, or otherwise handling paper, your paper work is more of a means to an end than an end in itself. Therefore, it should not take over or dominate your time.

If you are now—or ever will be—in a position of organizational or bureaucratic influence, I urge you to do what you can to eliminate unnecessary paper work, to streamline what is necessary, and to keep all of it in its proper place.

In the meantime, let's see what we can do about your particular pile of paper work.

Unnecessary Piles

Most of us tend to pile papers around us, on the desk, the credenza, the top of the filing cabinet, the coffee table, the stairs—anywhere there's a horizontal surface. This is so true I can often estimate an individual's ability to cope with their situation by glancing around their home or office.

A profusion of piles indicates to me a serious problem. An occasional pile shows me you need some help, but you're not a critical case. One accountant I know has covered every horizontal surface in his office, not with one, but with multiple piles! That's right! A bottom pile about six inches thick, bound in a rubber band or made up of uniform-size papers. Then on top, another pile bound in a separate rubber band or made up of a different type of paper. Sometimes, one pile is bridged across two others; in several cases, the piles are three or four units high. Some of them are UPOs—Unidentified Piled Objects. The man no longer knows or cares what is in them.

I know from my own excavations (when he wasn't around to become upset) that some of the papers are of absolutely no value. They date from well beyond any statute of limitations and concern clients who died and whose estates were settled years ago. This man loves his piles, far beyond any real value the information in them may command.

If you love your piles—if you have some psychological need to retain your paper work longer than it retains its value—I'm going to have a hard time helping you out of those habits. You may need a different kind of help, entirely.

But if your habits have developed out of neglect or lack of training, or if you honestly feel having those papers "right at your fingertips" helps you work more effectively, you can be helped, and right now!

The truth is, those piles are nothing but millstones around your neck. Face it! They don't help you work more effectively, any more than piles of old junky car parts help your garage mechanic do his job any faster or better. My grandfather used to save old calendars. He'd say: "If that year ever comes back, Rob, I'm going to be ready!" I guess it was a joke. But it was no joke living with a pile of musty, rolled up calendars waiting for 1943 to return.

Look at your piles. Then look at the facts. How many of those papers in your piles actually will ever be useful to you? If you are anything like the people I've worked with, about 75 percent of that stuff is junk. You'll never look at it, except in the course of searching for something else. You'll never miss it when it's gone. And while you're hoarding old Annual Reports and last month's reading matter, you're letting those papers get in the way of today's shot at greater effectiveness.

The Measles Syndrome

But don't believe me. You won't anyway. Use a trick I call the Measles Syndrome to spot your own problems with unwanted, unnecessary, and useless piles of paper.

From now on, every time you turn to one of your piles to look for something you need, carry a pencil or a fine-line marker with you. Put a light dot in the corner of every document you touch as you work through the pile. Put another dot on each document the next time you sort past it looking for something else.

Just for fun, write down your guess as to how many times you will handle the top sheet of each pile: I'm willing to bet your guess is much too low.

In a very short time, your piles will break out in "measles." You'll have more dots than you can shake a stick at. By some counts, some people handle a single piece of paper 137 times or more while it sits in a pile on their desk! And then it's still in the way! So start counting the number of times you handle those papers in the course of looking for something to work on. Once you're convinced your piles subtract from your effectiveness, you can take remedial action.

Clear Away Obstructions

Try to get in the habit of working with an absolutely clear desk. The only papers on your desk that are doing you any good are those that pertain to the one "most important" item on which you are working. Put everything else away.

"Out of sight, out of mind" applies here in a very literal sense. Most people keep papers in plain sight at least partly so they won't forget what the papers refer to. They're afraid if they file the paper away, the task or responsibility it represents will fade from their consciousness, with suitably awful consequences.

They may be right. But that's not a valid excuse for overburdening your desk. You don't have to live with your relatives to remember who they are, do you? What makes you think you have to live with all your paper work to keep it all in mind?

What actually happens with your piles of paper is that you have a hard time concentrating on that one "most important" task. Every time your eyes stray around your desk, anywhere you have your papers piled, your mind is wrenched off track by the memory of some other important item you must eventually work on. This is a valuable trick, one we'll use selectively to jog your memory regarding certain important items we want you to keep in mind. But the key word is selectively. This trick becomes counterproductive—as it probably has with your piles of piles—if you use it too often or too universally.

You become stuck in somewhat the same role as an overworked

salesman at a convention. You start talking to one potential customer. But just as you reach a crucial point in the sales process, you spot someone else who is fingering your merchandise. So you rush off to make a sale there. But before you get the signature on the order form, a third prospect grabs your sleeve and asks a hard question about a different item. In the middle of your answer, you remember a great sales point you want to tell a previous prospect, so you drop everything to make a quick phone call to get this point across before you forget it. But while you're waiting for that person to come on the line, someone new enters your sales booth and wants to know about your product.

By the end of the day, you've been busy! You've spoken to hundreds of prospects. But you haven't completed a single sale. Net score: zero!

This kind of Ping-Pong approach to accomplishment—played with half a dozen paddles instead of just two—is a guaranteed way to lose control of your time, your energy, and your efforts. When you surround yourself with $8\frac{1}{2} \times 11$ invitations to digress, you're asking for ineffectiveness. And you're going to get it.

The better alternative is to keep a clear desk. Put those papers out of sight, and let them stay out of your mind while you concentrate on your one "most important" project. And don't worry about forgetting what to work on next. You won't!

First, you will certainly remember the most important items on your agenda. For a variety of reasons, these items will come to mind the very next time you face your Basic Choice of "What to work on next."

And second, there are some very effective mnemonic techniques that will keep your agenda items in front of you without letting them block your forward progress.

Before long, you'll be in the habit of maintaining a written daily plan. This little slip of paper will take the place of your most relevant piles of paper work—without the bulk or the unwanted grabbing at your attention you get with your current piles. You'll read more about this under "Planning" later in this chapter.

An even more important way to avoid unwanted piles without sacrificing any of their memory-jogging power is through the use of:

The Daily Prompter

TV personalities face the camera armed with any of a variety of memory aids to help them keep track of what to say and do. Why should you make do with any less?

The Daily Prompter is a fancy name for a common device nearly everyone has used at one time or another to jog their memories and help them keep track of many details. Every time you note a doctor's appointment on a kitchen calendar, for example, you're setting up a one-day "prompt." The calendar itself is a kind of prompter, and it will work very well if you will use it. The only drawbacks to your kitchen or office calendar are: 1) it is probably too small to note fully everything you want to put in your Daily Prompter, and 2) it has no place to store anything bulkier than a brief, written message.

A Daily Prompter file is a much more useful device because it never goes out of date and you can have one with as large a capacity as you will ever need.

Physically, your Daily Prompter is a series of large envelopes, files, hanging file folders, binders, drawers, or boxes. Label each one with a number from 1 to 31, or with one of the 12 calendar months. For 12 months and 31 days, you need 43 containers in all.

In action, the Daily Prompter is the one place to store—and hence retrieve—all sorts of messages, paper work, and information you want to remember, but don't want to (or are afraid you may not be able to) hold in your brain until needed.

NOTE: To make your Daily Prompter a useful tool, get in the habit of going to it first thing every morning to see what you have filed for yourself under today's date.

NOTE: To make your Daily Prompter an *extremely* useful tool, get in the habit of putting into it everything you can possibly think of that: 1) you are holding, thinking about, or doing now, and that: 2) you will want to notice again sometime in the future.

For example, if you make an appointment for a shampoo, cut, and blow dry next Thursday, drop yourself a note about the appointment (or the crimper's card may be enough by itself) in your Daily Prompter for next Thursday's date. If the appointment is very early Thursday morning, you may want to leave the reminder in Wednesday's container, and move it to Thursday's once you see it again.

Or suppose you have a car payment to make on the twenty-fifth of every month. Put your payment book, or something to remind you of the payment coming due, in your Daily Prompter sometime before the twenty-fifth—soon enough so you can make the deposit to cover the car payment. Leave it there from month to month.

Now suppose you have a meeting to attend on the eighth, and you want to bring some important papers with you. Drop the papers, clipped to a note about the meeting (where, when, who, what, why) in folder "8." Sure, you may forget about the meeting and lose track of where you put its paper work, but if you only remember to check your Daily Prompter every morning, the paper work and meeting reminder will appear when you need them.

Now you can see why you don't need piles of paper work on your desk just so you won't forget something. Put those papers in your filing system (more details on that system coming soon), and drop yourself a note about where you put them and what you want to do with them under the appropriate date in your Daily Prompter. You can then forget them, supremely confident in your knowledge that—like Moby Dick—your paper work will rise again to beckon you, on the appropriate date, and no sooner.

You can leave notes and other items you want to see far in the future under the appropriate months. Then on the first day of each month, open that month's file and put the items into the appropriate daily files according to the dates you need them.

One thing I love about the Daily Prompter is how a small amount of energy expended to file items and check today's folder in the morning pays huge dividends all out of proportion to your investment. You get the peace of mind from knowing you won't forget anything; you get the use of the mental energy released from having to remember—it's now available for other work; you get the convenience of having your appointments, ideas, and paper work automatically leap into your hand at just the appropriate time; and you get the added effectiveness derived from keeping your commitments, not forgetting items, and clearing your desk. I believe the Daily Prompter is a tremendous way to boost your effectiveness at a very low cost of time and energy. Try one for a month or two, and see how beneficial it can be for you.

The Prompter is also a great way to keep tabs on your own activities, progress, or stagnation. For example, say you get the idea to begin reading books by Henry Miller, or to take a friend on a fly-fishing trip in Montana, or to sign up for a Cordon Bleu cooking course. Leave yourself a note in the Daily Prompter a month or two ahead. When it comes up again, you are reminded of what you were thinking back then. Either you have done it or you haven't. Either you still want to or you don't. Whatever the current picture, you get a strong sense of how you are changing or staying the same during a period longer than your usual span of recollection. And this may get you moving toward new projects and goals.

The Daily Prompter is one way to keep up correspondence with friends and colleagues. Instead of setting down their letters (perhaps to be lost forever amid your piles) with a vague intention of writing back—someday—you put the letter purposefully into your Daily Prompter some time ahead. When it comes up again, make a point of writing—or calling—to keep in touch. This really improves your ability to maintain contact.

Your Daily Prompter is a valuable tool in your efforts to make better decisions. It can curb impulse buying and give maturity to your judgments. For example, you get a mailing piece urging you to buy a video tape recorder for only $999, and you very much want to send away for it. Go ahead, fill in the order form, and address the envelope. Then put the whole package into your Daily Prompter a week or so ahead. When it comes up again, look it over. It may not look so attractive this time around. But if it does, you've already done half the paper work. You can send it and be more confident that your decision is one you'll be happy to live with.

Or say someone asks you for your opinion or judgment on a weighty matter. Instead of thinking about the question and responding off the top of your head, do your thinking and formulate your answer—for your eyes only. Put the question and your answer into your Daily Prompter overnight—or longer if possible. When you take it out again, you have a chance to reevaluate your previous judgment, almost as if it belonged to someone else. You will be surprised how many foolish, hasty, superficial judgments you will be able to keep to yourself by this means.

As you get more comfortable with your Daily Prompter, you'll find many other uses for this simple but effective tool.

Comprehensive Filing System

Most people start their piles innocently enough, but once started the little darlings tend to grow and grow until they are out of control and you can't find what you want without a lengthy search. I have noticed that most piles start for one of two excuses (I won't dignify them with the label "reasons"): 1) "there's no place else to put this for now," and 2) "I'm just going to leave it here for a short while."

If you cut off these excuses at the roots, your piles simply won't have a chance to grow. Two good ways to keep from growing unwanted piles are: 1) have a good place—and only one good place— for everything you conceivably might want to retain, and 2) keep everything in its place except during those moments you are actively working on it.

A Comprehensive Filing System is the masterstroke here. It gives you a place—an adequate space—for all your paper work. And what is more, it gives you confidence that you can find what you file when you want it again. That's a big psychological factor when it comes time to put your paper work out of sight.

Let's face it: A messy filing system is like a messy closet. You have to take everything out to find what you want. And every once in a while, you open the door and the whole structure collapses in your face. If your current filing system (if you even have a "system") is like a messy closet, you would have to be a fool to use it very often. No wonder you keep everything in piles all around you.

But a well organized filing system with room for everything you are likely to want to file is an open invitation to clear your work space and concentrate on one task. In fact, it's almost an indispensable tool for deep concentration and total effectiveness.

SIX MAIN PARTS

The system I use has six main parts. One part is the Daily Prompter I have already described. This part is intended to be an automatic system to supplement your memory—even replace it for 95 percent of the random, low importance material you encounter.

A second part of the Comprehensive Filing System is devoted to ongoing activities, programs, and projects. Every "thing" I am currently working on is represented in this part of the filing system with its own folder or file. In fact, I start a new folder in here as soon as I see I might refer to an idea or some information more than once or twice. Filing materials are cheap compared to the time I would lose looking for items filed within too big a group or category.

I keep these files organized according to how I think of the information they contain. For example, if I think of several people or items under one general category, I'll file them all in one folder. But if I think of the same items as separate but related, I'll file them in individual folders with cross-referencing notes, or I'll put the folders physically together. I don't stick with a rigid formula, but I do like my filing system to reflect my mental categories and my natural patterns of thought.

I may give complex projects several subdivision folders within a larger hanging file to facilitate better retrieval. I may group other projects into a single folder, particularly if I rarely work with these papers. I keep everything here in strict alphabetic order.

I won't suggest any hard-and-fast rules for you; a successful work file like this must be tied to your personal thought patterns and working habits. However, don't be afraid to start a new folder whenever: 1) you feel like you need it, 2) you have just spent more than three minutes finding a specific item in your files, or 3) you want to file an item that doesn't quite fit into any existing slot or category. Remember, file folders, supplies, and equipment are cheap when compared with the cost of the time you waste searching for items you grouped too closely or too generally.

CROSS-REFERENCING

The biggest problem with these individual files is that sometimes a single bit of information or a whole package of paper work really "belongs with" several other files. The logical solution is to make duplicates and file the whole package everywhere it belongs. But it's usually faster, cheaper, and easier to create cross-reference slips. Before you file the multiple-interest item, think of all the "key words" by which you might look for it later. Then make and file cross-reference slips under each key word, referring you to the file's actual location.

For example, a close friend approaches me with a proposal for a brand new publication. Because it's his baby, I want to keep the paper work with other items under his name. Because it's a good idea for a publication, I want it filed with other good ideas for future reference. The proposal is so far along it really deserves a file of its own. And because I promised to reply to him within two weeks, I need a reminder of it in my Daily Prompter. The problem of where to put the paper work is resolved via the cross-reference form (original plus—in this case—two carbons or copies).

I put the actual paper work regarding the proposal into its own project file. Each cross-reference form lists all the key words: my friend's name, the publication idea, date response is due, and the name of the proposed publication. I circle the name of the proposed publication to show myself that's where I put the real paper work. Then I slip the cross-reference forms into each of the relevant files: one form into my Daily Prompter, one form into the file on my friend, and one into my file on ideas for publication. No matter where I conceivably look for this paper work, I'll find it, or I'll find a cross-reference form sending me directly to it.

ACTIVE VS. INACTIVE FILES

I like to keep my project files lean and extremely current, so I move out information I haven't worked on in three months or more. I keep these "past project" files in strict order and readily accessible, but not mixed in with my active files.

The thinnest neglected files I cull are easy to handle: just pull them from the current file drawer and slip them in with other "past projects" in the next room. But when I finish with a long, drawn out, complex project that has three to six inches of material in file, I usually take a few moments to go through it and put the papers in sensible order.

1)   I staple all relevant correspondence together, in chronological order, latest on top.

2)   I substitute staples for paper clips throughout (to prevent inadvertent couplings among my papers).

3)   I remove unwanted duplicates and unused reference materials, notes, or whatever. I leave only what contributed to the making of the project, but I leave *all* of this.

4) I remove generally useful reference materials, leave in their place cross-reference forms, and file the materials where they should be in my system.

When I'm done, I have a comprehensive, but minimal file reflecting the work I put into the project, stacked in sensible order so I can leave it for five years and recapture what I did should I look through it again. I am free to forget the details of past projects, knowing I can (and frequently do) refresh my memory should I ever need to.

REFERENCE FILES

A third part of the Comprehensive Filing System is for Reading and Research. Here you can keep all the articles, books, graphs, and items of interest you hate to lose but can't live with underfoot. As with your "work" files, you organize here according to your own interests. Whatever the main topics of the items you want to file, create a category or subject heading for each one, or each homogeneous grouping.

Simply give each subject heading a number: 100, 200, 300, etc. Then number the items you want to save, in consecutive order within each subject heading. For example, articles you save under "Automobiles" might be numbered 101, 102, 103, etc. Items you save under "recipes" might be numbered 201, 202, 203, etc. File the items in consecutive order, but be sure to use a good storage method for each. For example, put articles in binders, folders, or closed boxes of some sort; books on bookshelves; oversize volumes where you have adequate room, etc.

Now comes a very good part of this system. List each consecutive numbered item in a subject index: a sturdy piece of paper filed by subject. Include a brief title, source, date, and synopsis or main point. Note the file number you assigned the item. Keep the index up to date and properly filed. This is a bit difficult when you are converting a messy-closet type of system to something a little more ordered. But it takes just a few minutes to number, index, and file new items. Even if you leave what you already have strictly alone, make the resolution to file everything new according to this system. The payoffs over the long run will be staggering.

Assuming you have some items filed this way, watch what happens when you want to find one of them:

You're sitting and reflecting on some topic that's important to you, say, beech trees. Suddenly, the light in your head goes on and you say to yourself: "Didn't I read something on this just a few months back? Or was that a few years back?" Armed with your new filing system, you pull the index sheets for "Beech Trees" (or "Trees" or whatever) and quickly scan the titles, synopses, or sources to refresh your memory. Yes! You find the item you want, number 379. Your brief synopsis shows you it's the item you were thinking of. You put back the index sheets and go right to where you keep item 379. In three minutes, you have found an article you haven't seen or thought about for three years! And you went right to it!

What would you do without this system? How could you have found this article? Would you have looked over seventy-nine articles in this subject heading to find this one item? Time consuming and boring. Hardly likely. And would you have recognized it if you had looked? Possibly not. Would you have remembered the critical information about this article well enough to have found it in some other library? Would you have taken the time and trouble to do so? Would it have been a worthwhile use of your time if you had? In my experience, most people would simply do without it.

And that's not entirely a bad idea, you know. I'm not proposing that you use this Reading and Research file to keep everything that ever crosses your desk that you might conceivably, sometime, possibly, perhaps want to look at again before you retire or die. No, that is not how we select the items we want to retain.

Too many people decide to retain reference material or interesting items on the basis of their answer to the question: "Could I possibly need to see this again?" That's the wrong question, because the answer will almost always be "Yes."

A more relevant and useful question is: "Should I need this (approximate) information again, how hard would it be for me to find it, assuming I don't save it?" Most of the time, you don't need to save items because you can replace them relatively easily with the same or newer items from library collections. Sure, it's a little less convenient to have to retrieve articles from distant libraries, rather than from your own collection. But we're concentrating here on making good use of your time, and you can usually do more productive things than play librarian, particularly when paid librarians are around to keep materials anyway.

Save yourself a lot of filing bother by getting a list of publications received by libraries to which you have access. Keep it around and don't save articles from those publications unless they are of extreme relevance and timely value. What you should save, though, are: 1) quick-reading items you intend to read, scan, or clip from and then throw away, and 2) unusual items you may not find in libraries readily available to you.

Another problem in deciding what to save and what to toss is that gray area of partially valuable material which you want to save because, now get this, you might not remember that it exists when you want information on that topic sometime later. This gray area has been bothering me for years, causing me to clutter my files with junk I never look at because I might want to look at it sometime—and how would I ever even know it's there unless I save it? I'm talking about booklets put out by the government or large corporations only for a short time because they cover a "hot" topic. A perfect example would be those late 1970s full-page advertisements paid for by oil companies to explain the energy problem to us consumers. They are listed in no public index or reference work I know of. Yet I might want them for an article or a book five years from now. So I have saved representative samples. Sheer junk!

Only recently has a workable solution to this problem occurred to me—so simple I wonder I never thought of it before. I merely take notes on the dates the ads appeared in various newspapers, with a brief synopsis of the explanation they offer, and file these notes under my "Energy" subject heading with a reference to them in my index. Now I no longer have to save the original ads. When I want them, I can refer myself to the newspapers in which they appeared, newspapers the public libraries are certain to have for me. *Voilà!*

PLANS AND DREAMS

Part Four of your Comprehensive Filing System is oriented toward the future. Here you keep track of your long- and short-range plans, your hopes and dreams, your random and/or brilliant ideas—anything you want to preserve for future refinement and possible implementation.

You can save all these items in chronological order by the date you first filed them. If there is just too much to leaf through conveniently, you can also sort them by category, by subject, and by level of refinement as you move the items along from initial conception to final implementation.

GENERAL REFERENCE

Another equally important section of your Comprehensive File is your General Reference: A–Z. Here you can put all those names of people you met at conferences and cocktail parties, those titles of books you mean to read, scribbled maps of how to get to your friends' houses, and little booklets you get at the tourist agencies or government offices. If you want to save it and you can't find a place for it anywhere more specific, you can always stick it in here with good hopes of finding it again.

Most of us lose things in alphabetic files as easily as we lose keys in the snow. But you don't have to. Simply get in the habit of filing (and retrieving) items by what they are about, rather than what they are.

For example, say you meet a congressman who promises to help you land a big government contract next time you are in Washington. Don't file his name alphabetically. You may not remember it when you're ready to leave for the Capitol. Instead, carefully place this name in your file under "Government," "Washington," "Sales," or "Congressman," depending on what mental road you will take when you want to retrieve his name again. To be safe, cross-reference this name all over the place.

Or say you are saving a booklet that tells you how to save money on your car insurance. Don't file it under Allstate or State Farm, where you'll never look for it. File it under "Insurance" or "Car." To be even more ingenious, place the booklet in your Daily Prompter timed to surface again a few weeks before you must renew your current auto insurance policy. Then you will see it again automatically when, and only when, you are likely to want to act on it.

What about the names of local baby-sitters? Under "B." Your family doctor? Under "D." What about that book you want to look for and read? Not under the title—you'll forget it. Leave it in your file under the subject, with a cross-reference to your Daily Prompter a month or so ahead. Use your Daily Prompter here only if you really want to get that book. Otherwise, you may be acting highly efficient, but you are certainly wasting your time by taking steps toward a goal you don't really want to achieve.

YOUR TRAVEL FILE

A file on travel information is the sixth part of the system, but only if you travel a lot, or enjoy it very much. This part of the system is strictly a place to keep track of facts, maps, and useful information regarding places you want to or are likely to visit.

For example, business travelers (and others) can keep a separate folder for each location they visit regularly, plus other folders for cities, counties, countries, or continents you hope to see someday. Store here all the interesting articles, relevant maps, tips from people who have been there, and (where possible) experiences you garner yourself—anything that can be of use to you en route to or in specific locations.

Bring the appropriate files with you when you travel. Then, when you're sitting in your hotel room, bored silly and desperate for something to do, you can turn off the tube and search your files for a nice restaurant, an exciting show or theater, a colorful district or neighborhood, or whatever turns you on. Keep track of your good and bad experiences in each location, too, so you can repeat those you want to and avoid those you don't, without wasting any time or effort the second time through.

CREATING A PAPER-WORK SYSTEM

Start with a Wastebasket

One of the best tools for cutting down the size of your paper-work pile is a large wastebasket. That's right, a large wastebasket, because a good-sized one encourages you to use it more than a small one, which may fill up too quickly. The wastebasket is the best place to put a good portion of the paper that comes your way. But once the wastebasket is full, people often find other—more lasting—places for perfectly good trash. This is a shame, since paper work you place in the wastebasket will not come back to haunt you, whereas paper work you store elsewhere will take up a tremendous amount of space and time, no matter how worthless it may be intrinsically.

A large wastebasket is also valuable as one part of a system for sorting your paper work. It's often useful to divide your incoming papers before you tackle them. One good system involves the following categories:

1) Handle Immediately—don't put it down without taking some action on it.

2) Interesting or Useful; Read and Save—your Primary Reading, good category for valuable materials you really should know about.

3) Interesting or Useful; Read and Discard—your Secondary Reading, a larger category in which to place materials it would be nice to peruse, but which may not make it because of other demands on your time. If you don't read it within, say, two weeks, out it goes.

4) File under ————, the place to collect your items for filing until there is enough to make you do it.

5) File 13.

This last is, as you may have guessed, your trusty wastebasket. And one rough measure of how well you manage your time is how large a proportion of all incoming paper goes directly here.

If you have someone to help you, let them sort your paper work before you see it, according to this or some other system that makes sense to you. If you have no help, take a few moments before you start your paper work to sort it thoroughly. Here's how:

a) Stack your incoming paper work on your otherwise clean desk or work surface. Let no other papers be present for this ceremony. Have your stapler and a bold-colored marker ready.

b) Pick up each item in your nonwriting hand, scan it quickly, and decide what to do with it. Let's assume you're using the five-point system above.

c) File your trash immediately. Have your trusty wastebasket close at hand. You can crumple the papers and toss them in, but I prefer to slide them in unfolded, unceremoniously, unworked on.

d) Make a quick note to yourself or your helpers regarding how to handle items for filing. Mark the file in which it belongs, plus other "key words" you think of to help in cross-referencing the item for later retrieval. Write all this boldly at the top, right on the front of the papers. If you don't want to mark it, staple (don't clip) notepaper to the front and write on that. Stack everything for the files in one place.

In this stack include reference material and other records for filing. Put your notes and original paper work earmarked for your Daily Prompter here, too. Basically, if the item doesn't require you to handle it immediately, put it here for filing so it will come up by itself just when you need it later on.

e) Stack up materials you want to read and then save. Put them in a convenient folder with the newest items on top. Take this Primary Reading file with you everywhere, and when you get a few minutes, pull off the top item and read it on the spot. Then mark it for filing, or toss it if you can.

Because this Primary Reading can be so important to what you are trying to accomplish, you owe it to yourself to put reading time into your schedule. Give yourself a few hours a week to start with. Then adjust your total reading time until it's enough to cover what's important, but no more. (Reading for pleasure is something else—can be handled the same way, but deserves a time slot of its own.)

When your Read-and-Save folder gets too thick, pull off items from the bottom and quickly reevaluate their worth before you throw them away. If you haven't read them by now, you probably don't have time for them. Besides, they may be out of date or superseded by other reading matter, or irrelevant to your current interests. Scan them. Don't read them to see if they are worth your time because if you do, you'll be intrigued (you were once before, when you first put this item in the folder, remember?). Or worse, you'll feel so guilty for not reading the item so far ("I really should read this") that you'll stop your really important work to read the thing right now. Retain only what you really want.

Incidentally, you can learn a good lesson if you pay attention to items you discard unread from your Read-and-Save file. Some you don't want anymore. Some are no longer relevant or useful. Some are just plain stupid. Pay attention to this phenomenon, and perhaps you can learn to put less into this file in the first place.

f) Do the same with items to be Read and Discarded, except this is a lower priority file from which to pull items to read. If this file gets too thick, simply pull items from the bottom and toss without looking at them. You certainly don't have time for this stuff, and almost certainly you don't even have the time to see whether you have the time for them. If you do find time to read something from this file, just pass the piece under your scanners, record what's relevant or useful in your brain (this happens automatically), and toss the paper out of your life.

g)   If you can't throw away paper work or file it, you probably will want to take some action on it. In that case, the best step is to take that action immediately. If it's a letter, reply to it right now. If it requires some fact-finding or planning, take the first steps right now. If it requests a decision, make it right now, or start the decision-making process as best you can.

If the paper work calls for a large project, begin it by making a step-by-step plan for completing it. Then get started on step 1 right now. If you are not ready to begin planning for the project, at least start the process of getting ready by involving other people, writing the preliminary letters or inquiries, making the initial phone calls, or whatever.

In general, you can make better use of your time simply by handling the paper in your hand, rather than by shuffling it hither and yon a few times before putting your mind in gear to "work" on it.

There are exceptions, however. For example, if someone sends you a book and asks you to read it, you don't have to finish all 592 pages before you pick up the next paper-work item. But even so, you should put the book where you can find it again, and make a mental or a written plan about when and where you will read it. That done, you can turn to the next item on your desk. At this point, I hope it goes almost without saying: If you make such a plan, you should follow it.

Eliminate Repetition

One source of paper-work drudgery is the need for endless repetition. For example, information from one report has to be reworked or copied over onto one, two, or three other reports. And this goes on every week, sometimes every day. Or you get frequent requests for the answers to the same questions. Or you have to make the same statements, or initiate the same requests, time and time again in the course of whatever you're trying to do.

You can save a lot of this "repeat" time with a few extra minutes to provide some alternatives.

Cheap printing services are a very good answer to some of these situations. I'm talking about both quickie offset printing and machine-made copies. For example, the first thing you probably need is stationery with your name (title, if any), address, and phone number. If you don't care to be fancy, you can buy personalized labels (you-lick-'em or pressure-sensitive) for a few dollars in your favorite stationery store, or even by mail order. Look around, you'll see the offers.

Even though you have stationery, personalized labels save you half a minute or more every time you have to give your name and/or address. Such labels are one of the most profitable $2.00 to $5.00 investments you can make.

For situations where you need to copy information, start looking for duplication equipment you can use. Make a machine copy and attach it to the new form, instead of copying the information by hand. Or make a machine copy and cut-and-paste the information you want to transfer. Not only is this faster, but there's no chance for hand-copying errors that can waste even more of your time when they come back to haunt you.

You can also make copies with carbon paper. Take a few seconds to stack all the sheets you need filled in, and inter-leave the carbons. Then one writing of the information produces all the copies you require.

Make it a policy never to handwrite the same information twice. Suddenly, you will find many opportunities to save time via mechanical copying procedures. These opportunities are worth looking for and using. You may save only a few seconds each time, but you will save hours, even days, of monklike copying by hand in the long run.

Cheap printing is also a great way to eliminate needless repetition of standard answers to questions people commonly ask you. The next time you write an answer to what seems like a standard question, make a duplicate before you send it off. File it where you can find it again. After you use it a few times, and you have refined it or simply like what you have, make several duplicates at one time. Then, next time that standard question comes in, just reach into your files for the answer, staple it to the question (if it comes via correspondence), and send it out.

Try the same procedure for standard questions you ask others, or for standard statements you make to others via your paper work. Print the question or statement, and you will never have to write or type or dictate the darn thing again.

If you want to get a little more elaborate, combine half a dozen or so of your standard "communiqués" on a single sheet of paper. Simply circle or check off the appropriate ones before you send it off. We've all received these forms from government agencies, banks, and other institutions. They are a little tacky, particularly where you want to make a personal impression, but, nevertheless, you can make a strong argument for using them to save your precious time.

A "Book" of Paragraphs

For semi-elaborate correspondence, you can usually save time by creating your own "book" of common paragraphs. Go through your past correspondence, or start fresh from today. Find your best paragraphs on every common subject that normally occurs in your writing. Compile them all into a loose-leaf binder, organized by subject or some other appropriate scheme. Give each paragraph a number. If you have a typist, make sure they get a copy of the binder with the exact same numbers on the paragraphs.

Now creating correspondence is relatively easy. Just leaf through your book until you find the paragraphs you want to use. Make notes to yourself for each letter you want to write, or specify the paragraphs to your typist by code number. Be sure to list the code numbers in the order you want the paragraphs typed. Now give the name, address, and subject heading (see Direct Writing Skills, page 108) and you're done. The letter will go out just as you want it to, in a fraction of the time it would have taken otherwise.

If you don't like your own writing or don't want to make your own book, you can buy books of letters on a wide variety of topics. Check your local business library for such books and give them a trial run before you buy.

Let Others Do It

A basic credo of maximizing your results, applied here to paper work, is to let other people do as much as possible for you. If you are spending too much time on paper work of too little importance to your goals, look around for opportunities to let other people do it: employees or subordinates, people who send you the paper work, people who expect the paper work from you, and payroll, accounting, clipping, reading, or other services that can do some of your paper work.

If you have a secretary, let him or her begin by sorting your mail. After a week or two of watching how you handle your daily mail call, your secretary can probably take over most of this time-consuming chore.

1) You need never see junk mail again unless you want to. Even then, your secretary can throw the stuff in a box in the closet, where you can dig through it for your own enjoyment when you're not busy with something more important. This makes a great change of pace from those hard-driving days under pressure.

2) You need never handle routine correspondence again. Your secretary can learn the responses to four out of five of the items people send you. Teach your secretary to give these responses, and you free yourself for more important activities.

3) You need never compose routine correspondence again. With the aid of your collected book of paragraphs, or with a little native writing skill and some direction from you, almost any secretary can compose a large portion of the letters, memos, reports, and other items required from you. Give up this chore—although you should probably supervise this work until you are confident it is going O.K. Incidentally, there is no need to handle routine work perfectly. Doing it adequately saves time with very little loss of effectiveness.

Even without a secretary, let people who work for you handle "your" paper work regarding what they do. For example, one department supervisor in a large manufacturing company had to spend hours every week filling in "production reports" which detailed how much each worker in his group had turned out during the preceding week. He began saving 80 percent of this time by letting each of these people keep track of their output directly on the forms. He merely checked over what they wrote. After a few months, he could keep the same level of confidence and yet make only spot verification checks, saving even more of this paper-work time.

In another situation, a group leader was supposed to read a long-winded article and pass on the relevant portions to his group. He saved thirty minutes off his paper-work time by refusing to do it this way. Instead, he simply clipped the appropriate paragraphs from the report and distributed them to the appropriate people in his group.

Whatever amount of help you have or don't have, here's something you can do: Write your response right on the originals sent you. Run a machine copy and send the original right back where it came from. If that isn't enough help, look for other ways to put more of the burden on the people who send you the paper work.

For example, a bank sends me an application form for a loan. I send it right back clipped to a copy of a previous loan application that has all the pertinent information. I include a little handwritten note: "Here is all the information I believe you need. Let me know if you need anything further." My idea is to let them neatly copy the details into those tiny blank spaces. I have more important things to do.

"Traveling Files"

Sometimes you spend more time filing and retrieving relevant papers you work on than you spend actually doing the work. If this happens to you, stop putting that paper back in the file. Keep the entire bundle clipped securely into a folder, and let it circulate—but not on your desk—until the project is complete.

For example, a proposed vacation schedule requires a lot of time gathering vacation eligibility data from dozens of scattered personnel files. Then you have to put everything back in the files while you pass the schedule around for verification and approval. And then you have to dig them all out again to make the necessary changes. Instead, simply copy the relevant paper work (less confidential materials, of course), clip it to the schedule and send it around as a package. When you get it back with all suggested changes, notices of conflicts, and requests for time in Somaliland, there comes with it all the reference paper work you need to complete the job. This technique saves so much filing and retrieving time, it's a wonder.

Of course, this method may not help you much when you have

reams of material, large circulation lists, classified data you cannot let out of your office, or projects where you work in long stretches with only short interruptions before the project is complete. But if you look for chances, you'll find plenty of opportunities to use this technique.

TIPS
FOR AN EFFECTIVE OFFICE SYSTEM

Physical Space

Paper work is a physical process, so don't overlook the need for adequate physical facilities to handle the paper flow. For example, if you look at blueprints or large layouts, you need a large expanse of work space on which you lay them flat. You need adequate lighting. And you probably need efficient storage for other large papers you want to keep around. Without adequate equipment, you're wasting your time.

If you receive large volumes of paper work each day, you need the physical facilities to store it, process it, and pass it along or file it. Take a few moments right now to trace the flow of paper around you. Check to see that at each step there is enough room for your normal flow of paper; enough supplies; enough work space; and enough storage for incoming and outgoing paper so you don't have to live with piles all around you.

Once you have everything off your desk, and neatly filed somewhere in your Comprehensive Filing System, you can turn your attention to the physical placement of all these papers. There's almost certainly not enough room to have all this material—in its filing cabinets or old shoe boxes—within arm's reach.

So separate your materials according to how frequently you turn to them. Files, reference materials, and current-project folders you use several times a day belong within easy reach—although not directly on your desk. A low table, cabinet, or set of shelves behind or alongside your work space can hold these items out of sight, but ready when you need them.

Other files, project files, and reference materials you use less frequently can be set up across the room from where you normally keep busy. Dead storage, and items you look at only once or twice a year do not deserve to be in your workroom at all. Keep them out in the hall, in an adjacent room, in a locked storage room, or elsewhere.

Try to arrange your paper work and materials roughly in concentric circles. What you need most frequently should be within arm's reach. The next group should be within a step or two. The next group within several steps, and so on right out the door. This way, you'll automatically save time and energy in the ordinary course of accomplishing what you want.

Time Limits Work

Self-imposed time limits are an excellent tool for reorganizing the goals you work toward.

Essentially, a self-imposed time limit is a figure you create as a maximum daily or weekly allocation to a specific kind of effort. In this case, you might decide to limit your paper work to five hours per week. This means you'll keep careful track of the time you spend on paper work, and when you finish your fifth hour of the week, you stop. That's it! No more! Any leftover paper work will have to wait until next week to receive your attention, or it will have to work its way into some other category in your time schedule.

For example, one shop manager limited his paper work to seven hours, and one week cut himself off before he had had a chance to review his inventories and order more raw materials. Two days later some of his unfinished paper work came back to him as an emergency shortage of raw materials. So that's when he handled it.

You can be a little smarter in setting your paper-work limits by evaluating your paper-work load and giving yourself enough time to do your important paper work—just enough! You reduce the value of your time limits if they give you enough room to include irrelevant or worthless activities.

Refer to a current Time Log to see how much time you are spending on your papers. Is your paper work really worth that much of your time? If you haven't yet done very much to let other people help you, to avoid senseless duplication, to clear your desk, and to sort before you work, you can probably set your paper-work time limit to half of what you currently spend on it. If this seems too drastic, try reducing your time spent on paper work by 10 percent a month for a few months. You'll be surprised how much time you can cut. Almost everyone I have worked with has safely reduced their paper-work time by 40–60 percent with no loss in final effectiveness.

HOW TO HANDLE
YOUR CORRESPONDENCE

Special correspondence is more than routine paper work. It's the unique letter, the original proposal, the personal reply, the expert analysis, the communication that can come only from you. You would have a hard time trying to standardize this material, and most likely it would not be very desirable for you to do so. But that doesn't mean you have to waste time or lower your overall effectiveness level when turning out special correspondence.

The key is to be as thoughtful and original in deciding how to get your special message across as you were in creating your message. For example:

Call, Don't Write

Sometimes, you can get the message across very quickly and effectively with a phone call rather than a letter. For example, when I was editor of a publication, I received dozens of letters from writers wanting assignments. I hardly ever took action on any of them. But I will always remember the impression one writer made on me with a phone call. I experienced her enthusiasm directly, and I found myself giving her extra points for having the initiative to call me, a total stranger. I gave her an assignment on the spot, whereas letter writers had to wait until I got around to them. The phone call worked out well for both of us, saving our time and reducing the demand for laborious correspondence, as well as serving to increase her effectiveness in getting what she wanted.

But in other cases, there may be a smaller time saving. For example, one man I know used the telephone very effectively to convince people they needed his services. But invariably, the last few lines of the phone conversation would go like this: "Gee, it all sounds great, Larry. Can you send us a confirmation letter on this?" "What for?" "Well, we can't make any decisions on something like you're proposing unless we have it in writing."

Larry got a lot of work as a result of his phone calls, so he used them effectively, but they did little to reduce his need for correspondence.

Evaluate each of your special messages, and then decide whether the telephone or the typewriter will be more effective. The phone may be faster—even cheaper if you add in the cost of your time. But you may not save as much if the message will require a letter anyway. A letter may be the better medium for your message if you want more time to think out and polish your remarks. You can rewrite what you say until you get it right. However, on paper you lose both the give-and-take and the emotional contact you can sometimes achieve via direct electronic connection.

The way to get more done in less time here is to be sure to pick the medium you want the first time around, and then to use it as skillfully as you know how, to achieve the success you want.

Let Your Secretary Write It

There's no doubt that you have to be the one to originate most if not all of the special correspondence you send out. That's the definition of special correspondence, in fact. But this does not imply that you must be the one to physically produce it.

For example, it's not unusual to think that letters going out over your signature are yours, even though you may not type them. If you have picked up some or all of the words from other writings and such, the letter is still yours, even though you may not be the writer. Let's take this principle a step farther. For example, a letter can still be yours even though you merely indicate to someone else how to write it. In fact, it can still be yours if you only indicate that your assistant should write it, even if you omit any directions or suggestions whatsoever. As long as *you* are satisfied with the result, you can use this technique to free a lot of your time for other work. Just be sure you *are* satisfied with the result.

To make this plan work, you will probably have to devote some time, initially, toward training the person who will be doing your writing for you. This can take a lot or a little bit of time, depending partly on them and partly on your skills as a trainer. You can start by showing your "correspondence surrogate" what you've written in the past. Indicate which items you think good, which not so good, which you would rewrite if you had to do them over.

Slowly introduce your surrogate to the job by letting him or her work with you to write a few of your special correspondence items. Incorporate her ideas, where appropriate. But stick with your wordings and pet phrases as much as possible. As you gain confidence in your surrogate's writing ability, let her handle some of your writing chores. But check everything before it is mailed. In the next stage, let her write more of your correspondence, and check it briefly just before you sign it. Finally, give all your special correspondence work to your surrogate. When you become totally comfortable with her judgment and her work, you might want to join the ranks of those few top executives who no longer sign or even see their own letters!

Handwritten Replies Save Time

Check out your letter-writing process from your initial desire to write, through first and/or second drafts, rough typing, rewriting, and retyping, all the way out the door. Is what you have to say in your replies always worth all this? If not (and who can answer "yes"?), try a quick solution: handwrite your brief letters and notes and send them off as is.

Sure, they may not look as pretty as formal typewritten letters. But in most cases they can get your message across satisfactorily in a fraction of the time formal letters require. And they can lend a desirable "personal" touch to an otherwise austere and cold communication.

To facilitate this option, keep some notepaper on hand—5½ × 8½ is a good size—and use it often for letters and notes you initiate. It can also work well for letters you get and to which you want to respond, particularly those from people you know personally. Write neatly on one of your notepapers, and sign legibly. Then make a machine copy and send off the original. Again, all this may save you just a few seconds each instance, but over the long run the time and personal energy savings will mount up.

Make It 90 Percent Perfect

This trick is guaranteed to make some of you angry, outraged, or at least upset. The idea is simply to reduce your standards for selected special correspondence from 100 percent to 90 percent perfect. Is that anything to get upset about?

Notice I'm saying "selected" correspondence. If you are writing a proposal for a multimillion dollar contract, you might decide to check every comma and question mark. You might want such a letter to be perfectly perfect. If it's 1776 and you are making a handwritten copy of the Constitution, to be signed by the Continental Congress, again you might want to start over a few times until you get it letter perfect. Thomas Jefferson certainly did.

But how many of those items do you write in a day? Most people pore over their precious prose as though it were timeless verse, yet it usually gets no farther than the local bulletin board, the desk of someone just as overburdened as you, or your mother's house. Except for your mother, does anyone care if you've mistyped "the" as "teh" and fixed it with a neat ballpoint? Believe me: no one will disparage you for a few timely xxxxxxx's, especially if they cover less than 5 percent of your letter.

You may not believe me, but take courage and try it. Be a little imperfect in your correspondence once or twice, and see if anyone even notices. And if someone should notice, ask if they mind. I'm sure you'll find you can cut some time off your special correspondence in this way with little or no reaction from your readers.

Direct Writing Skills

Direct writing is the art of saying what you mean, as accurately as possible, in a relatively short time and space. For letters, there's a direct writing format that allows: return address and signature to be typed from the left margin; no indentations for paragraphs; no flowery opening or closing paragraphs; and numbered listings of items if desired, rather than a narrative flow of words. All of this cuts some typing time, as well as time required to compose what's being typed.

You can do even better by adding a subject line instead of the famous "Dear——." I mean, how often are these people dear to you? And isn't it embarrassing when you can't tell if the person is a man or a woman from their first initial or first name? Omit the salutation we learned in high school. Substitute the effective "subject line." This line (you can type it all in capital letters) states very succinctly what the communication is all about. For example:

NOTES ON OUR RECENT MEETING,

or

RE: YOUR REQUEST FOR LEAVE IN SOMALILAND.

Once you get past the shock of seeing such direct communication in a letter, you begin to realize how beneficial the subject line can be. It not only sets the mood for the entire letter, it saves you whole sentences right away. Instead of:

Dear John:

I have been thinking very hard about your request for leave time in Somaliland, and want to let you know what I am thinking.

You can say:

RE: YOUR REQUEST FOR LEAVE IN SOMALILAND

No.

The art of direct writing is harder than it looks. The basic element required of you is practice. I have been at it a dozen years, and my writing showed noticeable improvement almost from the first. Now I find that a great deal of editing and condensing occurs in my head as I write. You can do the same. Your first step must be to declare your interest in writing directly. Then, simply practice every chance you get and you will gradually and continuously improve.

In this way, it's very much like touch typing: I first learned it in high school, almost as a joke, never thinking to use it as a skill. But from then on, whenever I typed, I used all ten fingers. After four or five years, I developed decent speed without any special practice sessions or special attention to what I was doing. Now, seventeen years later, I'm a whiz on the keyboard. I've saved years' worth of time, literally, over the old hunt-and-peck method (figures available upon request), all without any penalty or extra cost in time.

You'll find the same thing happens to you with direct writing. You'll get better and better, faster and faster, until a few years from now you'll habitually and automatically use your direct writing skills to save composing time on every written product you turn out.

IMPROVING YOUR READING AND WRITING

Modern Techniques Are Available

It's almost unbelievable, but the four popular ways people take in and give out information have remained virtually unchanged for a thousand years. We still do our reading, writing, speaking, and listening almost exactly the way our ancestors did them. And yet, consider how much more information we try to take in and give out in a lifetime.

We'll tackle the skills you need for effective speaking and listening when we discuss meetings, which are—in one sense—speaking and listening gatherings of various sizes. Here we can concentrate on better use of your time when reading and writing. It goes almost without saying that one basic way to improve your use of reading time is simply to read faster. This is not an endorsement of a speed-reading program. To my knowledge, speed-reading skills you might pay hundreds of dollars to learn are freely available in college and extension courses, textbooks on reading and learning, and mail-order learning programs of various kinds.

I suggest you learn these skills and use them where appropriate. It just doesn't make sense to read at 200 words per minute when you can gather the same information at 300, 400, or 500 words per minute. You may not be one of those rare people who reads novels at 1,000 words per minute with full enjoyment and comprehension, but so what! You do enough reading that even a 10 percent boost in reading speed will free up some time for other items on your agenda. That said, let's turn to some other techniques you can use to improve your use of reading and writing time.

Skimming and Scanning

The bane of most slow readers is their overwhelming desire to read every single word, usually in order. This will kill you. Imagine a situation in which your TV tuner is locked. You have to watch an entire day's programming on a single channel before you can switch one channel in either direction. It could take you a solid week just to move to the station you want! This would certainly discourage channel changing, and no doubt limit your enjoyment of the tube. Fortunately, you are perfectly free to change channels any time you like, as often as you like, as many channels in either direction as you like. Doesn't that give you a great deal of freedom to pick and choose the best of what is broadcast?

You get the same freedom in printed materials: the freedom to start on any page, read as much or as little as you like, and skip as far as you like in either direction as often as you like. So why limit yourself to plodding start to finish, word by word, page by page? When you break free of these limitations, you start skimming and scanning.

We can define skimming as the act of running your eyes quickly over a printed page, picking out headings, charts, and other eye-catching items. In skimming, you try to catch the main points of a printed page by reading only the prominent details. You can look at first and last sentences of paragraphs, too, since they usually offer good clues to the main points under discussion.

Scanning, on the other hand, is the careful examination of the outline or construction of a piece of writing, with a view toward understanding it without reading it. In scanning, you look at the table of contents, the list of illustrations, charts and/or tables, the index, and the appendices. You try to determine what the writing is about, and you try to zero in on the location of the juiciest meat. Only when you think you have located this meat do you turn there and begin to skim.

To save time, you do a minimum of solid reading. You go over every word only when you have trouble understanding the meaty parts on your first or second skim. In traditionally structured research articles, for example, you may read only the Summary. In other items, you may do no reading at all, or you may read the few paragraphs you have identified as being of most importance to you. This breakaway from word-by-word reading doesn't occur overnight. It may take you a while to break old reading habits, or to get comfortable reading so few words per page. Nevertheless, skimming and scanning are valuable means to cover more reading ground in a given reading time.

Collected Readings

Concentration is a basic principle for getting better results. Just as the assembly line helps people turn out larger numbers of similar items, concentrating or bunching similar tasks gives you assembly-line advantages. You can apply this to your reading by collecting materials you intend to read and sitting down to read them all at once. You can do even better by grouping materials on a single or small set of related topics and reading these all together.

Your "Read and Save"/"Read and Discard" files can be the places you collect your readings. Or you can create a set of special subject files in which you collect what you want to read for your next scheduled reading session.

The Reading Hour

Armed with a collection of similar items to read, and dedicated to your skimming-and-scanning tactics, your next step is to sit down and read. But here, too, you can get more done in less time with a subtle shift in old habits.

Basically, bunch your reading time. Sure, you can make five wasted minutes a little more fruitful by reading something from one of your reading files. But that's not the way to get all your reading done. Instead, dedicate one hour per week, or more, to pure and simple reading.

Find a comfortable location and secure yourself against interruptions for at least an hour. That's a good time period for deep concentration without fatigue. If you need more reading time and you can go longer at a stretch, do so. If you need less reading time, do the one-hour session less often. For the hour, sit comfortably with a decent light on your reading, and scan, then skim each piece. Make notes about relevant information right on the paper (unless it's a book you cannot mark up, in which case, make separate notes keyed to the book's page numbers).

Some people work through their reading faster if they use a timer to limit their attention on a single item to ten minutes or less (time limits, again). But this depends on your personal style. It doesn't matter how you do it, so long as you work through each reading item quickly and accurately. The notes save you time later by making recall of what you have read faster than if you had to rescan and reskim the item you want to remember.

Cooperative Reading

Some people have a great deal of "must do" reading: for their jobs, their hobbies, or personal interests and enjoyment. There just isn't enough time to allow such a big slice for reading.

The solution can be a cooperative reading set up. In this technique, you share your reading load with others who have the same or similar reading needs. For example, an engineering group at an aerospace company has more required reading to keep current in the field than they can possibly do. So they have formed a six-headed reading cooperative. Each member reads only one sixth of the journals and articles he would have to read on his own. Twice a month, they hold a briefing, where each member reports on the good items he found, and gives reference information so anyone interested can find and read the original piece.

Most reading cooperatives have a relatively large turnover of membership during the start up phase. Many people express interest and want to join, but after a few reading periods, most find it too hard to keep up their responsibility to the other members. Nevertheless, if you keep trying, you will find a group of readers with interests similar to yours, and forge a cooperative reading group that can cut your reading time significantly.

The Summary Statement

When it comes to reading and writing, one of the best ways to save everyone's time is to give and demand a summary statement. This is a short paragraph that summarizes the subject, facts, and conclusions of whatever piece of writing is to follow.

For best results, the summary statement should be set at the very beginning of the writing. In a lengthy report, you might place it on its own page. For shorter pieces, it might just be set off by separate margins on the first page. Wherever you place it, the summary statement saves the reader's time by providing the gist of the piece in a few seconds of reading. Then it's up to the reader to decide whether or not to continue.

The writer benefits, too, from the summary statement. Not only will the piece be read by more people, but it will probably be read sooner, because it's so fast to read the summary statement, and that's all most people want. If you're waiting for an answer to what you've written, your summary statement will facilitate both reading and responding to your piece. In fact, in some cases, you can write a good enough summary statement and leave off the main body of text. No one will miss it, and you'll save time in the writing.

Cook Before Composing

This is the secret of much effective writing. Not only does it make the writing process go faster, but it often results in outright better writing.

The secret is not to jump off too soon when it comes to choosing words. Instead, study the material you're going to write about. Take extra time to be sure you understand it. Then outline what you want to say, or at least make a note of what you want to achieve with your writing.

Now comes the cooking part: Put the work aside for a day or more. Let your subconscious brain (some would say the right half of your brain) ponder the problem and live with it. If you have enough time, don't rush into any writing. Wait for "inspiration" to strike you. Sure, writing is 10 percent inspiration and 90 percent perspiration, but you might as well have that 10 percent extra if you can get it. Even if you cannot wait for full "inspiration," the time you give yourself to "simmer" the material will result in a better blended, more effective piece of writing.

What actually happens is this: your brain (or brain half) takes real time to absorb new information, integrate it with older information already absorbed, and come up with a well-meshed synthesis of everything it knows. We call this synthesis "understanding." When you get it, very often the light in your head goes on and you feel a bolt of "inspiration" strike you. Suddenly, you know exactly how to write what you want to say, and the enthusiasm this generates makes you want to start right now.

To put this to use, all you need do is allow some elapsed time between the time you finish preparing to write, and the time you start writing. The more time you give your brain to "cook" the new material, the closer you get to understanding it well, and thus the better job of writing you can do.

Dictate, Don't Handwrite

If you're moving through this book in traditional fashion—word by word—you may have come across a section advising you to handwrite some or all of your correspondence. And now I'm telling you the opposite! Well, read a little farther, and you'll see that I'm talking about two different kinds of writing.

Here I'm discussing your longer writing projects such as reports, in-depth analyses, and proposals. In general, if it takes more than five or ten minutes to write it, don't write it at all: dictate.

There are at least three important advantages that dictating has over writing by hand.

1) You can talk two or three times faster than you can write by hand; sometimes this multiple climbs as high as five or six. There's a clear time-saving advantage here, despite the stop/start nature of most dictation.

2) You can dictate comfortably in situations where writing is impossible. For example, you can dictate while driving, in jostling trains, while walking, even lying in bed with the lights out.

3) Dictating is difficult if you are unprepared. Almost anyone can write pure emptiness without a moment's preparation, and some can even make it sound like it's on the topic. But few of us feel comfortable dictating unless we have a very good idea of the points we're trying to make. This means that dictating time has a higher chance of being useful time, while time spent writing may or may not prove worthwhile.

If you have a secretary, it's doubly advantageous to dictate to a machine rather than a person. This way, your secretary can stay busy while you get the material on tape, cutting required "people hours" by one third. And tests have shown transcription typing to be faster than typing from shorthand notes, so that's another time saver.

To make your dictation go smoothly, it's advisable to make some written notes prior to speaking your first word. Depending on your dictation skill, you will want anything from a total outline to a simple list of words to jog your memory. Whatever you have in front of you, follow it. Don't let the machine set your pace; make sure it serves you. Also, you might find it helpful to:

a) practice dictation a few times before trying it for real,

b) cross off items on your outline as you cover them to prevent repetition, and

c) review the whole tape before sending it for transcription.

It's most important, though, to think of your dictated material as a first draft only. This way, you won't be so nervous or perfectionist in the dictation process. It still saves time to dictate a first draft, then make corrections in pencil, especially when compared with the time cost of handwriting the first draft yourself. And don't forget, as you gain dictating skill, your first draft material will get closer and closer to final draft quality.

You'll find more dictation tips in Chapter 7, A Concise Program for the Busy Executive.

Professional Writers

If you have too much writing to do, and too many other demands on your time, consider giving your writing assignments to a professional. For example, corporate presidents and political candidates have long had professionals to write their speeches for them.

It could make sense for you too. Remember, you can achieve more if you steadily devote your efforts to what you do best, as well as what only you can do. You may be able to claim, legitimately, that the writing people want from you would best be done by others.

Professional writers demand a certain amount of your time in order to give you exactly what you want. But if you have a lot of writing to do, the time economics allow you to spend time selecting and working with writers and still come out ahead when compared with the time you would spend doing the writing on your own.

THE IMPORTANCE OF DELEGATION

If you have absolutely no one to help you do anything, and if you plan never to have anyone to help you, you can probably skip this section and not lose much. But for almost everyone else, delegation is an extremely valuable way to do more in less time. The guidelines for delegation give you a clear method for getting more done in less time by adding the energy of other people to your own.

But don't think for a minute that delegation is a way to shirk responsibility or get out from under a heavy work load. All it does is pyramid you and your efforts so you're in control of more than your own time. When you delegate, you gain influence over other people's time, as well. And that gives you the responsibility to try to use their time as well as you try to use your own.

Delegation properly done saves much more time and obtains just as satisfactory results as doing the work yourself. But to delegate properly, you need a basic pattern. Exhibit A shows you a Flow Chart of the delegation process. Keep this Flow Chart in mind as you proceed.

EXHIBIT A

Delegation Flow Chart

Decide to delegate task.
↓
Select appropriate delegate.
↓
Describe desired results, resources, contacts,
deadlines, and other factors to delegate.
↓
Listen to delegate's reaction.
↓
"Negotiate" delegation agreement.
↓
Agree on reporting method and schedule.
↓
Complete the project.
↓
Evaluate the project.

Plan First

Poorly planned delegation is often wasted time. Before you talk to that other person and get them working on your project, you had better know precisely a number of important details:

1) Exactly what do you want that person to achieve, and how will both of you know when it is achieved? How much room is there in this goal for modifications, additions, and deletions your "delegate" may want to install? What are the reasons for any absolute limitations you decree?

2) Exactly what resources (materials, budget, experiences, and power) can you give your "delegate"? Who should they work with? In what relationship? Is all this enough to achieve what you want? If not, what else has to be gathered, and how?

3) Exactly how much leeway can you give your delegate to implement his or her own ideas, plans, and methods on the road to the designated achievement? For best results, you should offer as much leeway as you can, and allow your delegate to take as much of this as he or she wants.

4) Exactly what deadlines apply to this delegated assignment?

5) Exactly what role do you wish to play in reaching the designated achievement? Why?

6) Exactly what method will you use to keep in touch with your delegate's progress?

Do It Right the First Time

Once you know all this, you can start talking with your proposed delegate and negotiate a satisfactory working agreement.

1) Can your delegate accept the goal you have in mind, and work toward it? Or if not, can you reach agreement on a goal you both will accept?

2) Can your delegate handle the assignment as it stands, with the resources you can make available? Can they gather on their own whatever else they may need? Can they work with the people they must, the way they must?

3) Is your delegate satisfied with the creative limits you are imposing?

4) Does your delegate appear able to meet required deadlines on this assignment?

5) Is your delegate comfortable with the role you wish to play? If not, can you reach agreement on a different role for you?

6) Does your delegate understand the reporting process you want to use on this assignment? Can you reach agreement on crucial phases of the project so you can time your progress-reporting schedule accordingly?

In the old days, many people assumed that delegation meant ordering someone meek to do exactly as you would do if you only had more time. But with the advent of assertiveness training, it's getting harder and harder to find such meek people. Besides, careful investigations seem to show that people give better results if they "own" a portion of the project. This is not Socialist propaganda. "Ownership" here refers to having a hand in the shaping of the project: being involved in planning it and having leeway in how you help carry it out.

Thus, modern delegation consists of negotiating a work agreement between you and your delegate so that: a) you set forth the skeleton of what you want to achieve, and b) your ideal delegate takes ownership through having the freedom to flesh things out to his or her own taste.

In reality, delegates run the whole spectrum from Bob Cratchit to Tom Sawyer. And so do delegators. So you have to modify the delegation process to meet whatever power and personal requirements may emerge. Any approach is O.K., just so you both agree on certain minimum performance parameters which are later met.

Delegate, Don't Dispose of

You may have noticed a certain insistence on some kind of prearranged reporting process in all of the above. This is to protect both of you during and after the delegation period. Reporting on progress is an important part of delegation from several standpoints.

1) The formal reporting process insures that you, as delegator, will keep in general touch with the project over the weeks or months it may run. Put a note concerning each task you delegate in your Daily Prompter so you are automatically reminded to keep on top of its progress and problems.

2) The reporting process encourages your delegate to think of you as backup, and to come to you when events start moving too fast.

3) You have smartly geared the reporting schedule to lag a few days behind crucial events in the project's development. This

way, if anything goes wrong, you will find out about it during the report, or by the absence or postponement of a report that's due.

Above and beyond formal reports, you retain final responsibility for what you delegate. This means you can't get rid of something unpleasant merely by delegating it. Even more important regarding your responsibilities is this: It's grossly unfair and often unethical for you to delegate certain of your responsibilities. Particularly in corporate or bureaucratic organizations, it's wrong to delegate within certain specific areas of your responsibility.

1) Confidentiality. If the material involved is confidential, you should not have a delegate handle it for you.

2) Discipline. You have to do your disciplining in person. Delegating this is both unfair and undesirable.

3) Morale. No one can be your morale officer. This is something you must keep high on your own.

4) Problems. It would be nice to have someone take your crises and emergencies off your hands, but they really belong to you. You can delegate specific parts of handling them, but you should keep the overall lead. If someone solves your problems for you, you'll lose points. If you solve them yourself, you'll gain. You'll even gain—posthumously—if you go down with the ship.

In addition to retaining what you must and receiving reports on a prearranged schedule, the good delegator does play backup. But it's important to draw the line between playing backup and playing nursemaid. In "nursemaid," no one makes a move without you, and you are far too indispensable to be out of touch for a moment. You haven't delegated here, you've merely taken on a few more arms and legs to direct.

When you play backup, you are available by appointment only to listen to your delegate's problems as well as suggested solutions. You help by asking questions, providing feedback, and offering encouragement where appropriate. You definitely do not allow yourself to be buttonholed on your way out of your office, or laden with chores at any time. In fact, a reliable indicator of how well you are delegating is who has the next move. If your delegate has it, you are on the right track. If you have delegated an assignment, but nevertheless you have the next move, something is wrong with your technique.

Upgrade Through Delegation

One of the most common problems preventing good delegation is said to be a lack of well trained, qualified people. The common refrain goes something like this: "I just don't have anyone I can delegate to." You may have joined this chorus yourself. But a lack of qualified people is not always the primary problem.

For example, in one Eastern big-city school district, the school board administrators were constantly pressured with too much to do and not enough people to whom they could delegate. They had the standard complaint: lack of trained, qualified people. But on looking closer, they began to see how their own poor delegation habits prevented their subordinates from acquiring the training or the qualifications. In some cases, administrators delegated so perversely they, in effect, prevented the school board staff from using the training and qualifications they already possessed.

Delegation is most often thought of and used as a tool to unburden you from unwanted work and time demands. But it works equal wonders when used as a tool to teach, provide experience, and through exposure to upgrade the people around you. In fact, the two uses go hand in hand.

For example, a typical overworked executive suddenly received authority to oversee considerably more of the operations within his organization. Since he was already working a full day, the only way to find time for the new activities was to slough off some of the old ones. Delegation was a good tool for this. In addition, the expansion of his authority put him in line for a move upward toward the company presidency. And that, he realized, could never happen unless he had one or more subordinates groomed to take his place. Delegation was a good tool for this, too.

In another situation, a woman home all summer long with her children began training them to: straighten their own rooms, make and pour their own drinks, change clothes themselves, put dirty clothes in the laundry basket, and select their own menus from what was available in the house. These were all tasks she could "delegate" to them first as a means of making better use of her time, and also as a way to "upgrade" her children's skills and abilities.

The "open secret" behind getting good, qualified people to support your efforts is to make the people around you more experienced, knowledgeable, and skillful. You do this by giving them plenty of tough practice under your watchful eye. Delegation is one of the best tools for this kind of training. Here's a proven method that may work for you:

1. Organize all the tasks under your control, in order of a) importance, and b) difficulty.

2. Cross off all the tasks now handled by other people, delegated, or otherwise not a time problem for you.

3. Begin delegating tasks from the bottom of what remains.

4. The first time you delegate a particular task to a particular person, give as much supervision and support as you feel that person will need to maximize the chances for success on the project.

5. Each succeeding time you delegate the same task to the same person, slightly reduce the support and supervision you provide. After a few trials, you will reach a stable, acceptable balance between the results he/she obtains, and the amount of time you give to supervising him.

6. Keep delegating more and more of the list until: a) you have delegated everything, or b) you have saturated the people around you and they cannot handle one more delegated responsibility.

7. While this only indirectly relates to upgrading through delegation, be sure to use the time you free up through delegation for the most useful, most valuable purposes you can find.

Shedding Through Delegation

Most people have a strong tendency to retain activities from their past even when these well-practiced actions are no longer useful, effective, or sometimes even appropriate to their new situation. You tend to get used to certain tasks. You come to enjoy certain others. And you keep giving time to them even though you have more important responsibilities on your mind. But as your life, career, and/or any situations develop, these comfortable actions tend to lose their purpose and provide less satisfaction than some of the newer tasks more appropriate to your position, skills, and abilities.

For example, a teacher was promoted to an administrative post in a very fine school district. But teaching was such a comfortable, habitual pattern of behavior that she spent a great deal of time on routine work with teachers. She went out of her way for such work as analyzing textbooks and supervising nearby classrooms because she was trying to relive her old job. Once she realized what her pattern of choices signified, she was able to delegate much of her classroom-related activities and replace them with new projects requiring new skills.

You can accomplish this process of consciously shedding old habits, tasks, and activities in favor of new and more satisfying replacements through delegation. In fact, delegation makes the process easier because you continue to supervise your delegate, so you tend to "cut the cord" more slowly. When the only other way to shed a task is to quit it abruptly, completely, and finally, you tend to balk. Delegation makes shedding such tasks a little more likely.

Schedule Your Delegation

While the process of delegation generally gives you more time for your most important projects, the act of delegating can sometimes disrupt your day. For example, say you receive a letter, memo, or some other reminder of a project you want to accomplish. But in the interests of better effectiveness, you decide to delegate it. Here's what might happen. First, you call for your delegate (disrupting their use of time). Then you think through the assignment you want to delegate very quickly (wasting your time and more of your delegate's). Finally, you make the assignment (spending time you could use more productively some other way). Even worse, you may repeat this pattern several times a day, wasting extra time on each occurrence.

The better way is to schedule a "delegation period" in advance. When you recognize a task for someone else to handle, make an appointment with that "delegate" to discuss the assignment. Then file the paper work in your Daily Prompter. You can make the appointment for later the same day if there is a rush. But most of the time, you can benefit from concentrating your delegation time. Wait until you have a few tasks to delegate, even if you're going to give them to several different people. You will make better use of everyone's time if you schedule a single delegation time for all the current assignments. This gives you an opportunity to think through the assignment(s) you want to make, and also puts the act of delegation in your schedule where you want it, not just where it pops up.

MEETING MADNESS:
HOW TO USE, EVALUATE,
AND AVOID UNWANTED GATHERINGS

Meetings are one of the best and most common methods of accomplishing any work. However, most meetings are boring, rhetorical, and long-winded, too lengthy, too crowded, and worst of all relatively unproductive. At one point, I had the firm policy of trying to avoid all meetings whenever and wherever I could. Now I have softened somewhat. I accept about 10 percent of my invitations to meetings, and I attend these with the knowledge that either: a) I will control the meeting and run it effectively, or b) I cannot control it, and so must facilitate the meeting as best I can and simply endure the rest.

If you are in the role of enduring your meetings, there are some points you can contribute to the smooth running and effectiveness of a meeting. Some of what a leader can do can also be done by an alert attendee. But if you are in or can take control of a meeting, there is a great deal more you can do to make that meeting exciting, effective, and extremely productive.

Here are some useful ideas:

Speaking at Meetings

Whatever purpose they serve or agenda they follow, most meetings respond to good oration. The smooth talker can sway a meeting far more powerfully than the person with better ideas who lacks speaking experience. For this reason, you can make better use of the time you spend at meetings if you practice and develop your speaking skills:

1. Know what you want to say before you open your mouth. Unless you are a natural orator, you can benefit from a plan. There is a novelty slogan I love that applies here very well: "CAUTION: Be sure brain is engaged before putting mouth in gear."

2. Jot a list of key words on a tablet in front of you to prompt your speaking. In many meetings it may be some time before you get the "floor" again, so list each point as you think of it, and make all of them when you have the chance to speak.

3. Don't bother with flowery phraseology or "housekeeping" comments such as: "In reply to what Mary said . . ." or "I know this has been said before, but I want to repeat it." Your meaty words will convey all this housekeeping information to anyone paying attention. (If you must repeat what others have said, and you probably shouldn't, just go ahead and do it. Why announce your lack of original thought?)

4. Be extremely concrete both in terms of the points you make, and the benefits you expect the group to receive if they go along with you. In general, anyone who can misunderstand you will almost certainly do so. But you can minimize misunderstandings in advance if you stay with specifics.

5. Say what you intended to say. Then stop. At the least, this tactic saves you some time and promotes a quick flow in the meeting. At best, your points seem more powerful and exert some "leadership by example" both for what you want, and for how you would like the meeting to proceed.

Listening at Meetings

The other half of the process at meetings is listening. This means paying active attention to all of what each speaker says, means, and privately thinks as evidenced by all that you know of him or her. Here are some useful techniques for listening at meetings:

1. Take brief notes on what each person says. Devote a whole page of your tablet, or a portion of the top page, to each attendee, depending on how much space you think you'll need. Then use

codes, abbreviations, and key words to record what they say every time they speak. You can then look at all their comments to understand any individual's point of view.

2. People speak slower than you can think. So you have "extra" time between words and sentences to analyze what they are saying. Do so.

3. Listen for the meaning of their words, and for their motivation. Apply what you know about the person to their comments and look for underlying ideas, attitudes, and feelings. This will help you understand them better, and may help you find a way to persuade them to do what you prefer.

Rate Your Meetings

The simple act of evaluating the quality and productivity of your meetings improves every meeting that follows. Here is a ten-item scale for rating any meeting you attend. Give the meeting a rating of 0–10 points for each item depending on how well the meeting fulfills it:

1. Starts on time?

2. Has a written agenda?

3. Everyone present and prepared?

4. Follows written agenda in order, without digression or backtracking?

5. Leader encourages participation?

6. Plenty of discussion of important points, without repetition?

7. General agreement or consensus by end of meeting?

8. Everyone clear regarding outcome of meeting, what they are to do as a result of meeting, and when they are to do it?

9. Agenda completed?

10. Ends on time?

Use Work Sheet 14 to keep track of these factors. Use a fresh copy for each meeting, and keep the completed ones as a record of your meeting experiences.

WORK SHEET 14

Meeting Rating Sheet

Meeting Leader: **Date/location:**

Purpose:

Attendees:

Rating Criteria	Rating (0-10)
1. Starts on time?	0-1-2-3-4-5-6-7-8-9-10
2. Has a written agenda?	0-1-2-3-4-5-6-7-8-9-10
3. Everyone present and prepared?	0-1-2-3-4-5-6-7-8-9-10
4. Follows written agenda in order, without digression or backtracking?	0-1-2-3-4-5-6-7-8-9-10
5. Leader encourages participation?	0-1-2-3-4-5-6-7-8-9-10

6. Plenty of discussion of
important points,
without repetition?   0-1-2-3-4-5-6-7-8-9-10

7. General agreement or
consensus by end
of meeting?   0-1-2-3-4-5-6-7-8-9-10

8. Everyone clear
regarding outcome
of meeting, what they
are to do as a result
of meeting, and when
they are to do it?   0-1-2-3-4-5-6-7-8-9-10

9. Agenda completed?   0-1-2-3-4-5-6-7-8-9-10

10. Ends on time?   0-1-2-3-4-5-6-7-8-9-10

Rate Your Meeting Leaders

If you rate a lot of meetings run by the same few people, you may
begin to notice that the meetings run by certain people consistently
score higher than those run by others. This is almost certainly a sign
of the meeting leader's skill. Make your meetings more effective by
using the highest scoring meeting leader available to run the important meetings that you call or control.

Calculate the Cost of Your Meetings

Many people like meetings so much that they convene them for little or no reason. For example, businesses very often hold regular
"department meetings" even when there is nothing important to discuss, or a decision maker will call a meeting to get five people's help
in making a simple choice. Some people even use meetings the way
some baseball players use chewing tobacco: as a habit. It has been
my experience that you need strong reasons to deter these people
from their chosen pastime. And one very strong reason can be the

prohibitive cost of a meeting that doesn't produce much value. You may not be able to get such people to dislike meetings in general, but you can get them to think twice about calling one particular meeting if you point out what it will cost in comparison to its likely benefits.

(Of course, this tactic is much less effective in situations where the cost of the attendee's time is hidden or minimized as with, for example, volunteers. In situations where someone volunteers time to help a cause, the people behind the "cause" have some moral responsibility not to waste that person's time in fruitless, ineffective, unnecessary meetings. You may not be able to make any impact with this argument. But again, you may. It's certainly worth trying.

(In situations where there are no hard-and-fast dollar expenditures for the attendees' time, the same principle holds. Whether or not money changes hands, everyone's time has some value if only because it could have been spent doing something more valuable than for what it was used. Dollar figures are simply the lowest common denominator we use to try to compare the values of apples and oranges.)

You calculate the cost of a meeting very simply:

1. Get the (contemplated or actual) attendance list. Calculate the rough hourly rate for every attendee. A person's hourly rate roughly equals their annual salary plus overhead (usually about as much as the annual salary) divided by 2,000 (the approximate number of hours people work in a year). You can express this mathematically as:

$$2 \times \text{Salary} \div 2{,}000 = \text{Rough Hourly Rate}$$

or

$$\text{Salary} \div 1{,}000 = \text{Rough Hourly Rate}$$

2. Add up the rough hourly rates for all the attendees to find the rough hourly cost of the meeting.

3. Multiply by the number of hours the meeting lasts (or will last) to find the approximate total cost of the meeting.

Now compare this cost with the benefits likely to result from the meeting. How you calculate these benefits will depend in large measure on the purpose of the meeting. However, think in the following terms to begin estimating or calculating the benefits of this meeting:

1. If this meeting were not held at all, what would happen and what would this cost? If this meeting is held, by how much can it likely reduce that cost?

2. If this meeting were not held at all, what will *not* happen and how much benefit might be lost? If this meeting is held, how much of this benefit can likely be obtained?

Now compare the cost of the meeting with its likely benefits. Is the meeting worthwhile? If so, hold it with confidence. If not, find some other, less time-consuming way to accomplish the same results.

How to Avoid Meetings

Meetings serve undeniable purposes. Most obviously, they let people make direct contact with each other. This in turn leads to other important interactions:

a) exchange of ideas and attitudes,

b) stimulation of thought and feeling,

c) sizing up of other people, and

d) establishing personal relations,

to name only a few.

However, many people call and attend far too many meetings in relation to what their meeting time accomplishes. You'll be safer if you know how to avoid any unwanted meetings.

There are four basic ways to avoid meetings:

1. Use telephones to keep in close contact with other people. This way, many of the interactions that meetings promote are already in progress. This means you may be able to accomplish some of your purposes without a meeting.

2. Use written communication in place of meetings. This works particularly well to replace "news conferences," or any meetings called to spread information and not intended for decision making, idea sharing, or stimulation. Many routine meetings—or portions of meetings—can fruitfully be replaced with a written report or summary.

3. Delegate your attendance. This technique does nothing to prevent the meeting; it simply pulls you out of it. Instead of attending in person, you send someone who: a) says what you intended to say, and b) reports to you what other people said and what they answered to any questions you submitted.

4. Substitute idea books for so-called "thinking sessions." Many times people call meetings to thrash out ideas, to "brainstorm," and to "bounce ideas around" in an effort to solve problems or originate actions. I firmly believe in such meetings, but sometimes you can use an idea book instead to save time or eliminate one of too many meetings.

The idea book is a plain notebook, titled with the purpose of the meeting it replaces. You leave the book somewhere accessible, so everyone who would have been invited to the meeting can spend time with it. Everyone on the list: 1) enters his or her thoughts, ideas, suggestions, and comments in the notebook on a regular basis, and 2) reads what all others have written before making new entries. Over a period of a few days or weeks, the idea book blossoms out with the same or better quality ideas and exchanges that might have occurred in a meeting. Sometimes it produces even better results because the elapsed time between each person's entries gives each of them time to consider many factors more fully in their thinking.

However, the black-and-white nature of an entry in an idea book may inhibit some people. That's why it's important that the idea book be as free and open as a brainstorming session: No criticisms, no judgments at all at first. Only after people have found a good number of options and alternatives should the idea book be thrown open for criticism, evaluation, and the creation of something practical and useful from the first set of entries.

One-on-One Meetings

Talks with one other person are not generally recognized as "meetings," but they contain many of the same time-wasting dangers, and they respond to many of the same useful techniques.

Make sure your one-on-one meetings:

1. Have time limits, and start and end on time.

2. Have agendas and specific purposes. Make sure that one or both of you have the resources, authority, information, and anything else you need to accomplish the meeting's purposes. If you don't have what you need, the meeting is a waste of time.

3. End with both of you in agreement on what was accomplished, if anything. Without such agreement, chances are that: a) the meeting did not accomplish what you or the other person thought it did, and b) you'll have to hold another meeting to clarify and redo the events of this meeting. It's obviously more effective to accomplish your purposes this first time.

Meetings for Planning

Meetings organized to plan an event or action require special handling to keep them running on track and working effectively. These meetings emphasize thought over action, situations, and circumstances as well as potential objectives. This means you have to discuss issues, considerations, and repercussions at great length with people representing all parts of the plan and interested in all sorts of special factors. The culmination of the meeting is very abstract, nothing more than a series of decisions that bring you to the best plan possible.

The planning process is cumbersome enough without gumming it up unnecessarily. To streamline and grease the wheels of your planning sessions:

1. Invite only those who can bring to the plan such necessary items as: authority, resources, and/or implementation.

2. Select a meeting leader powerful enough to control the people in attendance, but democratic enough to facilitate everyone's involvement. A planning meeting is not worthy of its name if one person "runs" it and forces his or her plan on everyone else.

3. Make the first item on the agenda the formulation of the plan's purpose: its goal. Once people agree on this, they can evaluate every aspect of the plan in terms of its contribution to or detraction from this purpose.

4. In general, the simplest plans are the best. If the plan becomes

unwieldy, encourage everyone to go back to the agreed-upon purpose and look for a simpler way to achieve it.

5. Spend as much time as it takes to get a useful, workable plan. While this process may be time costly, a useful plan saves you and everyone else involved a great deal more time when you put it into action.

6. Don't plan in a vacuum. Have people at the planning meeting who can verify that your tentative plans are workable. Otherwise, uninformed but grandiose thinkers will make plans that are tough to implement. And it works in reverse, too. Planning committees often get stuck for ways to do a job when anyone with the right experience knows four separate ways to do it fast, right, and inexpensively.

Action Meetings

You have to run things a little differently when the meeting is called to carry out a previously developed plan. The action meeting can be anything from an "envelope stuffing party" to a political caucus, from a friend helping you exchange sports car engines to a board of directors struggling for power in a penthouse suite. In such a meeting, the emphasis is on the results you can achieve. And to be highly effective you have to keep your eye on the likely outcome, no longer on potential, every minute.

To make your action meetings more successful and effective:

1. Invite only those who are needed. Too many people in the meeting will confuse everyone and create no time-saving or performance-improving benefit.

2. Select a strong meeting leader who can delegate assignments, make decisions quickly, and throw all effort and resources into effective implementation of the plan.

3. Start the agenda with a brief review of the purpose of the meeting, its goal, and the action required to reach that goal. Once everyone understands the purpose they are trying to achieve, everyone can work more effectively as the leader designates toward the common goal.

While you should always tell the people working with you what you want to achieve, in some circumstances you must be a little more discreet than in others. A political caucus is an example of a meeting where it is not always politic to announce your plan at the beginning. One reason is that the meeting's purpose involves more negotiation than simple action. Some of the people at the meeting are going to *act,* and others are going to *react,* often in unpredictable ways. In cases like this, it is often fruitful to have two meetings: First, a private meeting with your team at which you go over your agenda, specify your purposes and objectives, and make tentative work assignments; then, the working session in which the negotiation or action actually takes place.

4. Realize that few plans are carried out to perfection. In the heat of action, you will almost certainly have to settle for less than you want in some parts of the plan. In other portions of it, you may have to invent whole new ways to achieve the results you planned on. And in some cases, you may have to abandon the plan entirely and improvise as best you can.

For example, one group of parents had a plan to confront their children's teachers and insist on changes in some of the class curricula. But in the middle of the action meeting, the parents had to abandon their planned changes and work out a compromise that both sides could accept.

In another situation, a trade show display firm called a final working session to put together its product for a client. But problems developed and the final plans had to be revised on the spot in order to finish the display in time for the trade show. Be alert for such problems in your own action meetings. You may have to revise or even abandon your plans when you cannot achieve the results the plan calls for as readily as you expected. This "resistance" may be a sign that your plan needs settling, invention, or improvisation in order to yield an acceptable, effective conclusion.

News Meetings

These are briefings, announcements, and, to an extent, training sessions where the main thrust of communication is from the leader or a designated speaker to a theoretically receptive audience. To handle these meetings well, you must:

1. Have a complete and clear idea of the information, attitudes, and ideas you want to convey.

2. Have a plan for conveying what you want as clearly, accurately, and concisely as possible.

3. Use technology and techniques to get your message(s) across effectively. This means bombarding your audience with sensory material, including: spoken words, music, pictures, sound effects, items to handle and feel, written information, smells, tastes, or ideas that grab the imagination and excite the libido. Sex sells. And if your conscience will allow you, you can use it to convey your message, too.

4. Repeat your message at least three times: once in an introduction, once in detail, and once in a summary. Repeat it in three formats if you can: speech, pictures, and print. Research data show that people absorb very little of what they experience, and they retain only a small portion of what they first absorb. One key to communication is, therefore, repetition. You can almost never repeat a message too often. You can almost never repeat a message too often. You can almost never repeat a message too often! The trick is to do it without boring your audience into oblivion.

Surprise Meetings

These are more commonly known as interruptions. Your first reaction should be to avoid them. Refuse to be interrupted, or if you accept the interruption, refuse to spend more than 3–5 minutes away from what you were doing.

But sometimes the interruption is worthwhile: an old college chum pops in on her one day in your city, or a relative calls you with bad news or with a sweepstakes victory! Whatever the interruption, if you agree to participate in it, at least recognize it as the meeting it really is. Then use whichever ideas, principles, and techniques seem best suited to maximizing your effectiveness at the moment.

1. Establish time limits, and an agenda or purpose. Because this

meeting is a surprise, you cannot start it on time. But you can certainly set a time limit and end it on time. Do so.

2. Make sure the meeting is viable; that is, that the people and resources available at the meeting are sufficient to accomplish whatever purpose you have established.

3. Stick to your purpose. Resist digressions, discouragement, or efforts to start a new agenda before you complete the original one.

MAKING SUCCESSFUL, SPECIFIC PLANS: FOR A GROUP AND FOR YOURSELF

Planning is crucial to increased effectiveness, doing more, and shaping your results to meet your goals and your wants. It is the mechanism that lets you get out from under the crush and constant flow of events. Good planning puts you in the driver's seat instead of under the rear wheels. And best of all, good planners are made, not born. Nearly anyone can become a better planner simply by following the right principles and techniques. Try them, and you'll find this to be true.

Planning Teamwork

The planning process for work you do with other people goes through the same stages as the planning you do for working alone:

1. Put your goals in order

2. Develop a master plan

3. Establish specific steps

4. Schedule the steps in the best order

5. Follow your schedule.

Involvement

There are some important differences, most notably this: You must involve people in every stage of the planning process, and incorporate their values, goals, and ideas into your final plan, if you want to maintain maximum effectiveness. While many people view this as a loss of power, the involvement strategy actually has several very positive effects, as you'll see in a minute.

This involvement has to start at the very beginning of planning. To get people involved and eager to contribute, you must allow them a fair amount of influence over the selection of goals. The way people operate, it's inevitable that in most situations you will lose a great deal of motivation, ingenuity, creativity, and outright effort if you merely dictate goals and then expect others to attain them for you.

For example, in a large state institution, a department manager felt irritated by the cumbersome system his department used to keep track of its paper work. So he called a planning meeting and announced the goal of developing a plan to reorganize the paper work and computerize the overall system. The meeting did not progress well, and the plan took months to coalesce. All along the way, he met with stony silence, minimal cooperation, and active protests from some of the older department members. Eventually the department manager had to shelve the plan indefinitely.

From what I know of the case, he could have accomplished his purpose more readily by first calling a meeting to analyze paper-work problems. People would have raised plenty of problems and offered difficult piecemeal solutions. The idea of a totally new system would probably have evolved from everyone's comments and suggestions with very little guidance.

If you own and operate a small business, though, or you clearly control a small organization or group, you may be able to play a little more autocratic role. In situations where your leadership is well recognized and well accepted, it may be O.K. for you to lay down a specific goal as a means of establishing a common starting point.

For example, a woman who is the leader of her church's Auxiliary heard a lot of talk from the congregation regarding the shabby appearance of the building. Everyone seemed to want the place fixed up. She therefore decided that the Auxiliary would be the instrument to do it. She called a meeting of her most active workers, described the situation, and announced her intention of raising the money and having the needed work done. Everyone readily accepted her goal and began the planning process that would make it happen. In a case like this, where there's already plenty of involvement, simply dictating a goal to the people who will help you achieve it may have no undesirable side effects.

Complexity

Another important difference between planning your work alone and planning work for a group is the sheer complexity of the work, the effort to achieve it, and the plan that must account for it all. For example, a young carpenter who was used to working alone had developed the knack for planning his work in his head. But later, when he began hiring several other carpenters to help him, he found that his knack was not enough because simple plans could not cover all the work his men could accomplish. When you work alone, you need only plan for the small amount of work that one individual can accomplish. For a work group of five, however, there is five times the volume of work to plan for, as well as five times the communication, information, and activity. In addition, someone must coordinate some or all of the two-person, three-person, and four-person relationships that develop within the group.

Greater Planning Power

An offsetting difference between planning work alone and planning work for groups is that the group, which has greater need for planning, also has greater planning power. In other words, a work group of five must plan for more work, but it also has five "planners" who can develop a comprehensive and successful plan to direct and control their effort. This is a compensating factor that makes involving people in the planning process very satisfying. The involvement strategy actually lifts from your shoulders some of the burden of leadership, planning, and control.

WORK SHEET 15

Self-evaluation:
Organizing Goals

List your goals. Rank them in each column. When you are done, put them in overall order with the one you will feel best about accomplishing at the top.

YOUR GOALS	IMPORTANCE-URGENCY- VALUE-CHALLENGE-OTHER

WORK SHEET 16

Checking the Time You Save by Planning

Here is a simple form to help you calculate the specific amount of time you save by starting a project with the planning process.

FILL IN THIS SECTION BEFORE YOU START A NEW PROJECT—

1. Name of project:_____

_____

2. Goal, objective, or desired result:_____

_____

3. Estimated time for completion with conventional (non-planning

   or limited-planning) approach:_____

NOW GO THROUGH THE PLANNING PROCESS FOR THIS PROJECT—

4. Total time spent planning this project:_____

FILL IN THIS SECTION AFTER YOU COMPLETE THE PROJECT—

5. Total time spent working on the project. Get this figure from a
   Time Log or a diary you kept on this project. Exclude planning

   time in item 4 above:_____

6. Total of 4 and 5 above:_____

COMPARE YOUR ESTIMATED TIME IN ITEM 3 ABOVE WITH THE ACTUAL TOTAL IN ITEM 6

7. How much time did you save on this project?:_____

8. What is the ratio of time saved to time worked?:_____

9. What is the ratio of time saved to time spent planning this

project?:_____

10. What is the ratio of total time spent (actual) to estimated time?:

_____

_____

Planning Time Multiplies Itself

> Cast your bread upon the waters,
> and it shall return ten-fold.
> Spend your time in planning,
> and you shall save many times
> what you spend.

This is perfectly true. To prove it, go through this simple exercise. Work Sheet 16 will help you:

Pick a simple, ordinary project that is typical for you. Estimate how long it will take to complete. Now take this project through the full planning process. Then, work on it according to your plan. Calculate your planning time and your working time for the project. Compare your original estimates for the project with the total time for planning and doing it. You'll usually find that planning saves about twice what it takes. Thus, for every hour of planning, you probably saved two hours of implementation. Even though a good slice of your time is given to planning, your start-to-finish time is considerably less when planning is your first major step.

Practice Your Planning

Planning skills are like any others: They grow rusty with disuse; sharper the harder you work them. So it's worthwhile for you to practice your planning skills on literally everything. Before you mow the lawn, plan how you'll do it. Before you drive to the store, plan your route and your shopping list. Before you take your vacation, develop a detailed vacation plan. And don't worry about this being frivolous. Your planning efforts will multiply tremendously. You'll actually save thirty seconds here, a few minutes there, as much as an hour or two on your longer projects as you plan your way through your life. This extra time may be benefit enough for you to plan so frequently. But the bigger benefit is the development of powerful planning skills that allow you to take control of your life today, this week, this month, this year, and beyond. Watch how easily it can happen!

DAILY-WEEKLY-MONTHLY PLANNING

Your Daily Prompter is a good tool for implementing your daily, weekly, and monthly plans. Use the Daily Prompter to cue you with the items you have previously set aside to accomplish each day, week, and month. You can use the scheduling work sheets from Appendix D, instead of the Daily Prompter, if you prefer them. The basic point is to plan.

Use the planning process to break down every accomplishment you desire to a series of specific tasks. Schedule these tasks, and do them. You'll find that a few planning steps make up the entire process, and you can apply them again and again to plan the largest, the smallest and every task in between.

Daily Planning

On a daily basis, decide: a) what you want to accomplish this day, b) your priorities for these accomplishments, and c) what you can do to achieve them. Then tackle the highest priority accomplishment with the most direct task you can find. Work on this as long as you can, or until you complete it, then move on to the next highest priority. Plan a demanding schedule as far as the importance of what you do is concerned, but leave 20–50 percent of your time unscheduled. This allows for sudden shifts in priority, new tasks, and surprise items that disrupt your original plans.

You may notice that a well-planned day can uncrowd your desk. With every project and task accounted for, you don't need piles of paper to remind you what is pending. In fact, when one well-planned day follows another in a long series, you will find that very few projects get lost, fall behind, or remain pending very long.

Weekly Planning

Follow the same procedure week to week. Every Friday, for example, take thirty minutes to plan next week's work. Set up the goals you would like to accomplish, and establish plans for reaching these goals. Plan your weekends, too, if you like. Sort your week's goals into day-by-day accomplishments, and handle each day's work as it comes up in your schedule.

Monthly Planning

Follow the same procedure month to month. Use an hour or so of the last week each month to plan your accomplishments next month. Sort your monthly goals into week-by-week accomplishments, and break these down further as they come up in your schedule.

Remember to sprinkle in with your regular plans some of the items that will help you achieve the long-range personal and career goals you have established. Understand that you will never receive anything like this:

> You are cordially invited
> to include some of your
> "Long-range Goals and Objectives"
> in today's and this week's
> Regular Plans.
> The favor of your action
> is respectfully requested.

No one I know issues such engraved invitations to achieve your goals, although that might not be a bad service for me to provide.

Some people I have met indeed seem to be waiting for an engraved invitation to put some useful ideas, techniques, and principles to work in their lives. Please don't be one of them. Issue your own invitation, and accept it, right now.

Yearly Planning

This is the "annual time budget" for people who want to be more effective. Just as controllers across the nation assign dollar figures to every item in a Yearly Plan, you can assign time allotments to every item in your Yearly Plan. And, in fact, this is one of the best ways I know to make sure you find time for those most important, but easily delayed projects you wish you could get to.

For example, a young lawyer had the idea of buying a cabin in the woods and fixing it up as a hunting lodge and vacation home. But year after year, something always came up to delay the project. Finally, I gave him the idea of the Yearly Plan and its Annual Time Budget. He entered his cabin into his Yearly Plan, assigned it several weekends worth of work, and forgot it. But when the designated weekends came up on his calendar, this young man determined to follow his Plan. He pulled himself away from the "something" that had come up and went off exploring for his cabin. By the end of the year, he owned a cabin that pleased him and his family, and was well along in his plans to fix it up and use it.

The steps to make a Yearly Plan work for you include:

1. Set up a Yearly Plan that includes all the long-range projects you want to achieve or accomplish.
2. Allocate each one a fair amount of time: enough to make steady progress toward meeting your goal by the deadline you assigned it.
3. Make specific time assignments, so that you know exactly: a) what dates you will work on each of these projects, b) what you will try to accomplish on each of these dates, and c) how much time you will spend each designated date.
4. Follow the Yearly Plan.

It helps if you mark the Plan, or at least the designated dates, on the calendar you look at most often. Then, keep the written Plan handy, and review it frequently to note your progress, prepare for the next stage, and keep the importance of it firmly in mind.

MAKING USE OF TRAVEL TIME

Capitalizing on Travel

Most of the time you spend traveling is not physically demanding. Even while walking, you can carry useful items, think useful thoughts, and carry on a fruitful conversation. While driving you can listen to tapes, think, and talk out loud to yourself. On trains, boats, or planes you're usually free to read, write, think, and talk (quietly). All this translates into the potential to make good use of travel. Here are some techniques to help you:

Five-minute Tasks

These are the basis for much of your effectiveness during actual travel time. A "five-minute task" is defined as a self-contained task that you can pick up, understand, and accomplish in five or ten minutes. Tasks that require special equipment or reference to specialized sources of information do not qualify as five-minute tasks because they are not self-contained. However, modern dictation equipment and portable reference sources (print and electronic) vastly increase the range of tasks you can do on the run.

For example, the task of compiling a list of rug cleaners in your neighborhood might not be a five-minute task because it may require you to carry a heavy phone book or directory with you. But if you can tear out of the directory (or make machine copies of) the pages you need, you have created a five-minute task you can do on the run.

In another situation, an auto-leasing sales person carries a portable computer terminal with him as he makes his sales calls. Anywhere there is a telephone, he can call his home office and go to work. In just five minutes he and his terminal can turn out a neatly typewritten contract specifying every aspect of any proposed lease. This creates many portable five-minute tasks out of what used to be thirty-minute chores he could do only at his office. Now instead of waiting passively for people to see him, he borrows a phone and gets busy.

Other five-minute tasks include:

a) general reading,
b) routine writing assignments,
c) thinking over situations you have previously studied,
d) making decisions between alternative choices you have previously researched,
e) making notes on your last appointment,
f) boning up on details for your next appointment, and so forth.

Five-minute tasks not only keep you productive, they keep you flexible. For example, you can take a break almost whenever you want. You have only to finish the task you are on to be free with no loose ends, no strings left unfinished or unresolved. And you can choose from among all your five-minute tasks the ones that suit your mood, capacities, or available resources. These benefits give five-minute tasks significant advantages over longer projects, where you may take 15–30 minutes just getting set up to work, and where you cannot afford to quit or take a break for fear of losing your place or having to redo much of what you have already accomplished.

Once you begin to look for five-minute tasks, you will see plenty of them all around you. Save enough of them to keep you busy while you travel.

The Portable Office

This refers to a slim-line briefcase or other convenient container you use as your "portable office" whenever you travel. You put in all the essential equipment you need to get results on the run. Here are some tips on how you can furnish your own "portable office":

1. Collect useful chores, challenges, or five-minute tasks to do while you travel. If your local travel pattern is fairly well set, you will know approximately how much travel time you can devote to five-minute tasks every day. Be prepared with this much work. In fact, store your five-minute tasks in your "portable office" so you are always ready to work en route. You can even keep a work schedule or inventory of all these items in your "portable office" to help you organize and control your work.

2. Invest in equipment for your "portable office," such as a portable recorder for dictation or a portable cassette player. These help you make best use of your travel time. One man installed a computerized speed control in the car he called his "portable office" to make highway driving easier. With practice, he could soon concentrate much more than before on his five-minute tasks. Make arrangements to obtain worthwhile material on prerecorded tapes, educational programs from which you can benefit, and other materials to "furnish" your "portable office" and make your travel time more fruitful.

Use Your Seat as a Desk

Almost all commercial travel time is taken up with sitting: by car to the station or airport, waiting for the train or plane, sitting for the journey, by car from the station or airport to your destination, and the same sequence in reverse. If you will carry enough five-minute tasks with you when you travel, you can make all this travel time tremendously effective.

You can also make better use of the rest of your travel time if you use your sitting time to plan ahead. Instead of working on specific items, you review your itinerary, expand it or change it, then prepare for what's ahead. The more of your trip you plan, the more effective you will be. But it takes experience to know just how much you can ask yourself to do. Experiment to find the right amount: enough so you accomplish a great deal in each twenty-four-hour period, but not so much that you exhaust yourself and have to sacrifice some results to achieve others.

Using Local Travel Time

Local travel time is sometimes harder to use well than travel time farther from home. First, you usually have more local travel time, and you can run out of useful ways to fill it. Second, you are more likely to be driving or concerned with making your connections during local travel, rather than on one long hop. So it's harder to concentrate on work or anything other than the travel. Nevertheless, you can be extremely effective during local travel time, if you make use of it as consistently and frequently as possible. Here's how:

1. Make it a policy to use as much of your local travel time as you can. Local travel time usually offers very short opportunities for reading, writing, thinking, or planning. It's easy to say: "Well, never mind this opportunity, I'll take advantage of the next one!" But this attitude only grows worse. Instead, try to make a little use of every opportunity. The valuable minutes will soon add up to many valuable hours.

2. Plan good routes for your local travel hops, and stick to them. Once you establish your travel patterns, you can pay much less attention to the mechanics of getting there and concentrate more on accomplishing something useful.

3. Consider taking taxis, limousines, or public transportation for all or part of your local travel. Anything you can do to free your mind from routine chores will convert mostly wasted travel time to highly productive hours. Parking your car and taking other forms of transportation give you free time en route, and you can then use this free time productively.

4. Share your travel time. Car pooling or ride sharing is a great tool to make better use of your time. The people who travel with you can contribute to your knowledge, stimulation, and effectiveness if you all participate in a combined effort to make good use of your local travel time.

For example, a Los Angeles college student formed a car pool with classmates. Every day, one of the riders takes a turn lecturing on an agreed upon topic. The thirty minutes "lost" on the ride to school becomes a "found" study hour that directly produces better grades and more free time at home.

Using Long-distance Travel

One advantage of long-distance over local travel time is the amount of it you get in one unit. You may have two or three hours of available time in one piece, a dozen times as much as you usually get at home. In addition, long-distance travel isolates you: your family, friends, and common interruptions are usually far away. At least en route, you have fewer personal distractions and demands to pull you away from making good use of your time.

Whether you travel 50 percent of your time or less than once a year, your long-distance travel provides precious opportunities for effectiveness. Here are some techniques and strategies for making good use of this travel time:

1. Line up the important work or thinking you will do on your journey before you leave. You can either schedule as many important items as you think you can handle, or devote yourself to one super-important project. If you pick this second strategy, you will allocate all your travel time (one-way or round-trip) to the one super-important project you select.

2. Assemble the materials you will need in a briefcase or other accessible carry bag. Be sure to include writing materials, calculators, or any other equipment your tasks require.

3. Get a fast start. On each portion of your journey, find a good seat and get settled quickly. As soon as you're settled, open your bag and start working. Have a timer with you or a clock in view so you can count down to the next time you're scheduled to change seats (from waiting room to airplane, or wherever).

4. Wait until the last minute to break off your efforts. Then stuff your work into your carry bag and move on. Time yourself to make the last call for passengers, and work a few extra minutes so you will be the last one off at your destination.

5. Keep working on your important tasks or project at every opportunity until you complete it or run out of travel time. And remember, your successful completion of travel-time work entitles you to relax and celebrate. This is fair, because it helps insure that you'll work just as hard next time you travel.

Faster Than a Speeding Bullet

Here are some tips to help you slide through your itinerary like a hot knife through butter:

1. Prepack once and then leave it, ready to go. If you travel more than 15 percent of your time, or if you travel more than twice a year on short notice, a prepacked suitcase is worth its weight in gold to you. Prepack a duplicate of all your everyday toiletries, underwear, eyeglasses, and whatever else you take on a trip. Then the day you leave just add the appropriate outer clothes and you're ready.

2. Develop a relationship with a good travel agent, and "delegate" your booking chores. Travel agents do it better than you, as long as you tell them exactly what you want. And their services don't cost you a dime.

3. Leave copies of your itinerary at home and/or with colleagues, and take one with you. This makes it easier for people to reach you to communicate last-minute or emergency changes of plan. Check in frequently, too, particularly if you feel some of your plans are shaky or may change.

4. Keep money ready in your wallet or purse: a traveler's check and/or a blank personal check will do. Your hotel will cash this for you if you run short but can't get to a bank.

5. If you fly frequently, join one of the airline lounge clubs. They make the time you spend in airports more comfortable and productive, and eliminate waiting on many lines.

6. Fly direct. Flights that stop en route usually add between thirty minutes and two hours to your flight time. Extra landings and take-offs also increase your chances of encountering equipment problems and other delays.

7. Avoid checking baggage if possible. Carry-on suitcases are great because you save so much time. Checked baggage means a 20–40 minute delay, and is almost certain to create a longer delay at least once.

8. For international travel, make sure to have the local currency in your pocket when you arrive. Exchange some money while waiting to leave the previous country. This saves time at the airport or railway exchange booth, where tourists always form long lines. And you may even get a better exchange rate at a large bank closer to your hotel.

9. Pay for faster transportation. Sometimes an express train or a different flight arrives faster than a slower, cheaper excursion. You may be able to spend a little extra money and save a great deal of extra time.

Tips for Reducing Waiting Time

The best way to cut down waiting time is to schedule what you do for unpopular times. These so-called "off-peak" hours have far fewer and shorter lines than rush hours. Sometimes you avoid a line altogether. A few tested ways to avoid lines include: eat lunch at 1 or 2 P.M., "hole up" in cities during the rush hours, check out of hotels early, and pick up tickets or other items at odd hours. And these techniques work as well whether you're traveling around the block in your home town or around the world.

Here are some other techniques to help you avoid lines and many kinds of waits:

1. Consider getting others to wait on line for you. Many cities have services where young people earn three dollars an hour and up for waiting on line for other people. Be alert for this wherever you go, and use it where appropriate.

2. If you see a line where you want to go, try and reschedule your day so you can keep busy for now and come back to do this later. If you cannot reschedule, at least use five-minute tasks or other techniques to get something useful out of your waiting time.

3. Avoid bank lines entirely. Do all your banking by mail, or by teller machine at unusual hours. Also, spend as little cash as possible, and get what cash you need from stores, hotels, and others with whom you do business.

4. Avoid buying at stores, particularly during sales or busy seasons. You can buy more than 50 percent of the merchandise you want via mail order, catalog sales, and telephone calls to your favorite stores. One lady strolls through stores and writes down the locations, prices, and item numbers of what she wants to buy. Then she goes to a phone and has the order sent to her home.

    You can also place phone orders to stores and neighborhood businesses of all kinds for pick-up, or even better, for delivery. Many sandwich shops, grocery stores, pharmacies, hardware stores, and specialty shops will let you order by telephone. If they deliver, you save a great deal of time. But even if you pick up your own order, you save a significant amount of time over waiting to order, then waiting again for people to prepare it and ring it up. Get in the habit of shopping by phone as much as possible and you'll cut hours of waiting time out of your schedule.

5. Make appointments to the minute with everyone: including your crimper, doctor, dentist, and other people, too. When you call to make your appointment, explain that you're extremely busy and

trying to operate on a tight schedule. Offer to show up exactly on time for your appointment, but say you'll expect to be seen immediately. If necessary, take the first appointment of the day, and be there on time! Live up to your part of this bargain and encourage the other people to live up to theirs. Where possible, stick with the people who do.

Scheduling for Efficient Travel

The "great circle" route is the shortest distance between two points on the globe. While you may not want an authentic great-circle route for all of your travel, the concept is a big help to your effectiveness.

The idea is to save up your trips so you have several destinations each time you leave your home or office. You plan your route to touch all your destinations with a minimum of backtracking and redundant mileage. This kind of scheduling makes the average travel minute more effective because it reduces your total travel time without reducing results. And it works whether you're traveling thousands of miles by air, or less than a mile by bicycle. To schedule your own "great circles":

1. Look at a map whenever you plan your routes.
2. Mark your most frequent destinations right on the map so they're easy to find next time you look.
3. Follow the *fastest* route, not necessarily the shortest, between destinations. For example, the direct road from one destination to another may be a slow crawl with red lights at every corner. You may make better time by going three miles farther along a faster route. The only valid exceptions might be walking or bicycle routes you choose not for speed, but to avoid tiring hills or dangerous pathways.
4. Take the map with you when you travel. Be ready to change your route if conditions or priorities change.

THINKING AND CONCENTRATING SUPERCHARGE YOUR EFFECTIVENESS

Concentrating is a basic principle of top-level achievement. It's also a general guideline that saves you time and makes you more effective in a wide variety of situations. In this section, we explore some techniques for using concentration to increase your effectiveness and help you accomplish more of what you want.

Intensive Time Is the Most Useful

If you review your Time Log, or just think back on your own experience, you'll probably see that you have been most productive and most effective during periods when you were concentrating deeply. You can usually recognize periods of deep concentration by a variety of signals:

a) you lose your sense of time passing,

b) you experience a great deal of satisfaction,

c) you lose touch with sights, sounds, smells around you,

d) you become completely absorbed in your activity, thinking of nothing else,

e) you may neglect to eat, drink, or eliminate for several hours,

f) you operate at or near peak efficiency: analyzing accurately, thinking clearly, making top-notch decisions, and bringing a great deal of your experience to bear.

To make the best of your natural abilities, learn to recognize concentration when it comes, and also learn to set up your environment so you can concentrate for as long as possible.

1. Set aside time when you know you will not be interrupted. A "quiet time" is a good way to protect yourself. This is an established concentration period that you ask others to respect. Another way to gain interruption-free time is simply to note your least-interrupted times and to concentrate during them. For example, one writer I know works from midnight to 6 A.M., because that is the only time he is free of interruptions—free to concentrate.

2. Prepare your tasks so you can concentrate without interrupting yourself. Do all the preparatory work. Have all the reference materials and background information at hand. Familiarize yourself with your objectives so you know exactly what you are trying to achieve. Then, when you begin to concentrate, you won't need to break your concentration to handle basic business.

3. Prepare the people around you. Get them to leave you alone during your concentration. Put up a sign or signal that alerts them to your concentration, and obtain their cooperation so you can concentrate without being distracted or disturbed.

4. Prepare your work space. Sometimes, it is impossible to concentrate in a familiar environment with a million distractions littered around. Sometimes, it is impossible to concentrate unless you are in familiar surroundings. Try different places for concentration and see which ones you like best. You may even want to select different locations to concentrate on different tasks. The key item here is to find a place where *you can concentrate*. Once you find one, use it as often as you can.

How to Concentrate

Because your deep concentration time is so useful, you can boost your effectiveness if you learn to concentrate at will for long periods of time. Once you know how to reach and maintain a state of concentration, you can apply yourself when and where you wish.

Chapter 5 gives you a program for boosting your concentration time. This program really works. You can use it to lengthen dramatically the amount of time you can concentrate without a break. The basics of the program are these:

1. Measure your current concentration ability.
2. Practice concentrating as long and as hard as you can.
3. Reward yourself for any improvement in your concentration ability, irrespective of the results that concentration generates.

With practice, you can double or triple the length of time you can concentrate, and this translates directly into a tremendous boost in your effectiveness.

Quiet Hours for Concentration

Chapter 7, A Concise Program for the Busy Business Executive, gives you some tips on installing a "Quiet Hour" to increase your effectiveness. Quiet Hours are excellent opportunities to concentrate on one or two special tasks. And you can use Quiet Hours at home alone, or in cooperation with everyone in your office, or anywhere in between. The Quiet Hour is a device to augment your self-control. The "formality" of the time limits and the specific rules help you feel special about the hour you designate as "Quiet." And the same aspects make you feel better about enlisting others' cooperation. The result is to make every minute of the set-aside period count for more.

GETTING CONTROL OF YOUR TELEPHONE

Imagine a marvelous instrument you can use to converse with nearly anyone, no matter where in the world they may be. What a time-saver! In fact, the telephone may be the greatest time-saving invention developed in modern times. But that doesn't make it perfect.

The same telephone that saves you hours of traveling around your city practically every day of your life also:

- interrupts your bath,
- disturbs your evening meal,
- makes it easier than ever for you and people who know you to waste time in idle conversation, and
- inevitably gives you a busy signal or keeps you on "hold" when you are in a hurry.

This section is intended to give you techniques for controlling your telephone time so you can minimize the problems and maximize the payoffs of this marvelous communication system.

Get Right to the Point

Telephone conversations are strange combinations of one-to-one meetings and personal letters. You almost always have the urge to be friendly and conversational on the phone, even during business-related talks. Resist! You can save 10–30 percent of the time you spend on the telephone if you will limit your conversations just a little more to the purpose of your phone calls.

Follow these guidelines to keep your conversations short, sweet, and to the point:

1. Know what you want to say before you dial. Make a list of key words or main points and check them off as you cover each one. This telephone outline is a great time-saver for helping you get to the point and stay on it, and for eliminating unnecessary call backs to clear up the one or two points you missed in your original phone call. Work Sheet 17 gives you a form for your telephone outline and for the replies you get to each point. The scheduling sheets in Appendix D offer a similar opportunity to outline your phone calls in advance. Use whichever form seems most convenient and comfortable.

2. Refuse to tie up the other person. Try to cover the purpose of your phone call at once. When that's done you can socialize, if appropriate. But make clear you're ready to hang up the moment the other party wants to.

3. Protect yourself the same way. Insist on knowing the reason the other person called you. Try to take care of this reason quickly and effectively. Then socialize if you want to. But remember you have the right—and the responsibility—to end the conversation the moment you feel pressed by other things you need to do.

WORK SHEET 17

Telephone Outline

Phone call to:_____

Date:_____ Time:_____ Number:_____

My Points	Replies
1.	
2.	
3.	
4.	
5.	

6. _____ _____

7. _____ _____

8. _____ _____

   _____ _____

9. _____ _____

   _____ _____

10. _____ _____

   _____ _____

Cut Off Overextended Conversations

Long-winded conversations are not unusual, and they are one of the biggest dangers of modern telephone communications. For example, right in the middle of an important project, a friend may call who wants to fill you in on five years of his life, or you may get involved in an innocent conversation with a total stranger who is lonely and looking for telephone companionship, or a compulsive talker you know from any conceivable context may call for some slight "reason," then try to keep you on the line for an hour.

The cost for all three is the same: prohibitive loss of results and accomplishments. The antidote is also the same: firm action to end the conversation. The key to success here is your perseverance, and when pushed to the limit, your insistence on a quick end to the conversation. Bear in mind that no one can keep you on the telephone if you steadfastly refuse to permit it. You can hold firm, too, provided you have: a) raw courage, or b) a strong motivation that springs from your keen awareness of the importance of your goals and the limits on your opportunities to achieve them. If you feel short on (a), I hope this book at least has been able to help you with (b). Once you steel yourself to cut off the conversation, you'll benefit from some techniques to make the job a little easier. Here are four:

1. FIND A HOOK. This is the most subtle of the techniques. To work it, you probe gently at the beginning of every conversation for the "hook": a clue to what the other party was doing just prior to the phone call. For example:

OTHER PERSON: Hi, Jim.

YOU: Hello, Joe. Say, I thought you always went to lunch at this time of day.

OTHER PERSON: No. As a matter of fact, I was just balancing my checkbook when I thought of you.

"Balancing my checkbook" is the hook. Write it down or remember it for later, when you may need it to cut off the conversation. When you're ready to hang up, use the hook like this:

YOU: Well, all right, Joe. I'll let you get back to balancing your checkbook now. Thanks for calling. Bye.

Most of the time, the "hook" starts the other person thinking about what their next task should be. Your "hook" becomes a natural transition that eases them into hanging up quickly. But often they won't recognize the power of what you said.

2. MAKE UP AN EXCUSE. This is the most common tactic. For example:

OTHER PERSON: . . . so as I was saying . . .

YOU: Uh-oh. There's someone at the door. I'll have to hang up now. Bye.

Actually, I don't like the dishonesty of this approach, but it does work and it is used frequently by many people. You may as well have it in your arsenal of conversational techniques.

3. SET A TIMER. You can set a real timer or a mental one. Either way, you say at your first opportunity: "Listen, I have some things to do. I'll have to hang up in about five more minutes." This will often end the conversation on the spot. But when it doesn't, you merely wait a decent interval and say, firmly: "Sorry, Joe, but I've got to go now." If you wish, you can add the optional bonus: "I'll talk to you again . . ." (soon, later, tomorrow at 3 P.M., next year, etc.).

This technique is straightforward and honest. I like it. But to use it convincingly you must truly believe you actually have something more important to work on. That should be no problem for someone who has come as far through this book as you have!

4. SAVE THEM TIME. This is a reversal technique. Once you're ready to cut off the conversation, you say: "Gee, Joe, I know you must be busy. I can't take any more of your time. Bye." Sometimes Joe will protest by saying: "Oh, no problem, Jim. I've got nothing to do for the rest of the day." But you keep on with your tactic: "That's nice of you to say, Joe, but I just can't take any more of your time. Bye."

This technique may not work on the first try with everyone, but if you persevere, you'll turn the conversation onto a short track that dead-ends fairly quickly.

Have a Private Number

This is a valuable technique for making better use of the telephone. The private number excludes most people trying to contact you. They can call on your listed number. But since you know all the really important calls will come in on your private line, you can screen, divert to an answering machine, or allow your listed phone to keep ringing indefinitely.

Your private number gives certain people prime access to your attention. For example:

1. One magazine publisher gives people his private number and says, "Keep trying until you get me."

2. A movie producer answers his own private number, but has his secretary carefully screen the listed number of his office.

3. Your private number is an emergency hotline people "in the

know" can use to reach you no matter how busy you are, no
matter what the time or circumstances.

4. Your private number is a second line you can use to call out
while waiting for an important phone call on your regular line,
or vice versa. (Note: recently installed telephone exchanges offer
a "call waiting" service that eliminates this conflict, but which is
not available on every telephone number.)

The Telephone Hour

This is a designated part of the day or week in which you use the
telephone in a concentrated burst. Your telephone hour is perfect for
returning all your phone messages, making your important calls,
tracking down information or information sources via telephone, and
keeping in touch with other people on a regular basis. To set up and
use your own telephone hour:

1. Set up a comfortable telephone work space. Furnish it with a
good chair, and telephone table, writing tablets and pencils, a calendar, a clock, an alarm or timer system for reminders, and—of course
—a telephone.

2. Use your telephone work space for the bulk of your calling.
When your hand reaches for the phone at other times, other places,
think twice. Try not to call, but instead make a note about who you
wanted to call and the reason.

3. Find a good time of day for your telephone hour. Most people
are available during the first two hours of the morning, and the last
two hours of the evening. Try your telephone hour in this period. If
you get too many "no answers" or "will call you back" messages,
reschedule your telephone hour.

4. Save up your phone messages and return them all during your
telephone hour.

5. Keep notes on the calls you make, what both you and the other
parties say, and so forth. If you promise someone you'll "call back in
fifteen minutes," use the timer or alarm to remind you.

6. Obtain the best equipment. Automatic telephone dialers that

store phone numbers and dial at the touch of a button are great. Push-button phones are faster than rotary dialers. Portable phones let you wander and do routine filing or sweeping while you wait on "hold" or even while you talk. It's valuable to eliminate any repetitive chores you can from your phone hour, especially if a few dollars for better equipment will give you more time for accomplishing your goals.

Confirm Appointments

You can save yourself a lot of unnecessary travel time if you consistently use the telephone to confirm every appointment just before you leave. Ninety percent of the time, the appointment with your doctor, dentist, colleague, friend, or employer will be "on" as scheduled. Some people you call will even be surprised that you had any doubt.

But often enough to pay big time dividends, you will find that your appointment was:

a)   forgotten,

b)   cancelled "just a second ago," or

c)   "cancelled, but we forgot to let you know."

To make this confirmation habit easier, do this:

1.   When you make an appointment you must travel to keep, write down the telephone number at the same time and place as you write down your reminder of the appointment. This way, when your reminder comes up, you automatically get the phone number you need to confirm it.

2.   Reserve a few minutes before you leave for your appointment(s) to confirm them via telephone. It takes about two minutes each, and if you concentrate this telephoning, you may be able to confirm them even faster.

3.   As you confirm each appointment, ask: a) travel directions (if you have any doubts), and b) parking directions if you are going by car. This will save you additional time, as well as concern or worry when you arrive.

4.   Use this confirmation call as one last chance to remind the other

5

BASIC PRINCIPLES
OF EFFECTIVENESS

I pointed out earlier how increasing your effectiveness requires an effort something like the scientific method. And as with the scientific method, you get some general operating principles to apply to every situation. Efforts to accomplish more of what you want require a two-tiered discipline: On the first tier are literally hundreds of specific techniques for doing more in less time, eliminating tedious chores, speeding communications, and erasing other problems. You saw most of these in Chapter 4. On the second tier are a few basic principles that come together in varying combinations to generate those specific techniques. These principles, in fact, are often applications of basic patterns that work successfully in other aspects of life. The truth is, what works well in one area of life often works well in other areas of it. And your efforts to accomplish your goals are, after all, merely another part of the process of living.

In this chapter, we concentrate our energies on understanding these basic principles, or success patterns. Armed with these, you can literally invent a new technique to carry you through whatever unique chores, complications, or problems you may face. It's important to learn the principles for another reason: Without them, you are reduced to memorizing specific techniques, and your ability to accomplish what you want is limited by what you can remember. Once you absorb and understand the principles, however, you don't have that limitation. You'll have your memory and your creativity working for you: a one-two punch that can plug up most of the holes in a person's performance I've ever seen.

One caution, however. Don't be alarmed if some of these principles seem to set a pretty stiff standard of behavior. No one expects perfection. Because they are principles, not examples, I state them at full strength. If they are going to serve as beacons, let them shine out brightly. But don't let them blind you to what you can fairly expect from yourself.

Now let's go over these principles one by one:

ESTABLISH GOALS

This is so basic that I believe we have already covered the essential ground on this principle elsewhere in this book. I include it here only so Chapter 5 can be as complete as possible.

In essence, this principle tells you to start every day, every action, every project with a firm notion of specific accomplishments that will satisfy you. You need not satisfy other people to follow this principle, but if you fail to satisfy yourself, you cannot consider yourself to be reaching for the best possible goals.

For clarity, your goals should include the following details:

1. A description of the accomplishment you desire.
2. An objective method of measuring your accomplishment, together with criteria so you, or anyone else, can determine whether or not you have achieved your goal.
3. A reasonable deadline or general time frame to aid in making your Basic Choice and to insure that goals do not lie unused and unattained for too long.

In practice, the objective method and specific criteria for measuring your goals are most useful as tools for determining what you really want. To be objective and specific, you must know your goal in detail. But you, more than anyone else, measure whether or not you have achieved your goal. And since your satisfaction is your primary yardstick, objective measures can only be somewhat secondary.

WORK DIRECTLY TOWARD YOUR GOALS

This second principle is also a familiar one, forming the basis for much of what we have previously discussed. However, we can profitably add a few points of interest to what we have already said.

First, this principle contributes heavily toward the idea of priorities, and meshes well with the principle of "Finishing First Things First." The idea behind this principle is that, having established what will satisfy us, we can logically gain the greatest level of satisfaction by accomplishing as many of our goals as possible. And trying to do this leads us to:

1. Work as often as possible toward our goals.
2. Simplify and eliminate side issues and niceties if they hobble us.
3. Return to the direction of our goal(s) immediately after any and all detours.

You may want to think of yourself as a homing pigeon, in this regard. Despite the distance, the obstructions, and the dangers, you return to your basic course almost without thinking because it presents the straightest line between your present position and the place you would like to be. Persistence and perseverance are important elements in a long-range effort to accomplish the results you want.

WORK TO A FIRM DEADLINE

A deadline was once a line on a military prison floor. If the prisoners crossed it, they were shot. Today a deadline is a less dangerous time limit, but it retains almost the same ability to command your attention and force your compliance. The power of deadlines to make you more effective is immense. A deadline helps even a weak suggestion get action—whether you aim it at others or yourself. In addition, a deadline gives meaning to your activities, provides one basis for measuring your accomplishments, and helps you make your Basic Choice.

You have probably noticed how you work faster, more effectively when you try to meet a deadline someone hands you. You can give yourself the same benefits if you set and try to meet your own deadlines on all your projects. Even when you have a deadline set by someone else, you can add to its value by setting your own a few days earlier. If you supervise other people, you can help them improve their performance on any task by helping them to recognize and meet appropriate deadlines. And you get these results almost automatically.

For example, at home or with friends, how often have you asked someone for a favor, and had your request amiably shelved? You say something like, "Fred, would you bring back my garden hose, please? I need to wash down the back fence with it." Fred will say, "Sure," but he probably won't bring you the hose. Without a deadline, your request was just another line in the conversation, as quickly forgotten as your offhand comment on the weather.

Now look what happens when you add a simple deadline, "Fred, would you bring back my garden hose, please? I need to wash down the back fence with it *by Friday.*" The whole character of your request is different. Fred immediately begins thinking about how long it has been since he borrowed your garden hose, about whether he will need it after Friday, about how he can possibly get it to you by Friday, even about why you might need it by Friday and not Saturday. Your deadline gives life to your request, makes it more urgent, and opens a good deal wider the door to getting it done.

A deadline works the same magic on the job. You ask a supplier for a delivery of rubber bands, for example, and he says, "Sure." But you don't get them for a week and a half, maybe a month and a half! If you add a deadline to your request, you get a much better response. For example:

YOU: I need those rubber bands by the fifteenth, at the latest!

HIM: By the fifteenth, huh? Well, I got two trucks down and four men out sick, but I think I can drop them off myself on my way home. Yes, you'll have them!

You can drop a deadline on yourself, too. In fact, you absolutely have to give yourself deadlines if you expect "yourself" to get to those projects in the back of your mind, the ones that will take you toward your lifelong goals. Face the facts: You have been aware of some of these goals for a long while. And you are intelligent and practical enough to know some of the steps you must take to accomplish them. But you haven't done much about it. Why? Because there was no deadline.

Urgent items seemed more important. They had a deadline. Short-term important items seemed more urgent. They had deadlines, too. You have neglected your truly important tasks at least partly because it was never "time" to get moving on them. Nearly everyone else has done it, too. Without a deadline, you see, you can delay a hundred years and still not find the right "time" to get started. But one hundred years from now you probably won't be able to accomplish much, should you finally decide to get started. So don't wait. Use Work Sheet 18 to set some deadlines for yourself today. You'll soon see the difference they make.

WORK SHEET 18

Self-evaluation:
Five Deadlines to Live Up to

The object of this exercise is simply to have you establish for yourself at least five key deadlines for five projects that are important to you. The sooner you set some deadlines and make the personal determination to beat them, the sooner you can get the power of the deadline principle working for you.

I. List at least five important projects or activities you would like to complete:

1. _____

2. _____

3. _____

4. _____

5. _____

II. For each one, list the major steps you will have to complete in order to achieve your goal:

First project:_____

_____

_____

_____

Second project:_____

_____

_____

_____

Third project:_____

_____

_____

_____

Fourth project:_____

_____

_____

_____

Fifth project:_____

_____

_____

_____

III. Estimate from your own experience or just guess how many days must elapse between starting and finishing each step. Add up all the days to estimate each project or activity.

IV. Use the total elapsed time you estimate that you need for each activity to calculate a reasonable deadline for you to complete it. Take into account the order in which you want to tackle them, as well as your ability to work on several simultaneously. Enter your deadlines in the table below:

Project	Deadline
1.	
2.	
3.	
4.	
5.	

You'll probably notice that work you do to meet a deadline takes on extra meaning. It's one thing to paint your house yourself. It's something more to finish in time for the family gathering in June! It's nice to cook a delicious gourmet meal. It's more meaningful to get it on the table by 8:30, when your guests are ready to eat. You naturally set most deadlines according to when you need or want the results to be obtained. Therefore, meeting your deadline satisfies you twice: once by bringing you the basic results, and again by giving you the satisfaction of getting those results when you want them. You may even find a third satisfaction: the good feeling you get just from meeting a self-imposed deadline. All of this contributes to the meaning and enjoyment you find in accomplishing a specific task.

Deadlines also provide a convenient and objective method of measuring your accomplishments. It might be hard to calculate how well you're doing your job. But it's very easy to count up the number of deadlines you meet, the number you miss, and compare. It's just as easy to calculate the "time overrun" for each deadline you miss—both the number of days you overran your deadline, and the percentage of overrun on the entire project. Over the long term, deadlines provide a good way to measure your effectiveness.

At home, it's fairly difficult to check your progress on many or most of your projects. But a deadline makes it easier. Give yourself some specific deadlines for meeting specific objectives. Then count up how many of your deadlines you meet and how many you miss. But don't be a robot about this: give yourself humane and reasonable goals. Your diet? Give yourself some deadlines for reaching specific weights. Your social life? Give yourself some deadlines for meeting specific numbers of new people. Give yourself more deadlines for getting out of the house, seeing new movies, joining new clubs, finding new partners, or whatever turns you on. Physical fitness? Give yourself a deadline for getting in shape to jog a good distance, and another longer deadline for going that distance at a fast pace. Whatever you do, whatever you want to do, you can measure your performance (and make it more meaningful) if you set some deadlines and try to meet them.

Finally, a deadline is a useful criterion when you make your Basic Choice of "What to do next." Faced with a bewildering list of options and a confusing array of rewards, penalties, preparedness, and desire, you can often simplify your Basic Choice by considering deadlines. If everything else is equal or too confusing to cope with, you may decide to give your first attention to the item with the least time to spare on its deadline. For example, suppose you have to straighten the house for a party, clean the pool, do the marketing, and watch the NBA Finals on TV. You have until 6 P.M. when the market closes to go shopping, until 8 P.M. when your guests arrive to finish the straightening, until 8:30 or 9 P.M. when people will want to use your pool to clean it (I like to wait until the last minute, hoping someone else will volunteer to do it for me), and the Finals are on TV right now, 12 noon. Isn't it obvious? Watch the game now, then rush out to do the marketing (can you do this during halftime?), then straighten up the house, and clean the pool in whatever time is left over. Deadlines organize your day!

How to Use a Deadline

All you have to do to harness the power of deadlines is to respect them when they're given, and to set and respect them when they're not. Set deadlines reasonably far ahead: far enough so you can do the task without unnecessary rushing; close enough so you have little room for delay. Choose your deadlines from among the following four types:

Type 1: Ordered by someone, but negotiable. A moderately strong prompt, depending on just how "negotiable" it turns out to be. Examples: "George, I want you to finish this by Thursday." "Mayor Requests City Council Report Before Election Day."

Type 2: Ordered by someone and not negotiable. An extremely strong prompt, but can be too strong to use in certain situations. Examples: "If it's not received by Thursday, we cannot consider your application." "Send in your entries by midnight, Thursday." "Departure time: 3 P.M."

Type 3: Built into the task. A very strong, often imperative time limit. Physical laws and personal capabilities predominate here. Examples: Cooking four-minute eggs. Free-diving underwater (without an air supply).

Type 4: Added onto the task. A very strong prompt. Usually created by chronologically juxtaposing two separate tasks.

EXAMPLES: Using a rented car, due to be returned at 12 noon, to drop off your mother at her sister's house. Trying to become a millionaire by age thirty-five.

Any of the types will improve results, speed up action, and generally make you better and more effective at reaching your goals.

SCHEDULE IN REVERSE

As a basic principle, this two-part guideline has wide application. The key idea is to look first at where you want to end up, then: 1) analyze the work so you know how long each phase will last, and 2) schedule it backward so you know the "latest feasible starting date" you can use to meet your deadline.

Work Sheet 19 gives an example of a scheduling work sheet you might use to schedule in reverse.

WORK SHEET 19

Scheduling Work Sheet

Description of Step   **Required Time Per Step**

Step 1:   Time:

Step 2:   Time:

Step 3:   Time:

Step 4:   Time:

Step 5:   Time:

Step 6:   Time:

Step 7:   Time:

Step 8:   Time:

Step 9:   Time:

Goal: **Deadline:**

Complete Step 9 by:

Complete Step 8 by:

Complete Step 7 by:

Complete Step 6 by:

Complete Step 5 by:

Complete Step 4 by:

Complete Step 3 by:

Complete Step 2 by:

Complete Step 1 by:

Latest Feasible Starting Date:

For example, to complete a report by the fifteenth of the month, let's schedule in reverse. First, we use our experience and judgment to chop the task into short, manageable steps. Second, we start on the deadline date and count backward to allow time for each step. For this report, our steps (in reverse order) might include:

> final draft typing and proofreading (1 day),
> final draft writing and correcting (2 days),
> rough typing (1 day),
> rough draft writing and correcting (3 days),
> thinking and planning report (3 days),
> gathering materials (3 days).

It looks as though we need about thirteen working days to complete this report. By scheduling in reverse, we found our latest feasible starting date, plus starting and ending dates for each stage of the process.

Scheduling in reverse is more effective than scheduling with the flow of time because you get a more accurate picture of how to meet your deadline. Any way you plot a project's steps on your calendar, you're ahead of the game. But if you naïvely schedule your "Project A" from today forward, you can make mistakes:

1) You may neglect or delay other current valuable work because you are working too long or too hard on Project A. Better way: Schedule Project A in reverse, then delay or reduce your involvement

with Project A as much as possible—at least until you finish Project B.

2) You may rush to finish Project A too fast, then find yourself stuck with little or no other work to do. Better way: Schedule Project A in reverse, then work just enough on Project A to keep it afloat, and simultaneously look for other projects and opportunities to do now before they evaporate from neglect. For example, accept that honorary post you have been offered or someone else will, join that interesting committee or you may never again get the chance, work up the details on that new idea before you lose your enthusiasm, or offer to take charge of that feasibility study for the new product line. If you haven't analyzed Project A and you're unsure of how long you need to complete it, you may miss out unnecessarily on all your other possibilities.

3) You may finish Project A, then discover new information or learn a new trick that forces you to redo some or all of your work. Better way: Schedule Project A in reverse, then delay Project A until your latest feasible starting date. This way, you can bring to bear on Project A all your experience and the latest available information.

MATCH YOUR WORK TO YOUR CAPACITIES

This principle dictates that, ideally, you should try to: a) recognize the variations and changes in your capacity to do work, moment by moment, AND, b) select work that just matches your capacity of the moment.

The reason for this is simple: You are most effective when you are working at or near your full capacity. When you take on a task that's too easy, you are for the moment underemployed. When you try to handle one that's too hard, you are for the moment overemployed. Either way, you're less effective than your best. So the more consistently you match your work to your capacities, the more effective you'll be, overall. But don't be fooled. The simplicity of this idea doesn't make it easy to do.

You need practice to recognize your own capacity for work at a given moment. And you need a different kind of practice to make your Basic Choice at least partly on the basis of your current capacity to meet a task's demands. Let's look a little deeper into how you can put this principle to use.

Recognize Your Capacity

You've probably heard of many "cycles" that affect people. And you probably recognize that there are cycles within cycles within cycles. For example, there are: astrological cycles from less than a minute to thousands of years in length; lifelong cycles of development and decline; annual cycles; seasonal cycles; biorhythmic cycles; daily cycles of sleeping and waking, of full alertness and lethargy; and many more. Dr. Dorothy Tennov at the University of Bridgeport has reportedly discovered body cycles that influence our performance minute by minute!

Your capacity for work at any given moment is the "instantaneous" sum of all these cycles—what they add up to each instant. It's a tough trick to figure your capacity for work without a computer. But you can make your guesses more accurate with practice. Start looking for cycles in your Time Log. For example, try to find a pattern in your work on high-, medium-, and low-capacity tasks.

Pay attention to your feelings while you work, too. Begin to check yourself more frequently to see how you rate (1-low, 10-high) on each of the five "dimensions" of your capacity to work (see Work Sheets 20 and 22).

Use Work Sheet 22 to map your personal ups and downs for a while. Make plenty of blank copies and keep one handy to fill in. As you practice monitoring your capacities, you will soon begin to recognize your capacity fluctuations even without a work sheet.

Once you have a few filled-in grids, look at your high, medium, and low capacity efforts to see if they form a daily, weekly, or longer pattern. If you show one, you then have a strong clue to your capacity for work at any moment. The five dimensions of your capacities come together in various ways to influence your effectiveness at any given moment.

Your capacities not only shrink and grow, they lean and sway like a growing plant: first one direction then another as first one part of you is vigorous and strong, then another part predominates. And these cycles happen from year to year, day to day, hour to hour, even minute to minute in some instances. The story *Flowers for Algernon,* made into the film *Charlie,* with Cliff Robertson, was the exaggerated tale of a man who cycles from subnormal intelligence to super-intelligence and back in a few months. If you observe children, you may notice that a child who is vigorous, attentive, and smart as a whip one moment can be tired, cranky, and maddeningly slow to understand the next. Children's capacities vary much more rapidly than ours, but in the same general way. Our capacities cycle slowly enough that we can usually finish what we start. But if you're trying to maximize your effectiveness, don't leave this to chance.

WORK SHEET 20

Five Dimensions of Your Work Capacity

Low . . . High
1 . . . 5 . . . 10

1) Feeling strong, tireless_____

2) Feeling smart, creative_____

3) Feeling courageous, a leader_____

4) Feeling talkative, persuasive_____

5) Feeling warm toward others, understanding_____

WORK SHEET 21

Chart of Some Capacities for Work

FEELING:	BEST SUITED FOR:
Tireless, but timid	Paper work
Talkative and warm	Negotiations, Evaluations of others, Making personal contacts
Smart, but a follower	Meetings, Decisions by committees, Advising others

WORK SHEET 22

Self-evaluation:
Capacity Fluctuations

Begin paying attention to how you feel at various moments of the day and the week. Whenever you notice your capacities (see Work Sheet 20), mark the grid below: 1) at the proper location, and 2) with the point score you feel describes your capacities at the moment, from 1 (low) to 10 (high). Look for patterns in your scores, and try to take advantage of your strengths and compensate for your weaknesses as you notice your capacities fluctuate.

	Mon.	Tues.	Wed.	Thurs.	Fri.	Sat.	Sun.
8 A.M.	____	____	____	____	____	____	____
10 A.M.	____	____	____	____	____	____	____
Noon	____	____	____	____	____	____	____
2 P.M.	____	____	____	____	____	____	____
4 P.M.	____	____	____	____	____	____	____
6 P.M.	____	____	____	____	____	____	____
8 P.M.	____	____	____	____	____	____	____
10 P.M.	____	____	____	____	____	____	____
Midnight	____	____	____	____	____	____	____

Use All Your Capacity

Once you can size up your capacity of the moment, try to select the one task that suits you best. For example, if you are feeling tired and not too alert, don't start working on your tax return. You would be tackling a task way above your capacity. You'd drown in that sea of paper work like a poor swimmer in a rip tide. It would be a better choice to proofread a draft of a letter or report; it's a job you're more familiar with, less demanding than taxes. Wait until you're feeling tireless and smart to do your tax return.

On the other hand, it's not very effective to proofread that letter when you're feeling courageous and talkative. You'd want to rewrite the letter a whole new way. This is the time—if you're ever going to do it—to climb the north face of Mt. Everest or start negotiating with your boss for that long overdue raise!

Selecting a task to match your immediate capacities is a straightforward process:

1. Determine your current capacities, in terms of a numerical self-score on each of the five dimensions listed in Work Sheet 20. This takes about fifteen seconds, with practice.

2. Look over your list of tasks, and start making your Basic Choice of what to do next.

3. Just before you finalize your choice, determine the capacity demands of the task you have in mind. Give it a numerical score on each of the same five dimensions. This takes about twenty seconds, with practice.

4. If your score is within two points of the task's score on all dimensions, you are O.K. for that task right now. If the discrepancy is more than two points on any dimension, it's not a good match. Try to select a better one. In practice, take the task that matches your capacities the closest.

5. You should take on a terrible match in only two critical situations: a) important reasons make the task vital, and you must attempt it right now no matter how unsuited you are to doing it well; and/or b) you have no better choice.

Use Work Sheet 23 to help you find a good match for your current capacities.

WORK SHEET 23

Capacities Matching

SCORES:

DIMENSION	YOUR SCORE	TASK REQUIRES	DIFFERENCE
	( ) − (	) = (	)
A. Strong/Tireless			
B. Smart/Creative			
C. Courageous/Leader			
D. Talkative/Persuasive			
E. Warm/Understanding			

Let's go over an example: You have a choice of:
1) writing a speech to read to the Chamber of Commerce,
2) reading three reports on a complex and technical subject, or
3) visiting someone to win their support for one of your projects.
Your current capacities are:

Capacity	Your Score
A =	6
B =	7
C =	7
D =	5
E =	8

You rate the jobs as follows:

Required Capacity	Speech	Reports	Visit
A =	5	8	6
B =	9	6	8
C =	8	2	8
D =	8	1	9
E =	5	1	9

By comparing your scores with the scores you give each task on each category, you work out your matches as follows:

Speech	Reports	Visit
A & C	B	A, B, C, & E

On this basis, your capacities of the moment best suit you to the persuasive visit. Notice that there's no perfect fit. The best thing to do might be to find some fourth or fifth task to which you're better suited. But given the choices, you can maximize your effectiveness by making the visit and trying as hard as you can to use your capacities and overcome your deficiency of the moment.

This principle is often stated in a different form: "Do what you can do best, let others do what they can do best." The idea is the same. No matter what the form of this principle, it can help you reach more of your goals.

CONCENTRATION

Here is another fundamental success pattern that works wonders when applied to your efforts to achieve what you want. Concentration is the same principle that led to the development of the assembly line, where workers concentrate their skills and attention on performing a few tasks as rapidly and effectively as possible. It's a great idea. Unfortunately, many assembly lines generate some undesirable side effects when they require too much concentration on too dull and repetitive a task. But we'll avoid those drawbacks when we use this principle.

Concentration is also in evidence in most military campaigns. The winner is often the one who "gets there firstest with the mostest." This is a colorful way to speak of concentrating maximum military force at a single point. Concentration is the operative principle in effective football plays, weight-lifting regimens, laser beams, and ESP demonstrations. Nearly everywhere you turn, in fact, concentration is a powerful technique used to "soup up" effectiveness the way a turbocharger (which concentrates air) boosts the power of an engine.

Concentration in regard to your goals and achievements has four main variations:

1. Concentrating your ATTENTION so you are deeply involved with the task at hand;
2. Concentrating your TASKS so you work in a relatively long burst on many similar or linked tasks;
3. Concentrating your TIME by saving minutes here and there and pushing them together to make a block of time;
4. Concentrating your EFFORTS so you accomplish a single purpose despite a number of demands and opportunities.

Let's "concentrate" on these, one by one:

Concentrating Your Attention

You probably know how to do this without being told. I would bet you're concentrating your attention right now on "Concentrating Your Attention." This variety of concentration is widely used in a great many businesses and home-life applications. Think for a moment of the familiar comparison: how fast time passes when you're kissing someone you love; how slowly when you're holding your hand over a candle. But notice that whichever one you're doing, you're concentrating your attention on it.

Most of us can concentrate. Studying, learning to drive, listening to an interesting story all require concentration of attention. It's a very normal ability. But few of us have ever taken the trouble to practice the art of concentration and thus build up our ability to concentrate by conscious design. When you practice your concentration, you gain tremendous benefits:

1. You can concentrate for longer periods, up from the normal thirty minutes or an hour to as much as three hours of intense concentration at a stretch!

This results in a dramatic increase in performance. You see, you get more done "per minute" when you are concentrating your attention. You can prove this to yourself by measuring how well you do similar tasks, and how quickly you do them, at different intensities of concentration. The longer you can concentrate at a stretch, the more time you will have available at your higher levels of effectiveness.

2. You can concentrate in poorer situations: noisy, drafty, uncomfortable locations, for example; or under conditions of stress, deadline pressure, and/or illness.

Here again, this gives you a boost in performance. Since you can concentrate in a wider range of locations and conditions, you have more opportunity to work at your higher levels of effectiveness. You're less vulnerable to interruption. Thus, you can get more done.

3. You can dive into a deep state of concentration much faster, or stop concentrating for a moment, then get right back into it.

Again, this means more effectiveness. Getting into and out of a state of intense concentration more quickly means you exert a higher proportion of your total effort at your higher levels of effectiveness. The net result: You do more in less time, using your higher levels of ability and effectiveness more often.

Stretch Your Attention

You can stretch your ability to concentrate simply by practicing. At this point, you probably don't even know how long you can concentrate without a break. But you can find out easily. Here's how: Note the time and start concentrating your attention on a task. As soon as you lift your concentration, note the time again. Do this for a while and you'll get a feel for how long you can concentrate at a stretch. To expand this limit, strive to last for longer and longer periods without breaking your concentration. Set goals, and give yourself rewards for attaining them.

Notice two things here: First, how long you can concentrate depends partly on the object of your attention. For example, Johnny Rutherford, famous Indianapolis race-car driver, can concentrate for hours while driving a race or working on a race car. But he finds it harder to concentrate for more than thirty minutes on other kinds of situations and events. To make a useful study of your ability to concentrate, log yourself starting and stopping work on an important task or project that is very interesting to you. Second, when you stretch your ability to concentrate on one task, you can concentrate longer right across the board. This means you can practice concentrating your attention on just about anything, and know it will help you concentrate longer on your vital tasks.

Build Your Concentration

I can testify that six years ago the longest I could concentrate on my work without a break was one hour. But this wasn't enough because my work back then required heavy attention to make any progress, and I had a lot to do. So as I worked, I began a program to stretch my ability to concentrate. Here it is:

To START: Keep track of your concentration at least five times to measure how long you normally concentrate on something interesting without a break. Consider this your Base Period. From then on:

1. Whenever you settle down to concentrate, note the time.
2. Note the time when you feel your concentration break. This constitutes one Concentration Burst.
3. If you haven't concentrated long enough to satisfy yourself, try to start concentrating again. Do not quit just yet. If you cannot begin concentrating again within 3–5 minutes, consider this concentration session to be over.
4. String together as many Concentration Bursts as you can without a break. When you finally have to stop, note the full length of your concentration session. Take your break, and do it away from where you are concentrating.
5. Calculate how many "points" you earned in the session according to the following table:

   First Base period——earns 1 point

   Second Base period——earns 3 points

Third Base period——earns 6 points

Additional Base periods——earn 6 points each

In my case, I started out being able to concentrate for an hour. So the first hour of unbroken concentration was worth only 1 point; the second hour of concentration without a break was worth 3 points; and the third hour earned me 6 points!

6. Use the points you earn to "buy" the right to do something you enjoy. At the time, I was eager to get my faithful MG running again, so I made the rule that I had to earn 25 points to work on the car for one hour.

Today, I would pick a different reward, such as an hour of computer games, a ride in the country, or a swim in the pool. But the specific reward you choose is not as important as: a) scoring yourself honestly, and b) choosing a reward you really want. Given that, the process works by itself.

Concentrating Your Tasks

This is a great way to get more done more quickly. For example, if you return a good many phone calls, you can do each of them more effectively by saving up all your calls and making them in sequence. You tend to get into a rhythm, and to erase a lot of uncertainty about what to do next. As a result, you make each call faster and move on to the next one more rapidly.

You can get the same boost in effectiveness no matter what tasks you bunch together, from personal visits to letter writing, opening mail, or stuffing envelopes.

And this is a fairly easy idea to translate into action:

1. DEFER every task until you are up against deadline pressure.

2. ORGANIZE these deferred tasks in similar or related groups you can work on together.

In the next section, you'll see how to organize your efforts so you can work on these concentrated tasks.

Concentrating Your Time

Because the periods when you are concentrating your attention are your most productive, and concentrated tasks are the most efficient, it pays to work in 1–3-hour blocks, rather than 5–10-minute units. This aids your concentration and boosts your effectiveness. But most of us have to deal with dozens of distractions. In fact, if you are an executive, you probably average over sixty interruptions a day: one every 8–10 minutes. Many people in other occupations are interrupted even more. So unless you're very lucky, you usually won't find ready-made opportunities to work toward your major goals. The next best alternative is to create your own opportunities.

This can be difficult to do because time, unlike money, cannot be saved up easily or moved from one location to another. If you have five minutes to spare right now, for example, you can't put them in your pocket to use later on. You can't collect five-minute pieces and change them for a one-hour block at the bank. If you could, it would be a lot simpler to increase your ability to achieve the results you want. But there are some interesting possibilities, nevertheless:

First, although you can't shift around or save up time itself, you have considerable control over what you do. This means you have the chance to shift around and save up tasks, as above. And with the right manipulation of your schedule, you can get almost the same effect as moving blocks of time.

Second, while time itself is inflexible and marches on at a steady pace, it is also quite predictable. And that gives you an edge in your battle to accomplish more of what you want.

Third, the ability to create and make use of 1–3-hour periods is a skill. You can learn it, practice it, develop expertise. And you can get the benefits of your expertise in almost any situation. Some jobs, like foot patrolman, have opportunities to concentrate your time. Others, like high school teacher, are a little more tightly scheduled. Yet each of these, and most other life and work situations, will yield to the concentration principle to some degree.

The basic approach to "Concentrating Your Time" picks up where "Concentrating Your Tasks" leaves off:

1)   DEFER every task until you are up against deadline pressure.

2) ORGANIZE these deferred tasks in similar or related groups you can work on together.

3) JUGGLE your schedule to create long openings in your schedule: a) write on your calendar your most important tasks, b) junk your least important tasks, c) this should leave empty gaps on your calendar of commitments.

4) FILL THE GAPS by completing a whole group of similar tasks in one sitting.

You get an edge, too, because time is often so predictable. You can find and rely on patterns, which take place in time. One of the most common patterns is the bunching of activity. For example, you probably go through periods where all your frenzied activity is still not enough to get everything done. Then you go through other periods when you can't find enough to keep busy. These patterns exist on daily, weekly, monthly, and annual scales. You can use them to help you concentrate your time.

Retailers and the clothing industry, for example, typically have one or more "slow seasons" on a regular schedule. These are ready-made opportunities for people to concentrate time on cleaning up old business, reviewing and revamping procedures, and gearing up for the increased activity they know is coming. In your own situation, you may notice that Friday afternoons are exceptionally slow. This is your chance to create a "Quiet Time" on Friday afternoons, and be reasonably confident you won't have to turn away too many people.

The four points in the basic approach above will help you eliminate the little 2–10-minute items in your otherwise smooth schedule, and push the 10–30-minute units that occupy most of your day into a solid concentration session. This automatically leaves you with relatively large blocks of vacant time. Fill these with your most important projects.

You can think of this graphically as the process that loggers go through with their cuttings. Once the logs are cut and dumped in some nearby water, you have a pond or a river filled with logs and small chips of wood. After the loggers have been working for a while, the chips are gone and the logs are floating freely, but randomly, with open water between them. When the loggers are ready to float the logs to the mill, they have jammed the logs together into a tight pack, and the open water now surrounds all the logs together. In the same way, you clear out the chips and fragments of things to do, jam the big jobs together, and suddenly you have "open" time with which to work toward additional, more important, goals.

While the process of concentrating your time seems a little awkward at first, it becomes more familiar with practice. As you develop your skills and expertise, you'll find it almost second nature to defer, organize, juggle, and fill the gaps with big projects. And you'll be able to apply this basic principle in hundreds of different situations.

Concentrating Your Effort

This is the process of sticking to a single goal despite interference and temptation from a dozen different angles. This side of the concentration principle tells you to maximize your effectiveness by doing everything you can to achieve one goal, rather than trying to spread your effort too thin.

Some people work this way naturally. For example, one businessman I know has the steadfastness of a miller's mule. Hundreds of years ago, the miller's mule was an important source of power. When there was no running water to drive the miller's grinding wheels, the mule was hitched to a long post that pivoted around a set of gears. The miller's mule walked in a circle, turning the gears and grinding the grain. That mule would go nowhere, walking hundreds of miles around the circle, but he accomplished a tremendous amount of work.

In the same way, my businessman friend appreciates the challenge of sticking to one project until he accomplishes it. Too many projects going on at once make him feel uncomfortable. He would rather concentrate, than divide, his effort.

I prefer to have many projects happening simultaneously. I had to study the value of concentrating my effort. Eventually, I learned that if a project is the most important one for me to work on, it's often worthwhile to finish as soon as possible. And that usually means concentrating on it single-mindedly.

For example, a basketball coach may have ten or fifteen priority items to think about, such as: being fair about playing time, developing younger players, forging a cooperative team, and setting up next season's schedule, to name just a few. But when the championship games draw near, he's most effective by concentrating his effort on winning just the next game. Again, you may have half a dozen chores to get out of the way at home, but if you try to do them all at once you may accomplish none of them. You're probably better off concentrating your effort on the most important one until it's done, and so on down the line.

Of course, concentrating your effort is not always the best course. You may be under enough pressure that you must distribute your effort among several important items. The key is to concentrate your effort when one task meets the following criteria:

1. The results of accomplishing the task will be among the best results available from any task you're facing;

2. The task is set up so continuous effort will get it done sooner (some tasks, like photo developing, have built-in "process times" you cannot avoid or compress);

3. There is no other task that may "go critical" or cause problems should you concentrate your effort on something else.

FINISH JUST ON TIME

It's obviously an important principle to finish your projects by their deadlines, but it's not as well known that you should avoid finishing them early!

If you flip back to "Scheduling in Reverse," you'll see frequent references to the "Latest Feasible Starting Date" for a project. As you become more sophisticated in your achievement efforts, you'll realize that this is also the "Most Desirable Starting Time."

The reasons were hinted at in that discussion:

1. Finishing too early often means you have neglected other, possibly more important activities.

2. Finishing too early may "jump the gun" and force you to redo your work in the light of last-minute developments.

3. Finishing too early may be a waste because you may shelve the completed work for a while, then have to refresh your memory and recheck your work for accuracy before you execute it.

4. Finishing too early has no benefits, in most cases.

In fact, quality of work is much more memorable than beaten deadlines. No one will ever look at a project that took you two full months and say, "And it was finished so early, too!" Hardly anyone will know whether you beat a deadline by one hour or one year! And as long as you beat your deadline, you're on schedule. So there's no point in risking problems by finishing a project too early.

Thus arises the fine art of "cutting it close": starting a project just late enough to finish by the deadline. Here's where scheduling in reverse becomes a Golden Rule, worth its weight in golden hours you can save for better purposes. But note this: We're not talking about sitting through unwise delays that later force you to scramble and cut corners to meet your deadline. I've clawed my way through enough of those nightmares to have learned my lesson: I leave myself enough time to do quality work. But it's a challenge and a thrill to leave myself *just* enough time. Here are some tips that make finishing just on time a breeze:

1. Schedule in reverse, but add 10 percent or more for "contingencies" to your schedule for each step in the project.

2. Add another 10 percent to the project overall when you set your "latest feasible starting date."

3. Once you have your dates, follow them as strict guidelines. Stay on track from the first weeks of the project so you won't be too far behind at the end.

4. Listen to people who claim you're cutting your schedule too tight. This advice is right more often than it's wrong. Allow more leeway for any parts of the project in question.

FINISH FIRST THINGS FIRST

This principle emphasizes the need to establish priorities and stick with them. It almost doesn't matter how you establish these priorities. For example, your "first thing" may be a ten-cent project that's due tomorrow, or one that's worth a fortune ten years down the road. You may choose to finish first a simple chore that takes five minutes, or a complex project that requires hours of planning and preparation.

The principle merely requires you to know which among all your projects is of first importance, and to move that project as far along as you can before you work on any other. The more consistently you do this, the more your results will tend to come from your high priority projects. And since those results are by definition more desirable than results from lesser priority projects, you'll suddenly be more effective.

To put this principle into action:

1. Keep a current list of all the tasks and projects you could work on.
2. Give every project on your list a priority rating.
3. Move projects along toward completion in priority order, going as far as you can with the top priority project before you move to the second priority.

In practice, a current list of all your projects would be a book. It's better to divide this list into three parts:

a) "Everything I could work on, but probably won't." Keep this encyclopedia of responsibilities and opportunities in a closet somewhere. Review it only when you're looking for New Year's Eve Resolutions material.

b) "Projects and chores I'm going to do." These fifty or a hundred items deserve to be somewhat accessible, but don't look at them more than once a day; preferably once a week.

c) "Items I'd better do, because I'll be in the worst trouble if I don't and/or in seventh heaven if I do." These four or five items are your highest priority items, culled from the previous list, and kept in your pocket for ready reference all day long.

It's not so easy to give these projects and chores a simple priority rating, either. The ideal way would be to squint and "feel" the number, from 1 to 100, based on each project's: a) potential benefit when completed, b) potential loss if ignored, c) urgency or deadline considerations, or d) importance or long-range payoff. But since this is impossible, we mortals have to suffer along with a practical system:

Step 1) Go back to your goals and become familiar with them again. (If you're trying to set work priorities here, use your job description and your work-related aims along with your personal goals.)

Step 2) Try to connect every item on your list of projects and chores to be done with one or more of your goals.

Step 3) Determine how long you can safely put off each item, i.e., the latest feasible due date.

Step 4) Rank the items according to:

a)   how many goals they connect to, then

b)   how urgently you need to complete them.

For example, say you're trying to rank the following chores and work projects:

1.   Write a letter to an irate customer, responding to a nasty letter you received two weeks ago;

2.   Draw up a plan for moving ahead on a survey of people's opinions that you would love to have completed three years ago;

3.   Make plans to fly out of town for the next week to meet some people who may give you some lucrative business opportunities;

4.   Go next door and ask a crucial favor from someone you really don't like to deal with.

According to the practical system, they might rank like this:

Task Number	1	2	3	4
Number of goals met:	3	2	3	4
Number of days until due:	21	10	1	1
Overall Ranking:	#4	#3	#2	#1

The practical system may not give pleasant rankings, nor may it be entirely, perfectly, absolutely accurate. But it does have the distinct advantage of giving you some basis on which to make difficult if not impossible judgments.

Summary

In this chapter, I've tried to give you a basis for understanding some of the fundamental patterns that give you better control of your efforts to achieve the results you want. In review, they are:

ESTABLISH GOALS

WORK DIRECTLY TOWARD YOUR GOALS

WORK TO A FIRM DEADLINE—give everything a "due date," and you'll see how much more effectively you and others around you will operate.

SCHEDULE IN REVERSE—looking backward from somewhere in the future is a powerful method to plot the best schedule for each step in your plan.

MATCH YOUR CAPABILITIES—keeping yourself neither under- nor overemployed, minute by minute, keeps your effectiveness level near its maximum.

CONCENTRATE—your attention, tasks, time, and effort as much as possible to make best use of available limited resources.

FINISH JUST ON TIME—the key to brinksmanship is to start late enough so you have just enough time to do a good job.

FINISH FIRST THINGS FIRST—a call to prioritize and to follow your priorities when organizing your work and your life.

If you apply these principles wherever you can, they will give you admirable results. You will not only focus your efforts on work that achieves your goals, you will find yourself inventing many new techniques that uniquely, perfectly suit your individual needs for control, effectiveness, and satisfaction.

6

LEARNING TO WORK WELL WITH PEOPLE: AN ESSENTIAL INGREDIENT

When you think as much about effectiveness and achievement as you have in this book, you may begin to see it as something that has little to do with other people—a talent, a force, a kind of energy you possess with a life all its own. But this viewpoint is way off target. Your results are almost inseparable from other people's efforts. Other people are as necessary to your achievements and results as you are. And people bring their own abilities and capacities to a project, too. That is, five people coordinating their work on a single project can add their results together and accomplish more than one person working alone, just as five sailors coordinating themselves on the same rope can pull harder than one person pulling alone.

This requires us to study a broad range of people-oriented skills and techniques. Until now, we've concentrated mainly on your individual efforts. And we've taken for granted that the maximum results you can hope for in most situations are just what you can accomplish on your own. Now we have reason to explore the broader possibilities for managing other people's work in addition to your own. In effect, we can find ways to add their efforts to yours! If you can do it, you can move beyond the limits of individual effort to a higher level of achievement limited only by the talent, knowledge, and effort of the people with whom you work.

The range of options and opportunities for adding other people's achievements to your own includes:

> Delegating
> Asking Questions
> Consulting
> Proposing
> Controlling
> Leveraging
> Coordinating

Let's examine each one more fully.

DELEGATING TO THE RIGHT PEOPLE

Used well, delegation is a high art. In rough form, of course, it's a well known process that lets other people contribute their time directly to your goals and objectives. This was covered in Chapter 4. But when you concentrate upon, study, and apply the delegation process with more subtlety, you can transform it from a cut-and-dried management technique to a very personal process we might call "human engineering for results."

The key difference is the skill and sensitivity with which you delegate. To build your skill, you should concentrate on four important factors: relationship, assessment, motivation, and reinforcement.

Form a Relationship

This technique is basic to more effective use of the delegation process. Yet most people ignore it because you don't have to build a relationship in order to delegate. This may explain why so many people have so many problems delegating and getting good results.

For example, it's logically possible to avoid building any personal relationships at all with your delegates: You ignore the personal factors and simply command the use of their skills and abilities on behalf of your goals. It's logically possible, but not very productive. People use this style often in direct employment situations: where you own a company with several employees, for example, or where you hire someone to repaint your home. And you'll see this delegation style, too often, when both work for a distant boss who assigns one to follow the other's orders: where you head a department or supervise other workers in a large organization, for example. You can issue orders in these situations and have them carried out. But without a solid relationship, most people will do only what you tell them, not necessarily what you want. Without a relationship, expect very little interest or attention to detail from your delegates, and count yourself lucky if you get any more.

In contrast, consider delegating from the solid basis of a good working relationship. There is a common background here between you and your delegate, a history of good working relations. More than likely, you two know how to communicate well, and you like the idea of working together again. Your delegate probably feels well motivated, confident that you'll recognize and reward good effort because you have in the past. And your delegate may remember past good deeds of yours, adding to that motivation. Your personal relationship helps your delegate feel more involved and more interested in bringing the project to a successful conclusion. And his or her performance on the project usually reflects this. All things considered, delegating within a good working relationship is much more likely to satisfy you than any impersonal delegating you do.

But developing a good basis of working relationships is a tricky process. You have to draw and maintain a fine line between being personal enough and being too personal. There are obvious differences in the way you can and should relate to men and women, or people older and younger than you. You have to feel out the situation between you and every individual, and choose a warmly professional style appropriate for each one. Each relationship requires certain unique actions from you. However, there are four basic rules and guidelines that will help you in almost every situation:

1.   Be honest, frank, and straightforward as much as you possibly can. Show everyone a solid measure of respect as people and workers. Devious, dishonest, or manipulative behavior will show immediately, and will distort all your relationships with the people you delegate to.

2. Reveal only as much about yourself as you feel comfortable revealing. Then expect about the same level of response in return. Avoid excessively strong personal ties to people you delegate to. In general, the best work relationships resemble those between most cousins. Your special link gives you a basis for friendship, but usually there's not enough in common to make you best friends.

3. Avoid doing—and/or appearing to do—anything willful or harmful to the people you delegate to. You don't have to help them to your utmost ability if you don't want to. But neither should you cut any throats or stab any backs for your own benefit.

4. Give credit to delegates or share yours when you can; take blame from delegates or absorb some of theirs about as often. This policy will put you in solidly with the people you depend on, and is well worthwhile provided you don't carry it so far that you damage your reputation.

In most cases, if you are friendly and honest with the people to whom you delegate, you'll form the kind of long-lasting and valuable work relationships that will boost your delegation results.

Assess Others' Strengths

Some people think of delegation only as a formal process of getting others to contribute some time to their goals and objectives. For them, the particulars of who does the contributing can fade into the background. But when you, a dedicated time manager, seek to transform delegation into "human engineering for results," you begin to see the need for more careful selection of your delegate. You understand that the more demanding the task, the more skillful and talented your delegate must be.

This makes assessing your delegates' strengths and weaknesses very important. One ideal objective of delegation is to find a great match between the delegate and the demands of the task. In practice, you have to be satisfied with coming close. But either way you benefit from a careful appraisal of the people available to you.

You can make that appraisal much the same way you did in Chapter 5, when you were matching your work to your capacities via the five-step matching process and the Capacities Matching Work Sheet (23). Matching a delegate to a task is the same process as matching yourself to a task. The main difference is that when you delegate, you're looking at the outside instead of the inside of the person.

Use Work Sheet 24, the Delegation Planning Sheet, to match the demands of the tasks you want to delegate to the most suitable of all the people available to you.

WORK SHEET 24

Delegation Planning Sheet

Use this form to keep track of the capacities of the people to whom you delegate. When a task comes up, try to match the task to the most suitable of the people on this planning sheet. Make up similar forms to cover all the people to whom you delegate.

Name_____

Time Available:_____

Creative Ability:_____

Courage/Leadership Ability:_____

Verbal Ability/Persuasiveness:_____

Warmth/Understanding:_____

Name_____

Time Available:_____

Creative Ability:_____

Courage/Leadership Ability:_____

Verbal Ability/Persuasiveness:_____

Warmth/Understanding:_____

Name_____

Time Available:_____

Creative Ability:_____

Courage/Leadership Ability:_____

Verbal Ability/Persuasiveness:_____

Warmth/Understanding:_____

_____

A second quick way to assess your delegates' strengths and weaknesses is simply to keep track of how well they do the job. Each time you delegate an assignment, start a one-page log on the individual's performance. Add to the log after every briefing or report you receive, at every critical point of the process, and after the wrap-up. Keep these logs on file. Then scan them every time you plan to delegate, to pinpoint the one person who can do the best job for you.

Whether you do it by matching capacities or checking past performance, assessing your delegates' strengths and weaknesses lets you get the best help you can from your delegates and delegation. Because it's so crucial to good results, taking enough time to select the best delegate is a very good use of your time.

Motivate As You Delegate

You can be more effective with other people instantly, the moment you add motivation to delegation. Motivation spells the difference between so-so performance and exceptional results, between casual mistakes and attention to detail, and between uncertain results and success you can count on.

Here are some guidelines to help you add motivation to your good time management repertoire:

1. Reward People Before as Well as After Good Results—It's helpful to say nice things about a useful report or a job someone does well. On-the-spot compliments or congratulations make your delegate feel the work was well done and appreciated.

It's just as helpful to rekindle good feelings at the start of a project. For example, if I ask an associate to contact a client for me, I try to mention something similar that they handled well in the past. It comes out sounding like this: "Remember the Pyro Company you contacted last fall? Remember they asked us to come in and analyze their management system? Well, here's another company in the same position. I'd like you to give them the same kind of call and see if we can help."

By recalling your delegate's good feelings of success and satisfaction, you set the mood for continued good relations and a successful outcome on the new assignment.

2. Use a Motivating Style—Autocratic leaders have a firm style that motivates people for them. If you can project this naturally, you're O.K. Most of us are able to do more motivating with a "participative" style in which we invite people to contribute ideas, direction, and judgment.

For example, the owner of a Midwest printing company likes to stay in direct control of every phase of his business. He hires people who like to work for a strong boss, and he motivates people basically by smiling or frowning in accordance with how well he feels their work is going.

In contrast, an Oregon apparel manufacturer gives delegates much more leeway to take charge of their projects. And he is much less judgmental of their work in midstream. Like most participative delegators, he tries to specify the results he wants from a project, and the "out of bounds" limits beyond his tolerance. As long as his delegates stay within these bounds, he leaves them free to express their personalities in their decisions, use of authority, and choice of work methods and ideas.

To add motivation when you delegate, analyze your natural style and follow it. Use Work Sheet 25 for your analysis. Whichever attitudes or tendencies feel best to you, be aware of them and play them up or down with different people to make the most of your motivational possibilities.

WORK SHEET 25

Self-evaluation:
Delegation Style

Here are some questions designed to help you analyze your delegation style. Answer them honestly, and at the end read the comments to gain feedback on your delegation style. Keep this form confidential if you desire.

1. When you think of an assignment you might delegate, it is most often:
   A. One you hate to do anyway
   B. One that is too complex for others to do
   C. One that is too enjoyable to delegate

2. When you delegate an item, you like to:
   A. Spell out exactly how to handle every possible situation
   B. Forget it and go on to the next item
   C. Trust your delegate to do his or her best, and to ask for help if needed

3. Once you decide to delegate, you:
   A. Collar the first person you see
   B. Pick your delegate carefully, but outline the project only vaguely and leave him unaware of the results you want and what you expect him to do
   C. Pick your delegate and explain the project, but expect him or her to find his or her own resources and contacts without bothering you

4. At the conclusion of a project you have delegated, you like to:
   A. Move quickly on to the next item on the agenda, with hardly a murmur of "thank you" or "well done"

B. Point out how you would have done it, and the deficiencies of the results the delegate obtained

C. Rehash the good and bad points of the project, and offer positive and negative criticisms of your delegate's performance

----

Answers:

---

1. A. This may be a valid reason for delegating. Just be sure you don't dump only work without satisfaction onto others you depend on. They will eventually rebel.

B. This is your ego talking. Complex jobs may be simple to others, or may merely require additional training from you to be properly handled. And such complex jobs can be stimulating, challenging, and motivating to your delegates. You can use delegated work of this type to build a loyal team of competent people.

C.   You are entitled to keep a few low-value items for pure enjoyment and satisfaction. But these could conceivably crowd out your more important work, and earn you a reputation for delegating only "bad" assignments. As long as you keep these tendencies in check, you are O.K.

2.   A.   This is important when breaking people into new responsibilities. However, if you become overly detailed and dictatorial, especially with experienced people, you will unmotivate them and obtain poorer results than otherwise.

     B.   This tends to leave people feeling "abandoned" or "up in the air." Some strongly self-determined people respond well to this treatment. But most people want continuing feedback and comments from you.

     C.   This is appreciated by most people, but can backfire with those who cannot ask for help or admit their errors.

3.   A.   Haphazard. Tends to make people avoid you or stand near you, depending on their ambition and career objectives.

     B.   Leaves people with an uncertain feeling. Most will scurry for guidelines and objectives—if not from you, then from others.

     C.   Debilitating to your delegate, particularly if he or she expends hours to answer a question or solve a problem alone when the right contact could have helped a great deal. Also seems to say to them that you don't fully want them to succeed.

4.   A.   Misses a great opportunity to motivate your delegates. A few minutes of laudatory talk will usually lodge in the mind and heart, and result in better performance at the next opportunity.

     B.   Insulting at worst, pompous at best. Dwelling on deficiencies and "might have beens" makes delegates feel they can never do well enough to please you. Very few people are motivated to work harder by this approach.

     C.   This is a useful approach, and is worth the few minutes it takes. The indirect payoffs more than make up for the short lapse from direct action toward your important goals.

3. Show Confidence in Your Delegates—Confidence or lack of confidence is a self-fulfilling prophecy. More often than not, your delegate will live up, or down, to your expectations. So pick someone you have confidence in and let them go to work. You may have grown up with a certain belief in the ability of top performers to achieve beyond their capacities in order to "prove themselves" to the boss. But this is an American myth, much more often talked or written about than done.

In the practical world, you don't often get the best results from your delegates when you openly doubt them and defy them to prove themselves to you. You get the best results when you show your honest confidence openly and directly. Your style may lead you to demonstrate that confidence with action or to voice it directly. Either way works, provided you communicate to your delegates just how deep your confidence runs.

4. Spread the Good Word About Your Delegates—Take your delegate around to other people they may work with. Show everyone concerned your good feelings about the project and delegate. The more of these positive messages you give, the more you will nurture your delegates and improve your chances of getting good results.

5. Read Your Delegates' "Worries" and Satisfy Them—Most delegates have a few worries or concerns about the assignment at the start. Get these out in the open and take care of them.

For example, ask your delegate directly: "Are you concerned about any part of this project? Do you feel one or two parts of it may be much harder than the rest?" Use the answer to spot any special worries. Then make any changes you can to ease them. If, for example, your delegate is worried about other projects already pending, work out a plan for handling them. If your delegate is having a crisis of confidence, shore him up with your own positive expectations and evaluations.

Sometimes a delegate will have worries that he or she won't openly express. Here is where you have to "read" their faces and body language for tension or discomfort, very often clues to inner worries. By asking questions and noting the non-verbal reaction, you can often come close enough to the concern to guess at the changes you could make to ease the problem. Offer to make those changes. This is just another form of support that will help you in the long run get more effectiveness from your delegates.

QUESTIONING THE RIGHT PERSON

Asking people questions can help you get your work done, particularly when you ask for agreement or cooperation. But you can be much more effective in all your questioning if you make sure to question the right person.

"Qualifying" Your Contact

For example, one of the most valuable questions is to ask for agreement. All of us do it, although the most common instances of asking for agreement may be when a salesman asks for an order. This question is at the heart of a basic sales technique, and it works. But it's worthless if you ask for an order from a person who doesn't have the authority to say "Yes."

To avoid this problem, the most successful salespeople try to "qualify" a prospect right away. They want to know if you have the authority to agree to what they want. To find out, they look and listen alertly, and ask pointed questions if necessary.

You can apply this idea to get better results when you ask for agreement. Make sure very early that the person you are talking to has the power to agree to what you want. If not, save your breath for someone who can say "Yes" and make it stick.

Ask Cooperative People

Another category of questions are those asking for cooperation. For example, you have a lot of work due soon and you need help from someone to make sure you can complete it. Or you have made a mistake and need a favor in order to correct it without too much loss of time or money.

Favors like these are most difficult to obtain when you need help from peers, superiors, or other people in your life. You have little or no power to compel them to help you, as you do with subordinates or with people you can influence or control. You have to fall back on the good will you've accumulated, plus any inherent willingness to cooperate these people may feel.

You can accomplish more by concentrating on cooperative people. Cooperative people show their colors clearly by their friendly dispositions, professionalism, and general receptivity to your requests and appeals for help. Not surprisingly, uncooperative people usually "don't have time" to talk to you. They're less friendly, and frequently demand to know what they'll get in return for cooperating.

To double your effectiveness when you look for cooperation, follow these basic guidelines:

1. Keep in touch with people who have helped you before. They are the ones most likely to help you again.

2. Treat people nicely and leave a trail of good will behind you. This way, you're more likely to get help when you ask for it again.

3. Don't beat your head against a wall. If someone is aloof or hard to talk to when you need cooperation, look elsewhere. They will probably say "No" to your request anyway.

BUILDING A SYSTEM OF COOPERATION

In practice, getting people to cooperate with you involves setting up a web of relationships with all the people on whom you rely. For example, a clerk at a neighborhood dry cleaning store relies on specific people in the back room to help him keep his promises to customers. Without their cooperation, he'd be powerless to help special customers. The manager of a nearby all-night gas station relies on the day crew to finish repair work, routines, and cleaning up before six o'clock. Without their cooperation, he'd be overworked and beleaguered by unhappy daytime customers. An editor of a publishing company relies on sales and promotion people in the company to push a book he has fought to have published. Without their cooperation, his acquisitions would fall flat.

All of us rely on cooperation from others to do our jobs well, to enjoy our lives, even to survive. And most often, there is no way to command this level of cooperation from the people you rely on. Most of them are beyond your authority. So to make sure you will get what you want and need effectively, you have to use leverage.

Imagine yourself the fulcrum, and your energy and resources the lever. Leverage is the art of moving close to people you rely on and balancing the situation so they benefit from cooperating with you about as much as or more than you benefit from cooperating with them. This leveraging process turns one-way reliance into a two-way mutual cooperation pact that greatly helps you achieve what you want.

The basic techniques are simple:

1. Build genuine relationships with the people on whom you rely;
2. Use your power, influence, and resources to make their life easier or more satisfying—make them indebted to you;
3. Try to balance your reliance on them with their reliance on you. The more difficult it would be to get along without them, the more indispensable you should try to become.

In many service situations, like hotels and restaurants, a discreetly offered "tip" will go a long way toward balancing your reliance. But in most other situations, such a tip is unthinkable. For example, on the job you may rely on the typing pool to help you in critical situations. At school you may need tutoring from the class genius or need extra time in the language lab. At home you may need help waxing your car or need a partner for tennis or racquetball. In all of these situations and more, you can balance your reliance with the techniques outlined above. And the result will be a more even distribution of the benefits and hassles of effective cooperation.

Consult with Other People

Another very effective technique is to seek out people instead of books for vital information. It's much easier and effective to get high-level information, judgments, and conclusions from people than from printed matter. For example, suppose you want to find out about investing money. You can read up on the subject on your own and try to accumulate the facts you need. Or you can save yourself a great deal of misdirected research and learning time by talking to friends, college professors, local librarians, and other people who already know what you're trying to learn. They can ask and answer some useful questions, and steer you to informative materials you'd do best to study.

Unfortunately, you can waste a great deal of time and get a lot of misinformation if you talk too much to someone who knows a little but not enough. That's why you will get better information faster if you get it directly from the horse's mouth.

The trick is to concentrate first on finding the best source, rather than the right answer. In practice, this means putting your energy first into identifying the best available experts on the information you want, and only then contacting the experts and getting them to talk. Ask people, "Who are the experts?" rather than, "What are the facts?" You'll find that to zero in on the experts, you'll naturally have to specify what you want to know in great detail. But after you call or visit a few experts, you'll be conversant enough with the field to hold a useful conversation that helps you understand the information. And it has been my experience that a one-hour conversation with someone who really knows his or her field is more enlightening and educational than ten hours poring through books and periodicals. What's more, going this route will be considerably faster than doing your own research and then trying to teach yourself what you want to know.

You can get the vital information you want and need from experts and knowledgeable people if you follow the same three rules from the section above, with the addition of one extra technique:

4. Make it as easy as possible for these experts to help you:

   a) tell them what you want to know and why in easily digestible form,

   b) save them from any tedious computations or tasks your conversation may generate,

   c) travel to their place and be ready to help them minimize their time involvement with you in other ways.

You may be in a situation where you want to or need to pay an expert for the vital information and experience you wish you had. This process can be effective, too. The same rules apply, with one subtle difference: Since you're paying your own way and not asking for favors, you can demand more pre-performance promises from the expert and better cooperation with the way you like to operate. Otherwise, it's the very same ball of wax.

Propose Your Ideas to Others

This is a great way to identify early those options and plans that have no chance of working. If you're like most people, you can probably fool yourself quite often about the quality of your own proposals. But you'll find it much harder to fool the people around you.

In fact, if you want to be most effective, you'll go out of your way to develop and maintain relationships with people whose judgment you trust. These people give you a personal feedback system you can rely on. Use it! For example, one recent college graduate had the idea of looking for work with a social service agency. She felt a job like this would be a special opportunity for personal fulfillment and professional growth. Then she talked to several people she trusted before she accepted a job. They mentioned enough realities to change her estimation of the rewards and opportunities she was likely to find. Had she not consulted with her more experienced friends, she would have signed up for a job that could not possibly satisfy her particular interests.

Once you know some people whose judgment you trust, talk to them about your plans and ideas. Invite them to comment, criticize, and offer opinions. Realize that their comments are not always on target, but they can help you anyway. The biggest benefit is this: The more you share your ideas with other people, the more likely you are to spot flaws, problems, and overlooked items in your thinking. And spotting these rough spots before you take action will invariably improve your results and make you more effective.

Control Your Time with People

If you review the material on interruptions in Chapter 4, you'll find that one key idea is to take control of the time you spend with other people. For example, you take control of your time by refusing to let unimportant interruptions break up your day. You take further control of your time by carefully, conveniently, and effectively scheduling your appointments and meetings.

One key to good control is to think carefully about who has and should have a call on you. As an example, high school or college teachers have first call on their students. They not only compel attendance in class, they can create whole nights and weekends devoted to the projects they specify. Students, in turn, can call on their teachers only to show up in class, to grade any work turned in, and perhaps once or twice for a brief conference. It's much the same situation on the job: Your boss has first call on certain hours of your day, and sometimes overtime hours as well. You, in turn, have little or no call on your boss.

As you can see, there are two dimensions to calls on you and your energy: 1) the importance or rank of the call, as in first, second, third, and so on, and 2) the range such a call covers. Your spouse or lover may have first call on your attention over a broad range of your life, while a boss will have first call only during working hours and your child's teacher only rarely, or in extreme circumstances.

Most often, more than one person has a call on you. Exactly who, and what rank, depend on the specifics of your situation. The main reason you want to know the situation is to help you determine how you react to conflicting demands. For example, let's suppose you are working at a crucial point of an intricate task that you don't want to interrupt. Someone comes in to talk, or to ask that you stop what you're doing and start working on a different project. The best answer is most likely a solid "No." But the answer you actually give depends very much on whether or not that person has a valid and high-ranking call on you at that time.

What's more, some people have a stronger call on you than others. This makes for two kinds of uncomfortable conflicts: conflicts between others over us, and conflicts between ourselves and someone else. You'll handle both of these conflicts more effectively and more comfortably if you know who holds top rank and where you fit in the ranking. Most of us give ourselves too low a status in this area. As a result, you feel you have to give in to other people's demands. You neglect your own preferences, wishes, and goals in favor of the whims of other people, without considering your own agenda. While this may be a necessary tactic, it makes you less effective because it stops you from working toward your goals. And by definition, you measure effectiveness by your success in reaching your goals.

Keep out of this trap by making sure you know who has legitimate claims to your attention and who does not. Use Work Sheets 26 and 27—Interruption Priority Lists and Communication Priority Lists—to help you. When someone asks for your help, gives you an order, or urges you to change your agenda to accommodate some new demand, consider all this information before you accept or reject what they offer. Remember, whether you say "Yes" or "No" to what they want, you take control by making your own decisions about the goals you pursue and the achievements you complete. And when an inevitable conflict between you and someone else arises, you have a responsibility to yourself to make sure you resolve it with at least one eye on the personal and career goals you want to achieve.

WORK SHEET 26

Self-evaluation:
Interruption Priority Lists

Here's the place to codify all the people who have legitimate calls on you and your attention in a compact list of people you will allow, sometimes allow, or never allow to barge in and interrupt you. Even if you have no strong-minded person to enforce this for you, the process of making up these lists is valuable, and can often encourage you to act out what you have decided.

1. List all the people you are willing to see whenever they drop by your location, no matter what work or effort you are concentrating on at the time:

2. List all the people you are a) willing to see should they drop by when you are not making a special effort to concentrate at the time, but b) willing to consider seeing should they drop by even when you are concentrating heavily.

_____

_____

_____

_____

_____

_____

_____

_____

3. List all the people you are never willing to see whenever they drop by your location, no matter what work or effort you are doing, or not doing, at the time:

_____

_____

_____

_____

WORK SHEET 27

Self-evaluation:
Communication Priority Lists

Here's the place to codify all the people who have legitimate calls on you and your attention in a compact list of people you will allow, sometimes allow, or never allow to interrupt you by telephone or other communications device. Even if you have no strong-minded person to enforce this for you, the process of making up these lists is valuable, and can often encourage you to act out what you have decided.

1. List all the people you are willing to talk to whenever they call, no matter what work or effort you are concentrating on at the time:

2. List all the people you are a) willing to talk to whenever they call, provided you are not concentrating heavily at the time, but b) willing to consider talking to even when you are concentrating most heavily:

_____

_____

_____

_____

_____

_____

_____

3. List all the people you are never willing to talk to no matter when they call or communicate, no matter what you are doing, or not doing, at the time:

_____

_____

_____

_____

_____

_____

_____

_____

_____

_____

_____

Get People to Support You

There are positive and pleasant ways to get support from people around you; you don't always have to use the "three B's" mentality of Brute force, Blackmail, or Bribery. You can make a positive bid for support from others by following the "A,B,C's" of purposeful achievement efforts:

1) Ask for the help you want and need;
2) Be the first to offer favors so people will feel inclined to help you when you ask;
3) Create a situation in which helping you lets people help themselves, too.

The more directly you can change situations so people benefit when you do, the more support you will get from the people around you.

In general, working well with people entails being nice to get along with, being helpful, being honest, and being fair. The more often you find applications in your own situation for these basic behaviors, the better you will get along with other people, and the more effectively you will be able to add their achievements to your own.

7

A CONCISE PROGRAM FOR THE BUSY BUSINESS EXECUTIVE

This is a concise program to help the overworked executive do more in less time and direct his or her effort more accurately toward the most important goals and objectives. The value you obtain from this concise program depends directly on: 1) how much specific detail you use in your responses to the questions and, 2) how long you stay with any changes to which the program leads you.

This program is intended to be a step-by-step guide to take you from your present habits and work patterns to a more useful, more streamlined, more effective system. I suggest you go through the program slowly but steadily and complete each step before going on to the next.

For best results, make a note on your calendar to go through the program again in a month. It will go faster the second time, since much of the list preparation will be done and the concepts will be more familiar to you. Even more important, a month from now you will have a chance to see what improvements the concise program has given you. And you will have a chance to correct any errors or old habits that have crept back into your day.

MEASURE YOUR PRESENT RESULTS

STEP ONE: **List Responsibilities**

Go through your job description, your own career, and your personal goals to determine all the areas that deserve your best efforts. For example, if you are a sales manager, some of your responsibilities from your job description might include: supervising twenty-three sales people, approving expense-account expenditures, and helping set sales quotas. Your career goals might dictate responsibilities such as: keeping abreast of current developments in your field, preparing yourself for promotion, and developing relationships with key managers in your organization. Your personal goals might lead you to: stay in good physical condition, develop an interesting carry-over hobby for retirement, and read one new novel a month. Use Work Sheet 28 to list all the responsibilities you feel you should fulfill.

WORK SHEET 28

Your Responsibilities

Responsibilities from Your Job Description:

New # Hours Spent	Time Needs	Preference	Responsibility	Current Time

Responsibilities from Your Career Goals:

New # Hours Spent	Time Needs	Preference	Responsibility	Current Time

Responsibilities from Your Personal Goals:

New # Hours Spent	Time Needs	Preference	Responsibility	Current Time

_____

_____

_____

_____

_____

_____

List below any additional responsibilities you have but which, for one reason or another, did not show up in the three previous lists:

New # Hours Spent	Time Needs	Preference	Responsibility	Current Time

_____

_____

_____

_____

_____

_____

_____

STEP TWO: **Determine Work Patterns**

The most accurate way to spot your work patterns is through a Time Log. Details of Time Log techniques are discussed in Appendix A and elsewhere in this book. You can estimate these figures, rather than log them. An estimating procedure is given in Appendix C. However, your estimates contain both bias and factual errors that will distort the value of this concise program. Estimating is much more immediate, though, since Time Logs may take weeks to yield usable numbers. My recommendation is that you do it both ways. Go ahead with the concise program using estimates for now. Then work through this program again in a month with the benefit of your Time Logs and their more accurate figures. When you go through the program again, you can skip the estimation procedure and move right to the evaluation section that follows it.

HOW TO ESTABLISH YOUR PRIORITIES

STEP ONE: **Indicate Your Preferences**

When you are satisfied you know your patterns of work, go through the list again and indicate to the left of each responsibility (by "+," "−," or "0," for example) whether you would prefer to spend more, less, or just about the same time on that responsibility as you do right now.

As you indicate your preferences, take into account the present value of each responsibility: what it is worth to you when achieved; what payoffs or benefits you will receive when you fulfill the responsibility. Also include in your estimate any future value the responsibility may have: what it will be worth to you a year or more after you achieve it; any long-term skills, contacts, or other benefits that will stay with you long after the responsibility itself is forgotten.

STEP TWO: **Calculate Time Needs**

To the left of each preference write two other time figures for each item:

1) The MINIMUM time it is fruitful to spend on the responsibility each month—the figure below which it is just impossible to get anything at all accomplished. This may be zero for many items.

2) The OPTIMUM time it is fruitful to spend on the responsibility each month—the figure that balances the cost of your time with the benefits available from that item. This may be identical with your preference figure for many items.

For example, say you are considering your responsibility to oversee your credit union. This is a serious responsibility you want to fulfill successfully. The MINIMUM effort here might require 5 hours a month. If you give less than that, you have no chance to keep current with the credit union's outstanding loans and investments. The OPTIMUM effort, on the other hand, might require 10 hours a month. This is enough to handle everything that must be done, with a cushion for handling emergencies or some of the more desirable and important extras.

These figures will help you balance your new allocations somewhat more meaningfully. By considering them when you allocate your attention, you won't put too much or too little effort toward any single responsibility.

STEP THREE: **Re-allocate Your Time**

When you have studied your availability, your responsibilities, and the realistic requirements of each one, begin re-allocating your effort fairly among all your responsibilities.

To the extreme left of each item on your list of responsibilities note the new number of hours you want to devote to it each month. Make sure the new total for all responsibilities is close to your monthly responsible time. In actual fact, you will probably have more responsible time very soon without working longer hours, as the benefits of your new effectiveness training start to accrue. But it would not be prudent or productive to start counting these hours before they arrive. You can and should make adjustments to your allocations as conditions change, anyway.

Your allocation to each responsibility will depend on many factors, but most allocations will probably fall somewhere between the MINIMUM and the OPTIMUM, depending on how heavily committed you are elsewhere. This is good practice, in any case, since we know that you will get more done if you are slightly under pressure rather than under no time pressure at all.

HOW TO BEGIN PLANNING
YOUR DAYS AND WEEKS

STEP ONE: Block Out Big Efforts

Now that you have a list of allocations for your major responsibilities, you can take steps to put these responsibilities first. Get a large wall calendar with ample write-in room for each day. Go through your list of responsibilities and block out when you will make each effort—note the hours and dates exactly. For example, say a portion of your list of responsibilities has these new allocations:

1.	Weekly performance report	8 hours
2.	Monthly performance report	2 hours
3.	Development of product X	20 hours
4.	Coordinate departments	15 hours
5.	Test market product Y	8 hours

You might block them out as follows:

DATE	RESPONSIBILITY		HOURS
8/1	1.	Weekly Report	9–11
	2.	Monthly Report	1–3
8/2	3.	X development	9–11
	4.	Coordination	1–3
8/3	5.	marketing Y	9–11
	5.	marketing Y	1–3
8/8	1.	Weekly Report	9–11
	3.	X development	1–4
8/9	5.	marketing Y	9–11
	4.	Coordination	1–4

The pattern here is a good one. It includes 2- and 3-hour "blocks" reserved for specific important purposes. It leaves holes in the schedule for routines and daily activities, unexpected developments, and last-minute changes. Most important, it puts major responsibilities on the calendar first, before routines and "urgent" trivia can crowd them off.

Get and use a set of wall calendars, and fill them in to show your scheduled allocations for your major goals and objectives well in advance. Stay scheduled at least two months, and as much as a year, in advance if you can.

STEP TWO: **Follow Your Schedule**

This advance scheduling insures that you will work toward fulfilling your major responsibilities early enough to meet your deadlines. You won't have to disrupt the smooth flow of work to make a last-minute rush for completion.

But none of this will do much good if you allow yourself to fall back on your present work patterns and habits. Do what you can to mark your calendars, and to follow the schedules you mark.

STEP THREE: **Rate Your Performance**

Check yourself at the end of a month. See if you are working when and where you planned to. Check your results and achievements. Give yourself a rating from 1–10 for:

A.   Fulfilling responsibilities   _____

B.   Completion of work on time   _____

C.   Relevant allocation of effort   _____

D.   Satisfaction with new system   _____

E.   This month's accomplishments _____

TEN GREAT TECHNIQUES
YOU CAN USE IMMEDIATELY

1.   The Office Meeting—Coordination and cooperation is a big problem in most organizations. If one person doesn't get word of a decision or a vital bit of information, weeks of work by many people can go down the drain. Also, isolation and lack of communication can reduce morale, weaken loyalties, and seriously interrupt your unit's effectiveness.

The office meeting can be the antidote to all of this. It is simply a regularly scheduled get-together in your office or somewhere close by, where everyone has a chance to listen and talk about the work issues of current concern. In-group and out-group feelings can be short-circuited by inviting everyone to the office meeting.

The agenda for the meeting should be well planned to include:

Current items of interest

News everyone should hear

Brief reports from people on how their work is going

Discussions of problems coordinating people, and

Brief discussions of projects and problems to come.

The meeting should last just a few minutes, should start promptly on schedule, and should be conducted with a brisk air of busy people eager to get this accomplished and get on to something else.

Two variations on this meeting include the daily meeting with your secretary, and the weekly or bi-weekly meeting with your most important subordinates. Again, these are regular, brisk sessions at which the major business is to communicate fully and thereby coordinate the upcoming work.

2.   Wall Calendars—Already mentioned in this program, wall calendars are a valuable organizing tool for any executive with several irons in the fire simultaneously.

Post your wall calendars on the wall where you can see them without squirming, and write on them large enough so you can read them from your usual chair.

Fill them in yourself, or give your secretary or someone else the task of filling them in for you. Keep noting items on your calendars as far into the future as you can. Use pencil for tentative dates; bold marker for important objectives you want to meet. You can also use colors to designate certain standard kinds of work. For example: red for budget planning, blue for reporting efforts, green for appointments, and orange for reading or thinking time.

Check your wall calendars frequently to see what's coming up later this week and next. Use these cues to get mentally ready, to assemble needed materials and information, and to advise anyone you'll be working with of the upcoming scheduled effort. Also check your wall calendars before adding new commitments. This way, you won't overload a certain week and leave three others with virtually nothing important on tap.

3.   Quiet Hours—A great device for getting more work done in a given period of time. The whole key to every occurrence of the Quiet Hour is cooperation. The idea is that everyone within earshot keeps quiet for a certain period every day. Most Quiet Hours are established from 8–9 or 9–10 A.M., or later in the day from 3–4 or 4–5 P.M. The specific hours you choose don't matter, so long as you win cooperation from the other people around you.

The basic rules of the Quiet Hour are:

1.   No unnecessary talking, walking, or moving around. No loud noise of any kind.
2.   No incoming or outgoing calls or visits.
3.   Everyone concentrates on his or her most important activities for as long as the Quiet Hour continues.

Everyone should participate in the Quiet Hour, ideally, except for one receptionist who can turn away visitors and take phone messages.

There is a problem with the Quiet Hour, however. Many people do not like to be put off when they call you or come in. Whether they have nothing to say or a big emergency to deal with, every individual believes his or her message is important and deserves consideration now. You can overcome this problem, of course, but it takes a two-pronged effort of education and good manners to do so.

Print up notices to all the people who commonly call during your Quiet Hour. It can say something like: "We are instituting a Quiet Hour from 9 to 10 A.M. every day. During these hours, no visitors and no calls will be accepted. Our purpose is to concentrate our efforts and get more work accomplished. Since our Quiet Hour will result in better and faster service to you and anyone who does business with us, we hope you will understand our procedure and our need for it. Thank you."

In addition, you can make special arrangements for special callers who might have legitimate need to talk to you in an instant. You can have a special "hotline" which is answered even during Quiet Hours. Or, you can give your special callers a "code word" that signals your receptionist to put them through. Too many exceptions, however, will circumvent the whole purpose of the Quiet Hour.

4. Dictation Techniques—Dictating is three to eight times faster than longhand writing, depending on the speeds of your wrist and your thoughts. If you are dictating now, think about doing more of it. If you haven't yet switched over, consider it now.

Dictation is useful for:

a. writing reports
b. correspondence and memos
c. notes on phone conversations
d. notes on meetings
e. capturing random thoughts and "bright ideas"
f. giving instructions to distant staff
g. sending tapes directly to give a personal touch to long-distance communication
h. creating speeches by verbalizing instead of writing them
i. working while driving or otherwise traveling

. . . and you may find more uses, too.

The basics of dictation include good equipment. There are many dictating machines on the market, with many features and varying degrees of portability. Investigate and get a machine that does what you want and need.

Dictate from an outline, not off the top of your head. Make a list of points you want to cover, and then elaborate on each one in turn. Also, prepare in advance. Do your preparation, your reading, and your thinking before you turn on the machine. Then you'll have the ideas all ready, and have only to voice them.

Use dictation for an initial draft at first. You needn't make it perfect because you'll correct a typed transcript and polish your prose in print. But after a while, you won't need to review short items like letters, memos, and notes. If you have the knack, you may gain enough skill to write longer manuscripts right on your machine.

Take your machine with you when you can. The more you use it, the more effective you will be. Get in the habit of carrying a pocket-size version in your car, on walks, to the tennis court, even to bed—anywhere and everywhere your mind is active. Record any thought you think worth saving. Have them typed up for your later review, modification, or disposal.

5.   Preprinted Communicators—You can speed your communication efforts if you prepare preprinted versions of your answers to the most common inquiries. You can also print up: routing slips, inquiry letters, form statements of procedure, descriptive materials, lists of satisfied customers, and so forth. Anything that you write or say more than once can probably be effectively duplicated. See Chapter 4 for more details on this technique.

6.   Chart the Flow of Work—A visual representation of the work in your office can be a great help. It lets you smooth that flow, coordinate elements better, and plan your work so you are ready for each step when it's due. See the **Sample Flow Chart** (with deadlines) that shows the visual representation of a film project from initial concept through finished print.

To chart the flow of your work:
Take each project separately. Start with current status and results you want this project to achieve. Then list all the interim steps between. Put the steps in order, showing which must be in progress or completed before others can start. Consult your plans for the project to make sure you list all the steps. Convert this into a chart on a large sheet of paper as follows:
Place the results you want at the bottom of the paper. Put the first step or steps at the top. Organize the remaining steps between the two, well spaced out on the page. Locate simultaneous steps in horizontal rows, next to each other. Put continuing processes in vertical columns. Draw lines from earlier steps to show others that follow in sequence.
Post the charts around your office, and use bold color markers to indicate progress and highlight developments. Feel free to change, rearrange, and redraw your charts as often as new developments warrant.

SAMPLE FLOW CHART (with Deadlines) FOR FILM PROJECT

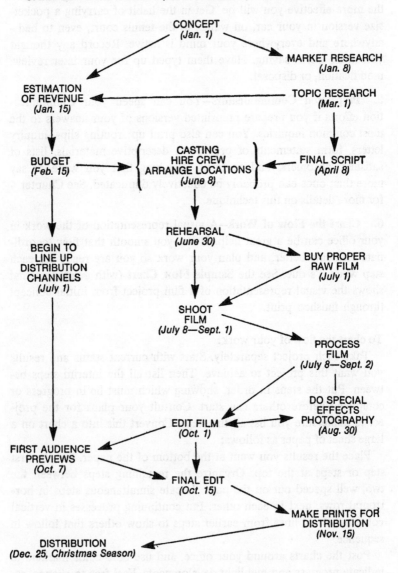

Work proceeds from appropriate starting date through given deadline

7. Eliminate Travel—This is probably the biggest, least productive part of your schedule. Count up all the hours you spend: walking to locations at work; commuting between work and home; going out for meetings, lunches, and inspections; traveling out of town for conferences, negotiations, more meetings, and other reasons. Whenever you can find a way to accomplish your purpose without traveling, you're streamlining your effort and arrowing toward the results you want a little more directly.

Save up your trips. Many face-to-face meetings—particularly around your office—aren't urgent. You don't have to walk down the hall to ask someone about a particular matter. You can save up several matters and handle them all in one or two trips a day.

Hold regular meetings. One meeting a week can substitute for a dozen quick trips down the hall or across town. Sometimes a regular meeting is not only easier, but produces better results. Everyone comes prepared and you're all concentrating on solutions, not improvising off the tops of your heads. But avoid the trap of comfortable meetings that serve no purpose. Cut out any regular meetings that regularly have nothing of importance on their agendas.

Use the telephone. You can eliminate unnecessary trips by using the phone more often. Sometimes the phone impedes communication more than enhancing it, but most often it's the other way around. You can make your telephone call quick and to the point, where a personal visit might require more socializing both before and after the point.

Out-of-town travel can be replaced with telephone, video, or computer conferencing—all techniques for transmitting information and ideas back and forth effectively between widely separate places. You can also save up your long-distance travel and handle several items in one meeting, or cover several locations and the work at each of them in a single trip.

In some situations, you can ask people to come visit you. Even if you meet them at the train or plane, and spend long hours with them (all unnecessary, in most cases), the entire process will work better for you than if you were the one to go traveling.

8. Train Your Replacement—This is a scary thought to some executives, who feel the only way to protect their position is to keep others in the dark about what they do. But in most situations, training your replacement helps you accomplish more of what you want, and boosts you toward promotion.

Once you have trained your replacement, you see, you have demonstrated your excellence as a manager. You have managed to fulfill your responsibilities almost totally through other people. Even more to the point, you are now free to move up. Your colleagues, who are heavily involved in their departments, are not good targets for promotion because their current assignments would fall apart without them. But yours, complete with your fully trained replacement, is perfectly able to run without you. And this makes your prime management talents both desirable and available.

But even more to the point of this book, a well trained replacement can handle a great deal more work for you than a poorly trained underling. Your well trained replacement can take much of the routine, maintenance, and general duties off your shoulders. This leaves you free to work on long-range planning and innovative projects that will bring in large returns and satisfaction.

The key to training your replacement is to pick one or more potential candidates. Then put your candidate(s) through a series of experiences that will: a) familiarize them with your responsibilities, b) familiarize them with the complexities of the decisions you are asked to make, c) give them the working and social contacts they will need to handle your job effectively, and d) give them confidence in their own judgment.

You can accomplish all this with a steady diet of delegated assignments. Hand out assignments in gradually increasing order of difficulty. And make them more useful as training exercises by holding a post-project discussion of each one: What went right? What went wrong? What can we do better in the future?

9. "Bump" Your "Last Job" Leftovers—Almost every executive brings along after a promotion some leftover responsibilities from his or her last job. After a few promotions, this collection of leftover assignments can become quite a load of baggage.

You tend to carry a few assignments with you on promotion for several reasons: a) they are fun to do, b) you are good at them, c) no one can "do them as well as you," and d) in the uncomfortable situation of your new assignment, it feels good to have a few familiar responsibilities to fall back on.

Carrying a few assignments along is O.K. But there comes a time when you don't need them anymore, when you are hanging onto old assignments more from habit than intention. When you realize this, you can dump them and make room for current and future responsibilities. Go through your list of responsibilities and see which you brought with you from previous jobs. Look also for others that came with the current job but can legitimately be "bumped" to make room for something better.

Make arrangements to bump these tasks to delegates, colleagues, or people in your previous positions. You'll free up new energy and enthusiasm for new and more exciting responsibilities.

10. A Paper-Work "Flow Through" System—You can shuffle through your paper work more effectively if you have a smooth system for processing paper work. Chapter 4 gives you a five-point system that works for general applications. See page 96 for more details.

But you may want to design your own. Here's how:

a) Sort your paper work into categories, according to how you handle it. Category 1 should be "handle immediately." The last category should be "trash." In between you may need 2, 3, or more categories to cover the way you handle your paper work.

b) Establish guidelines or criteria so anyone will know the category into which any item might fit.

c) Make sure you have convenient facilities for all the storing, filing, referring, reading, writing, and other paper work you do.

d) Train someone to sort your mail, discard the trash, and handle routine items as much as possible. Transfer as much of your paper work as you can to this person, retain only the more unusual, important, or difficult items for your attention.

e) Practice with your system for several weeks. Modify it as needed to minimize its demands on you and maximize what you can shift to other people.

8

A CONCISE PROGRAM FOR THE BUSY LAWYER, ACCOUNTANT, OR OTHER PROFESSIONAL

This is a concise program to help any overworked professional discover his or her current work patterns, and to provide suggestions, analyses, and techniques for achieving better, more desirable results in the future. The value you obtain from this concise program depends directly on: 1) how much specific detail you use in your responses to the questions, and 2) how long you stay with any changes to which the program leads you.

Many of the techniques and ideas in this book are generally applicable to professionals as well as others. However, professionals—who use very specific and detailed knowledge in their work, and who require concentration skills and familiarity with many details to be effective—deserve special treatment if they are to achieve their special goals and attain their special desires.

I suggest you work through this program slowly, but steadily, and complete each step before going on to the next.

For best results, make a note on your calendar to try this program again in a month. You will go through it faster the second time, since you will have done much of the list preparation and will be more familiar with the concepts. Even more important, a month from now you will have had a chance to experience some of the improvements the concise program gives you. That will increase your motivation. Finally, on your second and subsequent exposures to the program, you will have a chance to remedy any errors or old habits that have crept back into your day.

KEEP TRACK OF YOUR BILLABLE TIME

STEP ONE: List Clients and Accounts

The first step in any analysis of your current work patterns must be to keep track of the projects you work on and the goals toward which you strive. As a professional, you must start with a list of the people, projects, and responsibilities which claim your attention. You can get this information from your list of active clients combined with a study of your daily calendar, which probably reflects most of your activities.

STEP TWO: Add in Additional Responsibilities

In addition to your current clients and activities on behalf of them, you have professional responsibilities and routine chores. Be sure to include these in your analysis. You should note your responsibilities and practice-related chores on your daily calendar or Time Log. Fill in what you propose to do, in advance for planning purposes. Then also fill in what you actually do, for an accurate record. For example, if you make up bills, handle personnel or staff problems, oversee purchasing, or attend any non-professional meetings in your office, you might put your plans to do so on your calendar. Then, when you actually do each one, make sure to note when you start and stop working.

Any of your personal or career goals that may help shape your days should also go on your list. For example, you probably try to keep up with current developments in your profession, preparing for higher levels of certification, or moving into new areas of political, social, or economic activity. These activities probably are not usually

WORK SHEET 29

Your Responsibilities

Responsibilities from Your Current Practice and Active Clients:

Time Needs*	Time Preference	Responsibility	Current Time Spent

Responsibilities from Your Career
and Professional Goals

Time Needs*	Time Preference	Responsibility	Current Time Spent

Responsibilities from Your Personal Goals:

Time Needs*	Time Preference	Responsibility	Current Time Spent

---

List below any additional responsibilities you have or chores you undertake but which, for one reason or another, did not show up in the three previous lists:

Time Needs*	Time Preference	Responsibility	Current Time Spent

---

---

* See discussion on page 247. Leave this column blank for now.

STEP THREE: **Determine Current Patterns**

The most accurate way to determine your current work patterns is through a Time Log. Details of Time Log techniques are discussed in Appendix A and elsewhere in this book. You can estimate these figures, of course, rather than log them. A specific Estimation Procedure for professionals is available in Appendix D. However, your estimates will contain both bias and factual errors that will distort the value of this program. Estimating is much more immediate, though, since Time Logs may take weeks to yield usable numbers. My recommendation is that you do it both ways. Go ahead with the program using estimates for now. Then work through this program again in a month with the benefit of your Time Logs and their more accurate figures.

ESTABLISH PRIORITIES

STEP ONE: **Indicate Your Preferences**

When you are satisfied with your determination of your current work patterns, go through the list of responsibilities again. Now indicate to the left of each item (by "+," "−," or "0," for example) whether you would prefer to give each item more, less, or just about the same attention as you do now.

As you indicate your preferences, take into account the present value of each responsibility: what it is worth to you and your practice when achieved; what rewards or benefits you will receive when you fulfill the responsibility. Also include in your accounting your estimate of any future value the responsibility may carry: what it will be worth to you a year or more after you achieve it; any long-term skills, contacts, or other benefits that will stay with you long after the responsibility itself is forgotten.

STEP TWO: **Calculate Time Needs**

To the left of each preference write two other figures for each item:

1) The MINIMUM effort it is fruitful to spend on the responsibility each month, the figure below which it is impossible to accomplish anything at all. Some items may have no MINIMUM.

2)   The OPTIMUM effort it is fruitful to spend on the responsibility each month, the figure that balances the cost of your effort with the benefits you derive from it. This may be a little less than your preference figure for many projects.

For example, say you are considering your responsibility to keep up with changes and current developments in your profession. You obviously want to give this all the time it deserves. The MINIMUM effort here might be 5 hours a month. If you spend less, you may have no chance to keep current with developments and ideas relevant to your practice. The OPTIMUM effort might be 10 hours a month. This would be 1) enough for you to stay current with relevant changes and ideas of immediate use in your practice, plus 2) just enough extra time for you to stay lightly aware of trends and developments only possibly of value to you.

Setting up MINIMUM and OPTIMUM allocations of effort will help you balance your new allocations somewhat more meaningfully, more effectively. They define a range of TIME NEEDS that help you place your preferred allocation on target. By considering these two when you allocate your attention, you won't put too much or too little attention toward any single responsibility. The TIME NEEDS you set up help you work more often at an OPTIMUM level of effectiveness.

ALLOCATE YOUR EFFORTS

When you have studied your responsibilities, the realistic TIME NEEDS of each one, and your preferences, begin making decisions regarding how much attention you will give to each item. The idea is to devote yourself first to your most important responsibilities and opportunities. Then use whatever you have left to clean up the smaller items. Rather than let your work schedule be dictated by events or by the relative insistence of your clients, this method puts you in full control and helps you maximize the results you obtain.

STEP ONE: **Once Over Lightly**

Look at your preference, the potential, and the TIME NEEDS for each of your responsibilities. Then note the number of hours you feel you would like to devote to each responsibility, each month. This is a first approximation.

STEP TWO: **Make Immediate Adjustments**

Make sure your total allocations for all your responsibilities add up to your monthly responsible time. You'll probably have to make adjustments at this point. Try to insure good progress on your best opportunities and most important responsibilities by serving them as fully as possible, according to their TIME NEEDS.

The best pattern is to stay with OPTIMUM-size allocations. This is like running your car at its most efficient throttle settings. Over the long run, this policy saves you a significant amount of gas. And over the long run, OPTIMUM allocations move you ahead toward your goals much faster. The more you can optimize, the more effective you will be.

STEP THREE: **Make Later Adjustments**

Let your least important chores suffer from any current shortages. You will probably find more responsible time every month without working longer hours, as the benefits of your new effectiveness techniques and attitudes start to accrue. But it would not be prudent or productive to count these hours before they arrive. Instead, make adjustments in your allocations as your changing responsibilities and your available energy seem to warrant.

LEARN TO WORK IN CONCENTRATED BURSTS

Now that you have blocked out a program for meeting your major responsibilities, you can take steps to concentrate on them before anything else. Most professionals do their most important work in their heads, where mental continuity and concentration are central to boosting effectiveness. Your primary effort must therefore be to work first on your major responsibilities when you can presumably be most effective. The best way to do this is to set up your schedule to concentrate on these items regularly, and in quantity.

STEP ONE: **Work in Unbroken Blocks**

Block out your daily calendar at least a week in advance. Mark off periods to match your allocation for each responsibility. If you can't finish a responsibility completely in one sitting, then at least do a large portion without a break, and string together as many such working sessions as closely as you can until you are done. Then go on to the next responsibility.

For example, suppose your major responsibilities include three very important projects for clients, plus at least two hours a week of professional reading and thinking. You would arrange your work week to provide unbroken time for each of these projects before any others. You would fit other lesser responsibilities into your schedule around them. A sample schedule might look like this:

DATE	RESPONSIBILITY	HOURS
8/1	Ferguson report	9–12
	Lunch	12–1
	Ferguson report	1–3
	Other routines	3–5
	Leave office	5?
8/2	Penny data	9–11
	Other routines	11–12
	Lunch with Sam	12–1
	Kilpatrick project	1–4
	Prof'l reading	4–6
	Leave office	6?
8/3	Shearson work	9–12
	Lunch alone	12–1
	Shearson work	1–3
	Other routines	3–5
	Dinner with Fred	5:30?

The pattern here is a good one. It includes 1-, 2-, and 3-hour "blocks" reserved for specific clients. It leaves room in your schedule for routines and daily activities. Most important, it puts major responsibilities first on your schedule and first in your mind. Routines, interruptions, and so-called "urgent" trivia have less chance to crowd into this schedule and absorb too much of your energy and effectiveness.

STEP TWO: **Stick to Your Schedule**

This pre-scheduling of sizable and unbroken working sessions helps you handle your major responsibilities when you want to, usually early enough to meet your deadlines. With this method, you'll be able to maintain a smoother flow of work and avoid (if you want to) most of those last-minute rushes for completion.

But you won't get any of these advantages unless you 1) start scheduling yourself this way, and 2) adhere to your schedule despite interference, objections, and interruptions.

There are several techniques to help you do this:

1. Refuse to work on an item unless it is first marked on your calendar. This initially appears somewhat arbitrary, and very often results in scribbling in items as you decide to work on them. But you'll soon form a strong association between items on your calendar and work you actually concentrate on. From there it's a short and inevitable step to develop strict habits of planning.

2. Make tomorrow's schedule before you leave the office tonight. If you want to obtain more results, consider that your workday is not complete until you have created the basic structure for tomorrow's efforts. Make this a strict rule for yourself, and you'll begin to see the benefits very soon: greater control over your days, less pressure, fewer unpleasant surprises, more accomplishment per day.

3. Say "No" to everything while you are concentrating on a particular project or case. Refuse to be interrupted, and leave strict instructions to hold all calls and intercept all visitors. If you show that you mean business about concentrating, people will accept it. But if you constantly make exceptions to the "no interruptions" rule, people will accept that, too. To compensate for when you are not available, arrange to be freely available during specific hours. If you can somehow hold off interruptions for the first few days, you will begin to enjoy the freedom and the effectiveness you suddenly find. This will boost your motivation and help you develop even greater willpower to resist interruptions.

STEP THREE: **Rate Your Performance**

Check yourself at the end of a month. See if you are working toward the goals you want. See if you are working in concentrated bursts rather than the pattern of fits and starts that probably dominates right now. Check your results and achievements against what you might expect with your current pattern of work. To be more exact, give yourself a rating from 1–10 for:

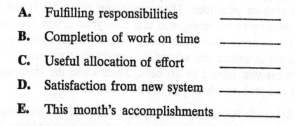

A. Fulfilling responsibilities   _____

B. Completion of work on time   _____

C. Useful allocation of effort   _____

D. Satisfaction from new system   _____

E. This month's accomplishments _____

If you are satisfied with your initial results, stick with the program and see how much more you can achieve by directing your efforts toward the goals you really want.

TEN GREAT EFFECTIVENESS BUILDERS YOU CAN USE IMMEDIATELY

1. Screen Out Interruptions—Train someone to screen your interruptions effectively. Give this assistant three lists of people who might want to interrupt you: people you never want to see, people you don't want to see while you are concentrating, and people you are always ready to see. The same lists probably hold true for both phone calls and personal visits, but if there are any differences, make two sets of lists.

If you work without an assistant, invest in a phone answering machine that can transmit two or more messages. Have a standard one for after-hours answering. But have a special one to use during the day that says you are "in conference" or "with a client." This will allow you to avoid answering the phone while you concentrate, without offending anyone.

If your practice involves emergencies, you might consider having a second telephone line and giving that number out "for emergencies only." It's a compromise because some people will call you on your second line who don't have legitimate emergencies. But it will keep you available for emergencies even when you are not answering your regular phone.

Avoid interrupting yourself, too, by taking notes. For example, you may be concentrating on the Williams papers when you get an idea for the Johnson situation. Instead of dropping one client's work and picking up another's, simply jot or dictate a brief but sufficiently complete note on your idea. Then, when you get to the Johnson situation, according to schedule, you can take your bright idea and run with it. These notes also work when you are interrupted by others. Take a moment before you accept the interruption to note where you are and what you intend to do next. Then when the interruption is over, you can pick up where you left off much faster.

2.   Fill Schedule Blocks by "Grouping"—The idea of blocking out a schedule for specific clients' work and other responsibilities can be carried another step. Notice how, in the sample schedule you saw earlier in this chapter, every day is fully blocked out. The idea is to work only in blocks, even if you have only 5- or 10-minute chores to do.

The secret is to "group" these quick chores into similar or related packages that will fill out an entire block. For example, instead of signing three checks at a time, ten times a week, you can sign all the week's checks at one sitting. In the same way, you can glance through all your new periodicals on Friday, instead of leafing through them individually as they come in the door.

You can group short tasks, chores, and responsibilities if they have any or all of the following characteristics in common. They require:

a)   the same mental processes, judgments, or faculties;

b)   the same physical equipment, location, or facilities;

c)   the same actions, routines, or procedures;

d)   the same reference material, forms, information, or contacts.

3.   Delegate Your "Semiprofessional" Work—You can be much more effective and achieve better results if you concentrate on work only you do best. Find someone else who is reliable to handle the routine, preparatory, and concluding portions of each item. For example, a legal assistant may be able to help a lawyer prepare contracts, do research, maintain and update files, keep on top of correspondence, and file papers. A semiprofessional assistant can help a CPA organize paper work, transfer work sheets to reporting forms, and handle other routines. You will then be freer to devote yourself to the truly professional work that is your specialty. And you can accomplish more of what you want via such concentration than if you allow yourself to be distracted by less demanding chores.

4.   Closely Monitor Your Progress—The more closely you monitor your progress, the more progress you seem to make! Just as a thrifty person saves more than a spendthrift, and unlike the proverbial "watched pot" that never boils, the professional who keeps a close eye on work attempted and completed does more than the professional who never looks back.

To put this technique into action, take notes on your efforts. Write down what you work on, in detail. Categorize what you do and how you allocate your attention. Compare the value of your effort with the value of what that effort produces. Do this for each category, each activity, each portion of the day or week. Devise methods and techniques to make this monitoring process easier and more convenient for you. Keep monitoring your efforts and your achievements for the next three months, and see what changes occur.

The Time Log is a good tool for all this (see Appendix A). But whether or not you use a Time Log, you can and should reflect on your efforts and achievements fairly often. For example, whenever you make your Basic Choice of what to do next, ask yourself: "Have I been working toward a valuable goal? Did I have a more valuable goal?" You can ask the same questions as often as they pop into your mind. And you should answer these questions from the broad perspective of your overall goals and responsibilities. Here's why this is so important:

If you simply take a few moments to register in your own mind your level of satisfaction with your current or past performance, very soon you'll notice a change. It's automatic. You'll begin to experience a growing willingness to abandon less important projects. You'll develop a sixth sense that sniffs out the most valuable project around. Within your own system of values, you'll move from whatever pattern you now show to a brand new pattern that makes you more effective and helps you achieve more of the results you want.

5.   Standardize and Simplify—Many professionals engage in repetitive actions that result in little or no progress toward their desired goals. For example, your first interview with a client probably is designed to elicit certain information and establish certain basics in your relationship. You can probably learn more, more quickly if you start using a standardized "first interview" sheet to guide your questions, comments, and statements.

Additionally, you can use the "boiler plate" idea for many of your less important actions. Routine communications to clients and to government agencies, your own notes, and client-related files are some examples. You can create standardized messages to cover the bulk of your routine communications, notes, and file information. Even if you have each of these messages hand typed, you need never compose them again.

You can probably find other uses for standardization in your practice, as well, if you make the commitment to look for them.

6. Recycle Past Efforts—Make more than one use of whatever you conceive, write, do, say, or send. While it's probably impossible to recycle all your professional work, you can make multiple use of a good portion of it. For example, if you succeed with a certain approach or solution to a problem, immediately look for elements in your approach or solution you can apply elsewhere. One lawyer found a tortuous argument that won a landlord-tenant case for him on appeal. He subsequently began to specialize in such cases and built a strong reputation in his town as the best one to see for that type of work.

An architect found a certain combination of structural elements that worked well together and also pleased his aesthetic sensitivities. He soon found five other projects where he could use the same ideas and elements effectively.

Most professionals make the mistake of putting aside their recent ideas and solutions to problems too soon. They "clear their minds" and approach new cases "objectively and professionally." But this isn't the only way to be professional. You can often do more or give your client better results by doing the exact opposite: looking intentionally for ways to utilize successfully your recent ideas and solutions in whatever new situations you face.

7. Keep Only Current Files on Hand—Files you turn to quite often should be readily available and physically separate from files to which you rarely refer. Most professionals seem to neglect this chore. But they pay a costly price because they must pore through mounds of paper work to find a single important item, and too often cannot find what they want when they need it.

You can save your efforts for productive work by flagging important files as you use them. Staple a colored tag to the file, for example, or use color-coded folders to enclose the entire file. When you are done with the paper, you (or have your assistant) return the file to the appropriate storage location. Some convenient categories might be:

a) **Red:** referred to once or more a day—store within arm's reach.

b) **Green:** referred to once a week or more—store within two steps of your chair.

c) **Blue:** referred to once a month or more—store outside your office where you or your assistant can retrieve it as necessary.

d) **Yellow or White:** referred to once a year or more—store in a separate file room with an index to help you locate items you have "forgotten" that you have.

See Creating a Paper-work System in Chapter 4 for more details on how to categorize each of the items you handle.

8. Use Linear Daily Scheduling—Straight-line scheduling methods let you tackle one problem, one case, one client at a time. Simply select your most important item and take it as far as you can go. Then select the next most important item, and take that one as far as you can go. Continue this pattern as long as you can.

Obviously, you can rarely start one project and take it all the way to completion before starting another project. To maintain a successful practice, you must have many projects going at once: some just starting, some midway, and some nearing completion. So you need to use split scheduling to juggle many simultaneous projects in your week-to-week and month-to-month schedules.

But in your daily schedules, split scheduling techniques tend to tie you in knots, prevent any long bursts of effort or of progress, and reduce your satisfaction to near the burn-out level. Linear Daily Scheduling gives you tremendous satisfaction from the large jumps you make in each case, and allows you to become involved with each case so you can do your best thinking, planning, and professional work.

Blocking your schedule and concentrating will help you develop habits of Linear Scheduling. But in addition, you must practice working as hard as you can as long as you can on the one case in hand at the moment. You will soon develop stronger concentration ability, and that will give you the stamina to take each project from where you pick it up to a point of maximum progress.

9. Cut Your Losses Early—This technique is very useful in many situations, particularly when you first try to improve your results and achieve more of what you want. The idea is simply to stay close to your daily schedule, even if you have to cut several items from your list and delay your work on them.

For example, suppose today you planned to handle three important projects in one hour each, and then after lunch to review some important materials for a meeting tomorrow morning. After completing your first project, you look up to see the clock at 11 A.M. You could plow ahead with the second and the third projects, but alternatively you can choose to cut your losses here. To do so, you simply skip in your schedule to the project you planned on starting at this point in your day. Everything you skip gets pushed down for handling later in the day or tomorrow, during one of the gaps you left in your daily schedule.

While this technique does not directly help you handle more projects, it does help you stay on schedule. And your schedule presumably reflects your most important opportunities and objectives. Your entire chain of scheduled activity does not suffer because you fall behind early in the day, or early in the week. Only one or two items get bumped, because you jump ahead almost as soon as you fall behind.

10. Do Work Right the First Time—Sounds simple, doesn't it? If you are one of the few people who insists on doing work properly, completely, and accurately the first time through, you already know the benefits of this approach. The rest of you can learn it quite easily.

You see, you are more effective when you finish correctly what you start, than when you speed through a project only to return later to correct your mistakes. Calculate your results versus hours of effort. You'll find that preparing and then doing your work right the first time comes out the big winner. The basic technique here is not to start until you are prepared, and then to work quickly, but thoroughly, on the item. For example, instead of roughly outlining a purposeful letter and later filling in the facts, wait until you have the facts and then outline the letter. If you don't, you probably won't be able to use some or all of your first attempt and will have to redo the thinking you have already done.

To make sure you get your work right on the first try, follow this step-by-step procedure as much as possible:

a. Grasp the project fully before you plan or take any steps.

b. Consider in full detail the effects of the steps you contemplate.

c. Listen when people object or suggest ideas. They may know or remember something you have overlooked.

d. Check your thinking with someone you respect, particularly when your plan of action is not routine. A mentor can help sharpen your wits, or you can develop a group where mutual exchange of ideas helps all of you get better results. When you explain your plan out loud, you (more than anyone else) have a good chance to pick up any problems, errors, or miscues it may contain.

e. Carry out your plan in full. The few items you leave undone or "for later" may undo or destroy the good effects of all the rest of your effort.

9

A CONCISE PROGRAM FOR THE BUSY "AT HOME" PERSON

Whether you sunbathe all day, or run three businesses out of your spare room, there are techniques to help you. The value you obtain from this concise program depends directly on: 1) how much specific detail you use in your responses to the questions, and 2) how long you stay with any changes to which the program leads you.

This program is intended to be a step-by-step guide to improve the results you obtain from your efforts, and to help you achieve more of what you want. Go through the program slowly but steadily, and complete each step before going on to the next.

For best results, make a note on your calendar to go through the program again in a month. It will go faster the second time, since much of the list preparation will be done and the concepts will be more familiar to you. Even more important, a month from now you will have a chance to see what improvements this concise program has given you. And you will be able to spot and fix any of your old habits or behavior patterns that have eluded your first attempts to be more effective.

DEFINE WHAT MUST BE DONE, WHAT YOU WILL DO, AND WHAT OTHERS MUST BE INDUCED TO DO

This is a great way to get more and better results. Whether you manage a home, go to school full time, or single-handedly have a career and three kids to raise, you probably never made a complete list of the goals you expect to accomplish. Make one now! To do so, start with the goals you developed in Chapters 1 and 2 (see pages 10, 16, 33, 39, 51). Build on these to create a complete description of the responsibilities and projects which you feel deserve your best efforts. Then add on all your routine chores and responsibilities that are part of your life, as well.

For example, if you have certain career aspirations, your list might include going back to school for a specialized degree, or moving up in (or out of) your present job. Your personal goals might lead you to stay in good physical condition, develop an interesting carry-over hobby for retirement, and read one new novel a month. Your routine responsibilities might include laundry, cooking, shopping, and child care, too. These are just examples. You undoubtedly will have more and different items on your list.

Whatever they are, use the column labeled "Responsibility" in Work Sheet 30 to list everything you currently work on. The next few pages will show you how to fill in the first two and the last columns.

WORK SHEET 30

Your Responsibilities

Requirements from Your Current Commitments and Responsibilities:

New # Hours	Time Needs*	Assigned to Whom	Responsibility	Current Time Spent

Requirements from Your Career and Professional Goals:

New # Hours	Time Needs*	Assigned to Whom	Responsibility	Current Time Spent

Requirements from Your Personal Goals:

New # Hours	Time Needs*	Assigned to Whom	Responsibility	Current Time Spent

_____

_____

_____

_____

_____

List below any additional requirements you have or chores you undertake, but which for one reason or another did not show up in the three previous lists:

New # Hours	Time Needs*	Assigned to Whom	Responsibility	Current Time Spent

* Note: This column will be discussed later. Leave it blank for now.

IDENTIFY
YOUR CURRENT PATTERNS

The most accurate way to determine your patterns of behavior is through a Time Log. Details of Time Log techniques are discussed in Appendix A and elsewhere in this book. You can estimate these figures, of course, rather than log them. An estimation procedure is given in Appendix E. However, your estimates contain both bias and factual errors that will distort the value of this program. Estimating is much more immediate, though, since Time Logs may take weeks to yield usable numbers. My recommendation is that you do it both ways. Go ahead with the program using estimates for now. Then work through this program again in a month with the benefit of your Time Logs and their more accurate figures.

DEFINE WHAT YOU WILL AND WON'T DO

STEP ONE: Select Your New Agenda

When you are satisfied you have established all the goals you now pursue and the effort you give to each one, go through the list again. Now indicate to the left of each item (by initials or other codes you like) whether you would prefer to do the work yourself or to have someone else do it for you. Keep in mind the many ways there are for getting out of work:

1. Children can help with a lot of household responsibilities, everything from taking care of smaller children to cleaning up their own and others' messes. You just have to insist, and train, and reward them for jobs well done—and wait for them to get older.

2. Paid help can take a lot of the burden off your shoulders. This includes everyone from "domestics" to appliance repairers.

3. Friends and neighbors can help you either as a favor, or as an exchange of favors. Talk to the people around you and you'll probably find several willing to *exchange* responsibilities on a serious, regular basis.

As you go through your list, stay aware of the value of your time, energy, and effort, of your financial situation, and of the cost of having someone else do it. You simply may be unable to afford hired help for an obnoxious chore. You will do it yourself or it will go undone. But more often you can afford to hire someone if you want; you just don't consider the value of it in terms of the results you can then achieve.

You can perform many complex comparisons between intangible values of satisfaction, free time, personal growth, and so forth. I encourage you to do this on your own. However, I will only attempt a method for comparing more tangible values. In this country, money is the basic measure of comparison: $10 worth of apples are easily compared to $10 worth of oranges. In the same way, we can measure $10 worth of your time and effort against $10 worth of time and effort you pay for from others.

There are two ways to calculate the monetary value of your time and effort that are relevant here. Go through them both to begin learning how to value your time more accurately than you probably do now.

HOW TO PLACE A VALUE ON YOUR TIME AND EFFORT: METHOD #1:

This method involves adding up the value of all the services you perform around your home, and either averaging them into a single figure or using the various figures wherever they apply. For example, my own estimate of a "housewife's monetary value" would be something over $40,000 per year, for about fifty hours each week of services like laundry, meals, clean-up, health and medical, taxi, gardening, shopping, and child rearing. This doesn't include the hard-to-pin-down prices for the companionship, advice, sympathy, and all the rest.

The average hourly wage for such a person, in my estimation, would be about $15.38, not including taxes and benefits, uniforms, sick leave, or paid vacation. But the hour-to-hour wage would vary from about $4.00 for menial chores like clean-up, to about $10 for tougher jobs like weeding the garden, to a high of about $100 for medical diagnosis and primary health care.

HOW TO PLACE A VALUE
ON YOUR TIME AND EFFORT:
METHOD #2:

This second method is my favorite. You simply ask yourself: "What is the least payment that would make me feel good about doing the job at hand?"

For example, if you have a choice of fixing a broken toilet on your own or calling in a plumber to do it, use this special question to resolve the choice. "What is the least payment that would make me feel good about fixing that toilet?" If your answer is higher than the plumber's charges, pay him to fix it for you. While the plumber is working, you have the chance to work toward an important goal. But if your answer is lower than the plumber's charges, go ahead and fix it yourself. You are "paying yourself" those plumber charges to do the job, and getting more than your "feeling good minimum" for the effort.

Here's another example: Suppose you have a chance to clean your own house after work or to pay someone to do it for you. Ask my special question again: "What is the least payment that would make me feel good about cleaning my house after work?" If your answer is higher than what you would have to pay, let someone else do the job for you.

I hope these two methods have helped you gain some perspective on the true value of your time and effort. With this new perspective firmly in mind, review your assignments of all the work that must be done. Keep in mind that the more of your routine, tedious, and unsatisfying work you can assign to other people, the more you will be able to concentrate your efforts on the unique, exciting, and satisfying possibilities around you.

STEP TWO: Calculate Time Needs

To the left of each assignment write two other figures for each item:

1) The MINIMUM effort it is fruitful to spend on the responsibility

each month; the figure below which it is impossible to accomplish anything at all. Some items may have no MINIMUM.

2) The OPTIMUM effort it is fruitful to spend on the responsibility each month; the figure that balances the value of the time and effort you put in against the benefits you produce from that effort. This may be a little less than your preference figure for many items.

For example, say you are considering your responsibility to keep up with personal letters and phone calls that you owe. You want to be sure you stay in touch with the people who are important to you without getting bogged down in endless letter-writing chores. The MINIMUM effort might be 1 hour a month. If you spend less, you may have to get new friends and family! The OPTIMUM effort might be 5 hours a month. This would be a) enough for you to stay current with people you care about, plus b) enough extra time for local phone calls and chores you might normally neglect.

These MINIMUM and OPTIMUM numbers are merely guidelines to help you balance your new allocations more meaningfully and effectively. They define a range of "time needs" that help you optimize the attention you give to each responsibility. With these "time needs" established, you can take care to divide your efforts fairly among all the goals and objectives you want to achieve. The "time needs" help you operate more often at your optimum level of effectiveness.

STEP THREE: **Parcel Out Your Energy**

When you have studied your responsibilities, the realistic needs of each one, and your preferred occupations, begin making decisions regarding the goals and objectives you will work toward first. Write down the new number of hours you would like to devote to each item, each month. This is a first approximation only. Make sure all your time allocations add up to your monthly responsible time. You'll probably have to make adjustments to make the totals fit.

The idea is to spread your effort around so you achieve your most important objectives for sure, and your lesser objectives if possible. Setting your own allocations gives you more control over your results, and helps you maximize the results you obtain.

Try to accomplish more of your most interesting, exciting, and/or satisfying objectives by blocking them in on your calendar before any others. Use their "time needs" as guidelines. The best pattern is to stay with your OPTIMUM-size allocations as much as you can. This is like running your car at its most efficient throttle settings as often as you can. Over the long run, you'll save a significant amount of gas. And over the long run, OPTIMUM allocations help you achieve more of what you want. The more of your effort you optimize, the more effective, productive, and satisfied you will be.

STEP FOUR: **Make Adjustments as Needed**

Work toward your best opportunities and most important responsibilities. Let your least important chores suffer from any current shortages. As you become more effective, you will probably find more responsible time every month without any longer hours. But don't count these hours before they appear; just make adjustments whenever your changing responsibilities and your schedule seem to warrant.

MAKE A SCHEDULE AND STICK WITH IT

Now that you know how much attention to give each item on your list, take steps to concentrate on the most important of them before anything else. Most people find that they have at least three classes of responsibilities:

1. Responsibilities to yourself and your future—opportunities you must take, and work you must accomplish, in order to realize your potential or follow your desires to a fair conclusion. Examples: dance class, going back to school, starting your own business, spending time with the kids.

2. Primary responsibilities to yourself and others you care about—these are often as important as category one, and include whatever is on your list of requirements that is satisfying, exciting, interesting, or otherwise worthwhile to you. Examples: taking the kids to the beach, entertaining, or gardening.

3. Drudgery—these are the chores, the routine jobs, the never-ending backbreakers that you don't really care about, but which somehow got on your list and seem never to get off. Examples: carpooling, laundry, cleaning, straightening the house, gardening (for those who hate it).

Since most of us have never had proper effectiveness training, most of us work too hard on category three, and not hard enough on category one. We usually make no special effort for jobs in category two, but at least we enjoy those a bit more than the rest of our day's responsibilities.

Right now I'm giving you a firm command: devote more of your attention to category one, and emphasize category two as well. Do as little as possible in category three, either by letting others do those items for you or just by letting them go.

To make this stick, create a schedule for next week, next month, and eventually the rest of your life. Arrange to control your efforts according to the goals you want to reach, and sure enough, you will reach those goals.

HOW TO GET YOUR LIFE UNDER CONTROL

STEP ONE: **Schedule Large Units**

Block out your daily calendar at least a week in advance—farther if you can. Try to mark off periods that match the full allocation you set for your category one responsibilities. If you can't finish a responsibility completely in one sitting, then try to do at least a large portion without a break, and try to string together as many such sessions as you can until you finish. Then block in the next responsibility.

For example, suppose your category one includes accepting the presidency of a local service organization you believe in, and investigating a potentially profitable investment, plus one hour a week of dance or physical exercise. Try to arrange your week so you have unbroken time to explore the investment, more time to concentrate on your presidential duties, plus free time for the dance or exercises you enjoy. These are most important, so schedule them first. Then, fit your category two items into your week where you can. And finally put category three items in, but only enough to fill in the time left over.

Your schedule should include routines and daily activities, of course. You cannot neglect paying your bills or feeding the cat. But neither should you let your whole life revolve around "feeding time," and what comes after. You owe it to yourself to put category one items first on your schedule and first in your mind. Everything else, including routines, interruptions, and so-called urgent trivia will then have less chance to crowd into your schedule and take you away from the pursuit of your important goals.

STEP TWO: **Stick with Your Schedule**

This pre-scheduling helps you handle your most exciting and satisfying work when you want to. With a schedule like this, you'll be able to maintain a smoother flow of work and effort, and avoid (if you want to) most of those last-minute rushes for completion.

But you won't get any of these advantages unless you a) start scheduling yourself this way, and b) stick with your schedule despite interference, objections, and interruptions.

There are several techniques to help you do this:

1. Mark everything on your calendar in advance. Try very hard not to take up an item or change your plans on the spur of the moment. At first this will seem awkward. You'll start scribbling in items as you decide to work on them. But stick with this rule; try not to wiggle around it. You'll soon form a strong association between your schedule and your activity. From there it's a short and inevitable step to strict habits of planning.

2. Schedule in advance—a week or more is best. If you want to be more effective, you must take responsibility for controlling what you work on. And, in fact, your scheduling efforts are among the most important actions you can take. Make this a strict rule for yourself and you'll begin to see the benefits very soon: greater control over your results, less pressure, fewer unpleasant surprises, and more desirable accomplishments every day.

3. Say "no" to new items while you are busy with something else. For example, once you start a thinking session, don't interrupt yourself to put the clothes in the dryer. Once you start a trip into town, don't stop to chat idly with a neighbor. Refuse to be interrupted and show that you mean business about concentrating on one item at a time. People will accept it. If you make too many exceptions to this "no interruptions" rule, people will accept that, instead, and you'll have a harder time finding uninterrupted periods. To compensate for when you are not available, arrange to be freely available on a schedule. If you can somehow hold off interruptions for the first few days, you will begin to enjoy the freedom and the effectiveness you suddenly find. This will boost your motivation and help you develop even greater willpower to resist interruptions.

STEP THREE: **Rate Your Performance**

Check yourself at the end of a month. See if you are devoting your energies to the goals you planned to accomplish. See if you are working in concentrated bursts rather than the pattern of fits and starts that probably dominates right now. Check your results and achievements against what you might expect with your current pattern of work. To be more exact, give yourself a rating from 1–10 for:

A. Fulfilling responsibilities _____

B. Completing work when wanted _____

C. Useful allocation of effort _____

D. Satisfaction from new system _____

E. This month's accomplishments _____

If you are satisfied with your initial results, stick with the program and see how much more you can achieve through effective control of your effort and your results.

HOW TO SAY "NO" FIVE EASY WAYS

Saying "No" judiciously is one of the unsung skills of high-powered effectiveness. It's the perfect defense against people who want to buy, beg, or borrow your time against your will. But for reasons of politeness, manners, inner guilt, and much more, many people are reluctant to assert their right to say "No." So here are five simple techniques to help you:

1. Just say "No." Actually, saying "No" is easy: just open your lips and speak the word. But you probably feel you can lose a lot of friends and acquaintances if you say it too often. And "too often" probably translates into "once." Nevertheless, saying "No" and meaning it is an extremely useful skill. So practice saying, "I'm sorry, but no" to yourself in the mirror. Look yourself right in the eye and say it. Repeat two dozen times. After several such sessions, you become more used to the sound, and you'll find it easier to say "No" to someone else when appropriate.

2.   Say "No" with a reason. This is easier for other people to swallow than a "No" that stands alone. For example, you're asked to speak at a neighborhood meeting or work for some volunteer cause. Say "No, I'm busy then." Three out of four times, the other person will not press for details. And if you make sure you are busy then, preferably doing something you value, you needn't feel guilty about it.

3.   Say "No" with a stronger reason. This is the response when you are pressed for details. You probably don't have a detailed plan to cite, because then you wouldn't have such a hard time saying "No." But cite one anyway. Say, "No, I have an appointment with my lawyer." This sounds so official that most people will stop right there.

4.   Say "No" for their own good. Once in a while you must cloak your "No" in a principle to avoid a chore you don't want. Say "No, I couldn't give you the quality of results I would want to deliver." This way, you don't reject the other person's values or commitments. You merely state your inadequacy to serve them properly. Despite any objections, you can usually be stubborn about this reason. You'll not only avoid the unwanted chore, you'll earn the reputation of one who likes to do a job right or not at all!

5.   Say "No" for your own good reasons. This is the final tactic, a "tough guy" attitude that no one can argue with unless you let them. Say "No, that's not on my list of priorities." You may lose a friend (or gain one), but you will never be thought of as wishy-washy. This statement takes getting used to, particularly when you're the one speaking it. But it is a stopper, a strong exit line that can save you from most unwanted chores, and even from being asked.

All of these variations on "No" require your willpower. Start with the first one, then say no more. Refuse to back it up with explanations, qualifications, ramifications, ifs, ands, or buts. If you do, you'll be back in the same one-way argument you were in before you said it.

If the first line doesn't end the pressure to say "Yes," move up. Escalate your response as high as necessary to shut off the other person's persistence. If all five won't work, still refuse to say "Yes."

272 A CONCISE PROGRAM FOR THE BUSY "AT HOME" PERSON

Then console any guilt or discomfort you feel with the knowledge that the other person is a boor who would say "No" to you if the situation was reversed. And that's probably true, too.

DECIDE WHAT YOU HAVE TIME FOR

Despite every general rule, there will inevitably come invitations and pressures you have the urge to accept. But to do so unthinkingly can destroy your control. Future commitments are like vegetable gardens: They start as little buds, but they soon grow into immense vines, booming squash plants, and tangled tomatoes. They require endless pruning and care, and can last a whole growing season, or longer. Today you may O.K. a quick commitment, but by next Monday that commitment may grow to a full day's effort. And by the time you finish (if you ever can finish), you may have given more to the project than you can ever get back.

There are two ways to avoid this problem. First, make sure you get a clear understanding of your total commitment before you accept it. For example, if you are thinking of hosting a get-together in your house, develop a clear understanding of what you will have to supply and what others will bring. If you accept it, be ready to object the moment your commitment exceeds your understanding. It will do so as often as you allow it, and the sooner you object, the sooner you can work toward your own goals again. Your objections may not save you much on the first commitment, but people will soon discover you cannot be imposed upon so easily.

Second, perform this little test before you accept any commitment for the future. Simply think about working on this commitment tomorrow, in place of a goal of your own. If you would prefer your own goals tomorrow, say "No" to the commitment. You will prefer your own goals just as much on that day, however far away it seems right now. You see, days get more crowded the closer they come. The commitment date will be just as full as tomorrow when it arrives.

CONSERVE AND PLAN YOUR TRAVEL

Most stay-at-homes don't stay at home completely. You're out running errands, picking up and delivering people, papers, and things more often than you probably realize. If you conserve on travel, you'll be able to expand your work toward important goals. Here are some techniques:

1. CONSOLIDATE YOUR TRIPS. This saves more than gasoline. It lets you concentrate on achieving results you want rather than getting to some destination. Stop running to the store for one item, or to the main street or mall for a few things you need. Make one trip a week, or at longer intervals, to the prominent places you now go quite often. Keep track of the items you need, and get them all on your next scheduled trip.

2. PLAN YOUR ROUTE to cover several destinations on one trip. For example, go to three stops on one trip rather than take three trips. Save even more with this technique by making your stops in order, minimizing repetitive mileage back and forth. Facilitate this technique further by marking a map with your frequent destinations, and by keeping a list of their opening and closing times nearby.

Additional Consolidation Techniques

Controlling your travel is only the beginning. There are several more consolidation techniques you can use. Here are three that work quite well:

1. CONSOLIDATE STORAGE. Keep all cutting tools on the wall in the garage or workroom; all pots in one drawer, all pans in another. Store all paper work, important records, and pending correspondence together in bundles. This way, you can find what you want in a hurry. You will eliminate long searches for what you want and be able to concentrate on using tools rather than finding them.

A good variation of this is to establish work centers, places where you have all the tools and space you need to perform a particular chore most effectively. A well arranged work center can speed your efforts by 10–30 percent or more.

2. DO ONE ACTIVITY IN ONE PLACE, and only one place. This is a trick that works mentally, as well as physically. The idea is to open your mail, for example, only in one spot in your home. Read a book only in another. Whatever your responsibilities, pick a convenient place for each one, and stay in that spot while you do it.

Here's the advantage: the place becomes associated in your mind with the activity. From then on, as you approach the spot, your mind starts focusing on the associated activity. By the time you settle in, you are concentrating hard on the activity before you, and automatically shutting out other thoughts and possible interruptions. The result is greater concentration and more effective performance.

You can combine this technique with the work centers above to establish a set of unique places where the equipment, facilities, and your mind merge perfectly to support and sustain your ability to achieve the results you want.

In addition, you can establish specific times for specific chores: Monday mornings for one thing, Tuesday afternoons for another. This way, your mind stays clear all week, knowing the chore is accounted for. And you quickly learn to concentrate very deeply on each task. Thus, you minimize your receptivity to interruptions and interference.

3. DO ROUTINE CHORES TOGETHER. You can combine a series of tasks into a solid block of effort and do more in less time two ways: a) you sustain a pace that facilitates your effort and speeds results on every chore, and 2) you eliminate the "start up" and "clean up" routines at the beginning and end of every job. By putting several tasks together head to tail, like beads, you streamline your effort and give yourself clear sailing from start to finish of all your beaded responsibilities.

TWO WAYS TO FASTER SHOPPING

If you go shopping more often than anyone else in your household, you can organize it your way to make it go much faster.

1. CREATE A MASTER SHOPPING LIST. This is a single sheet of paper that contains all the items you commonly keep in the house. Make the list once and from then on, make a bunch of duplicate copies for a few cents each. Keep one copy posted conveniently. As shopping needs develop, simply check off the items on the master list. When you're ready to go shopping, take the marked-up list with you. You're armed with a complete rundown of everything you need to bring home.

2. GEAR IT TO STORE LAYOUT. This adds a second level of sophistication to the preprinted shopping list. Arrange the items on the sheet according to the layout of the store you commonly use. This way, you can march up and down each aisle, and quickly pick the items you need, without ever having to retrace your steps. It goes almost without saying that you organize your shopping trips to hit the stores when they're least busy, but still fully stocked. That makes the process go faster, too.

DO FIRST THINGS FIRST

If you have been reading through this book, you've seen a lot of information on Priorities. Putting first things first is how to use them.

1. Look at Chapter 5, on Principles, and Chapters 2 and 3, on Goals and Priorities. Then go over your own list of responsibilities and rank them. Considering all the satisfactions and rewards each can bring you, which is most important to you? Which is least important? How do the others fit in between?

2. Now make your Basic Choice of what to do next in the light of these Priorities. Other factors may intervene temporarily, but not for long. For example, your highest Priority may be to paint a masterpiece that will hang in the Museum of Modern Art. But first get something to eat because you're hungry. My first Priority today is to finish this book for you. That's the truth. But first I have to pick up my son from the school bus.

When the intervening factors are disposed of, always return to one of your highest Priority items. Any other method is bound to yield fewer and less satisfying results.

10

A BASIC ACHIEVEMENT PROGRAM FOR EVERYONE WHO HAS A DREAM

If you've read through this book from the beginning, you now have some strong ideas on how to control your results by working first and foremost on your most important and satisfying opportunities. And this only scratches the surface of the ideas, principles, and techniques revealed between these covers. If you haven't read the whole book, you have a great deal of useful material to learn. This chapter synthesizes and incorporates much of the book's material into a specific procedure you can use to accomplish any goal you have in mind. Appendix B gives you blank forms and work sheets to help you carry out the steps and instructions of this procedure.

Summary Outline of Program:

1. Define your dream
   a. clearly
   b. deadline

    c. set up firm yardsticks
    d. rewards you will obtain

2. The Major Steps needed to achieve your goal
    a. put them in order
    b. find a reward from each accomplishment

3. Organize each Major Step
    a. set a deadline
    b. break down into Minor Steps
    c. put Minor Steps in order
    d. find or establish a reward from each Minor Step

4. For each Minor Step
    a. break down into one-day (or better yet, one-hour) tasks
    b. put tasks in order
    c. find or establish a reward from each task

5. Schedule each one-hour task
    a. one per day is enough
    b. but do one every day
    c. take the rewards you earn

6. Cross off the Steps you have completed
    a. this rewards you again

7. Share your method with others
    a. this stimulates you, wins you admiration and, thus, more
       rewards

8. Thoroughly enjoy the goal when you achieve it.

As long as you follow the principles and ideas in this book and apply them and the techniques to your special situations, you WILL achieve your dream. I guarantee it! Here's what you have to do:

KNOW YOUR GOAL

Your goal is the key to achieving your dream. Impossible goals doom you to failure; a goal you can reach is obviously much closer to success. But a reachable goal is not by itself a guarantee of success. There are a great many motivational and self-image considerations that strongly affect what you achieve, when, how, and why. Without attempting to dictate your answers, the first part of this goals-achievement program seeks to explore your relation to your goal. There are no "right" answers, just honest ones. Here are the steps to take to start achieving your goals:

1. Define your dream quite clearly. If you cannot define it, it is probably an impossible dream.

For example, a certain eager businessman got the idea for a new and extremely useful household appliance. Instead of selling separate electric can openers, blenders, food processors, mixers, and coffee grinders—each with its separate small motor—this businessman would sell all the appliances together as attachments to one very powerful and efficient motor.

He found investors and put up his own money to pay for the needed research and design. Very quickly the team moved close to a marketable product. But then his dream underwent a change. "Why settle for five attachments?" he thought to himself. "Six would be even better." So he convinced his investors to put up more money and sent his people back to the drawing boards to develop a way to add a meat grinder to the whole package. Again they made progress, and again the product took shape. But again the businessman found his dream undergoing changes. "Why mount the motor on a heavy stand that takes up counter space?" he asked himself. "It will be a better product if we sell it as a built-in." It took more money and more time to incorporate these new changes, but again the designers made progress. And again the man's dream metamorphosed.

The process went on and on for months until some of the outside investors began to suspect that the businessman's dream could, and always would, outstrip whatever the designers produced. They had no chance to achieve their goal because the goal was receding as fast as they made progress.

To protect yourself against the dangers of receding or other impossible dreams, define your dream quite clearly. Settle on something that will satisfy you, and describe it in detail at the beginning of your quest. Then if your dream moves out of reach, you may recognize what is happening. You will still have to choose between grabbing the satisfying goal you defined and which you can reach, or continuing to go after the impossible dream you cannot. But at least you will have the choice.

2. Set up a deadline for achieving your dream. Make it realistically far away, but near enough that you feel some pressure to start toward it now. Try several dates in your mind until you find one that feels just about right for this dream.

3. Settle on some specific criteria so you will recognize your dream when you achieve it. The more concrete, specific, and objective you make these criteria, the more sure you can be that your dream will not recede as you approach it.

For example, a newly married couple had the dream of "being rich." They settled on a goal of a yearly income which they thought, at the time, would make them happy. But with inflation, even a fabulous income doesn't go as far as it did a few years ago. Luckily, however, they had established other criteria to measure their "richness": a) feeling comfortable hiring domestic help, b) feeling comfortable dining in the most expensive restaurants in town, c) not feeling concerned about money in amounts smaller than $250.

Seven years later, both partners in the marriage were successful in their fields. They now earned the fabulous income they had wanted, but they knew it didn't buy as much as when they had first established it as their goal. On that basis alone, they had no way to judge if they had achieved what they set out to do. That's when the other criteria became helpful. Because they really felt comfortable enough to meet those criteria, they knew they had reached their goal!

In another case, an athletic young man wanted to "learn" hang-gliding. He set up some specific criteria for how long he wanted to stay in the air, how far he wanted to fly, and so forth. Years later, when he could meet his own standards, he knew he had done what he wanted.

4. Calculate the rewards your dream achievement will bring you. Dream Goals are usually not easy to reach. You need extra motivation, perseverance, and determination if you really intend to reach yours. You can get more of all three by calculating everything good that will flow to you once you achieve your Dream Goal.

For example, if your goal is great wealth, think about everything your wealth will bring you. If your goal is fame, think about all the glory and glamour of great popularity. More than likely, you do this already. It's the natural way that most people cherish their Dream Goals. But this is a more practical step. You've already defined your goal in more detail. Now define the rewards that flow from achieving it, again in more detail. And write them down on Work Sheet 31 too, so you can use the list to spur your motivation whenever you need a boost.

WORK SHEET 31

Define Your Dream

INSTRUCTIONS: Use the spaces below to record one of the Dream Goals you plan to achieve. Use a separate copy of the Work Sheet for each Goal.

1. Define your Dream Goal clearly:_____

_____

_____

_____

_____

_____

2. Specify a deadline by which you feel you can achieve your

Dream Goal:_____

3. Specify "objective" criteria so you or anyone will recognize when

you have achieved your Dream Goal:_____

_____

_____

_____

_____

_____

_____

4. List below all the rewards and benefits you expect to receive (and enjoy) once you achieve your Dream Goal:_____

_____

_____

_____

_____

_____

_____

5. Consider what will happen if you change your mind or abandon your Dream Goal before you achieve it. List the effects you think

might occur:_____

_____

_____

_____

_____

_____

6. Consider what will happen if you achieve your Dream Goal but do not like the results and the benefits you obtain. What effects might this have on you?:_____

_____

_____

_____

_____

_____

_____

5. Consider the possibility that you will abandon your Dream Goal before you reach it. This may seem unlikely to you now, but many, many people drop their Dream Goals before they have a chance to achieve them. To consider this possibility, you actually have to consider several separate questions:
   a. How much do you really want this Dream Goal now?
   b. How will you feel if you want it less later?
   c. How will you feel if you abandon this goal before you achieve it completely?

6. Consider the possibility of achieving your goal and still not getting what you want. Very often your estimates of the rewards from your goal are way off. And even when they are accurate, there may be powerful penalties and drawbacks you can't fully appreciate until you experience them. How would success without satisfaction affect you?

For example, a great swimming star spent years training for his ultimate competitive event. Without revealing his identity, I can say that he achieved all he wanted, and a great deal more. But two days afterward, he began feeling depressed, bored, and empty. His goal did not give him the satisfaction he had dreamed of. And it brought him responsibilities and burdens he didn't enjoy. Perhaps if he had thoroughly explored his own expectations, and the objective pros and cons of his goal, he might have been better prepared for "success."

SPECIFY THE MAJOR STEPS

You have explored your attitudes, expectations, and feelings about your goal. Now you can turn to a more active phase of the achievement program. Use Work Sheet 32 to list all the major accomplishments that together add up to the achievement of your goal.

For example, one famous actress felt strongly that she wanted a chance to direct feature films. She listed the major accomplishments necessary to this goal as follows:

a. Gain credibility as a director via academic credentials and practical training.

b. Make two or three short films to practice techniques and prove my talent.

c. Find a good story or script.

d. Use my contacts and knowledge of the industry to get a major producer to back me.

e. Make the film.

WORK SHEET 32

The Major Accomplishments of Your Dream Goal

INSTRUCTIONS: Use the spaces below to identify and organize the Major Steps required to accomplish your Dream Goal.

Dream Goal:

1. List below the Major Steps required to accomplish your Dream Goal.

_____

_____

_____

_____

_____

_____

2. Put the Major Steps in chronological order. Make two separate lists: one for Steps that must be done in order, and a second for Steps you can try to do anytime.

       Chronological Steps   Unrelated Steps

_____

_____

_____

_____

_____

_____

_____

_____

_____

_____

_____

3. Number the Steps above, and for each number, specify a reward
   you will receive from each accomplishment:

_____

_____

_____

_____

_____

_____

_____

_____

_____

_____

_____

If you have little or no experience in planning, you may be stymied at this point in the program. You needn't be. Breaking down large goals into smaller ones is a very simple and direct process. Here's one way to dissect your goal into Major Steps:

1. Specify the people, resources, equipment, information, skills, facilities, space and/or locations that are necessary to achieve your goal.

2. Acquiring or accomplishing each of these is a Major Step.

3. Putting all the elements together to achieve the goal in reality is at least one more Major Step. The difference between the Major Steps and the Minor Steps (which you'll specify later) is subtle but definite:

A MAJOR Step is an accomplishment or achievement that brings certain desired results. For example, it would be a Major Step on the road to the Presidency to become governor of your chosen state. It would not be a Major Step to run for election and lose. Several sets of results from Major Steps combine to give you your goal.

A MINOR Step is an action you take toward achieving a Major Step, and counts without regard to whether or not it brings you the results you wanted. For example, a Minor Step on the road to the Presidency would be undertaking an expensive publicity campaign. That action remains a Minor Step whether or not the campaign is successful. For this reason, you may have to take an unlimited number of Minor Steps to complete one Major Step.

Describe each Major Step as fully as you described your original goal, with a detailed description and several "objective" criteria so you'll know when you have completed it. Once you have a list of Major Steps, put them in chronological order. You'll find that some of the Steps obviously fit before or after certain others. But you can try to accomplish other Steps almost anytime. For example, the screen actress had to establish her credibility before she could expect to get backing from a producer. But she could reasonably expect to find a good story at any time. She didn't have to wait to establish her credibility to start looking for her "vehicle" to a directing career.

To handle this slightly confusing situation, make two lists of your Major Steps. The first list should contain all the Steps that are strictly chronological. The second should contain all the Steps that you can reasonably do at any point in the process.

Now refer to Work Sheet 32 and to your own imagination. Try to tie each of your Major Steps to a satisfying reward you will get when you complete it. This motivational gimmick really works. And while it may seem a little silly, tedious, or contrived, you will never know its value until you put it into action. Believe me, it will work.

PLAN EACH MAJOR STEP

Each major accomplishment or step deserves its own mini plan. Just as you did for your major goal, establish a directed series of efforts for each of your Major Steps. Use Work Sheet 33 to help you create:

a. a deadline for completing it

b. a series of Minor Steps required to achieve it

c. a chronological order for the Minor Steps

d. a satisfying reward you will receive when you accomplish each Minor Step

You can find the Minor Steps of your program by looking for actions you must take to achieve each Major Step. For example, if a Major Step entails contacting people and persuading them to approve your ideas, the Minor Steps might be:

1. identifying the people to contact

2. putting your ideas on paper

3. writing the letter or making the phone call to establish contact

4. transmitting your ideas

5. evaluating their response

6. visiting them to win their approval

. . . and so on.

WORK SHEET 33

Organizing Each Major Step

MAJOR STEP:_____

TOWARD DREAM GOAL:_____

INSTRUCTIONS: Use the spaces below to organize one of the Major Steps toward your Dream Goal. Use a separate copy of the Work Sheet for each Major Step.

1. Set a deadline for the achievement of the Major Step:

_____

2. List below the Minor Steps you must take to achieve the Major Step desired:

_____

_____

_____

_____

_____

_____

_____

_____

_____

_____

3. Put the Minor Steps above into chronological order. Make two
    lists: one for Steps that must be done in order, and a second one
    for Steps you can try to do anytime.

        Chronological Steps   Unrelated Steps

    _____

    _____

    _____

    _____

    _____

    _____

    _____

4. Number the Steps above, and for each number, specify a reward
    you will receive (or give yourself) from each accomplishment:

    _____

    _____

_____

_____

_____

_____

_____

_____

_____

PLAN EACH MINOR STEP

Repeat the same process with your Minor Steps. Now you can be much more specific, because the Minor Steps are action steps. Use Work Sheet 34 to help you break down your Minor Steps into simple tasks you can accomplish in a single day or, better yet, in a single hour.

Put these tasks in chronological order, and again find a satisfying reward you can tie to each one. Sometimes, though, the task itself is not rewarding. For example, one plan I once established for myself involved stuffing five hundred envelopes, addressing them, and mailing them. Another time, I had to hand staple two thousand, forty-eight-page magazines! Neither of these tasks was a lot of fun, but they were essential to the accomplishment of my Major Step and my goal. You tie rewards to such Minor Steps by creating them out of your imagination. For example, when I finished with the five hundred envelopes, I took the rest of the day off and went for a long ride in the country. When I finished stapling magazines, I treated myself to a meal in a fancy restaurant where I ordered the best food and wine on the menu. Your tastes for pleasure may be different from mine, but they are undoubtedly just as strong. Tie them to the Steps in your plan and you will make great progress toward your Dream Goal.

WORK SHEET 34

Planning Simple Tasks

INSTRUCTIONS: Use the spaces below to break down each of your Minor Steps into simple tasks you can do in a day, or better yet, in an hour. Use a separate copy of the Work Sheet for each Minor Step.

Minor Step:

Toward Major Step:

Toward Dream Goal:

1. Set a deadline for the achievement of the Minor Step:_____

_____

2. List below the simple tasks you can take to achieve the Minor Step desired. Try to break down the Step into small enough pieces so you can finish each task in a single day, or better yet, a single hour:

_____

_____

_____

_____

_____

_____

3. Put the simple tasks above into chronological order. Make two
   lists: one for tasks that must be done in order, and a second one
   for tasks you can try to do anytime.

   Chronological tasks   Unrelated tasks

   _____   _____

   _____   _____

   _____   _____

   _____   _____

4. Number the tasks above, and for each number, specify a reward
   you will receive (or give yourself) from each effort:

   _____

   _____

   _____

   _____

   _____

   _____

PUT EVERYTHING
ON YOUR SCHEDULE

Look how far you've come from idle dreaming about your goal!
You have a goal firmly in mind, fully described in detail, and you

have it broken down into Major Steps, Minor Steps, and single tasks you can do in one sitting. Suddenly the goal looks a lot closer than it did when it was nothing more than a dream. But you're not there yet. To make this Dream Goal a reality, you need to use every possible technique for increasing your effectiveness and shaping your results to what you want. And that includes scheduling.

Get out your calendar and begin scheduling each task in your overall plan. But don't burn yourself out by scheduling them all in a row for the next three weeks. This Goal is probably fairly large, and you have other responsibilities and other Goals to pursue. Schedule one of these goal-oriented tasks a day, or one every other day, as far in advance as you possibly can. Then do what you schedule, without fail. The object is not to get there as fast as possible, but rather to sustain your effort and get there for sure. The best rule to follow is "Slow but Steady Wins the Race."

As you complete each task, be sure to take the rewards you have tied to their completion. These rewards serve a very real and important purpose. You, like millions of others, may have trouble being nice to yourself or giving yourself a reward. Do it anyway. Learn this important skill, because it is an essential ingredient in any long-term effort toward a Goal.

MARK YOUR PROGRESS

Cross off each of the Steps as you complete it. And use a flow chart or a graph of some sort to keep your progress along the plan in full view as much as possible.

The graph of your progress is another reward that hits you where it helps whenever you see it. Don't hide the chart away or keep it a secret. You may be mistaking modesty for a self-defeating attitude that robs you of the fruits of victory even as you reach out to touch them. If you are working toward a Dream Goal you really want, and if you are making good progress, you deserve to feel good about your work and to share your good feelings with others.

SHARE YOUR METHODS
WITH OTHER PEOPLE

The Program for Everyone Who Has a Secret Dream should not be kept a secret. Share your success, and your successful methods, with the people around you. Unlike competitive situations, there is no penalty to you if other people achieve their dreams. You have nothing to lose by sharing what you know with others. And, if you can progress to the point where you can cooperate with others to achieve even larger Dream Goals, your sharing the method may even be a Major Step toward the biggest and best Goals you dream of.

APPENDIX A

A Time Log Form With Instructions

The Time Log is widely recognized by experts and other people who have used it as one of the most valuable and important tools yet discovered for helping you become more effective. It is effective at least four ways:

1. It helps you recognize your current work patterns.

2. It helps you identify improvements you can make in your current work patterns.

3. It motivates you to change your patterns, by making clear to you just how much of your effort goes for few if any results.

4. It provides feedback on improvements and any continuing need for improvements in your work patterns, when used at regular intervals over a period of a year or more.

When you start to work with a Time Log, you will experience two revelations: First, you will simply not believe how much time goes for trivial occupations. Second, you will come to believe your Time Logs and to be excited by the possibilities they show you for increasing your effectiveness.

Many people who recommend Time Logs suggest you keep filling them in for a week, two weeks, or longer. I prefer a simpler and more direct approach: Keep filling in your Time Logs until you believe what they tell you. For some people, one week is enough. For others, four weeks are just the beginning. But the value of the Time Log lies in what the completed forms tell you about yourself. And what they tell you will have no value until and unless you believe it.

Once you accept your Time Logs as accurate, you are ready to analyze the Time Logs and find ways to achieve more of what you want.

TIME LOG

NAME _____

PROJECTS &
ACTIVITIES ——▶

HOURS ——▶

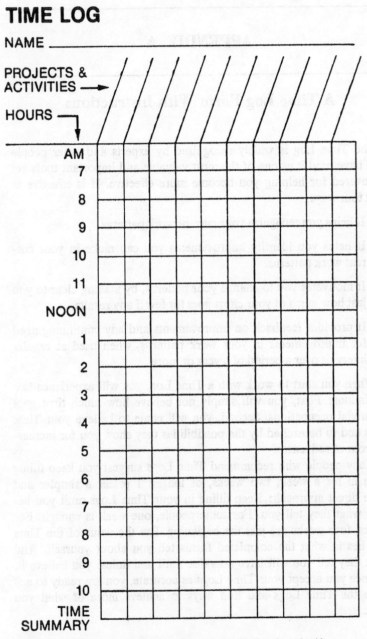

AM 7							
8							
9							
10							
11							
NOON							
1							
2							
3							
4							
5							
6							
7							
8							
9							
10							
TIME SUMMARY							

Instructions: Each 5, 10, or 15 minute interval (by the clock),
place a ✓ in the column that best describes your activity.

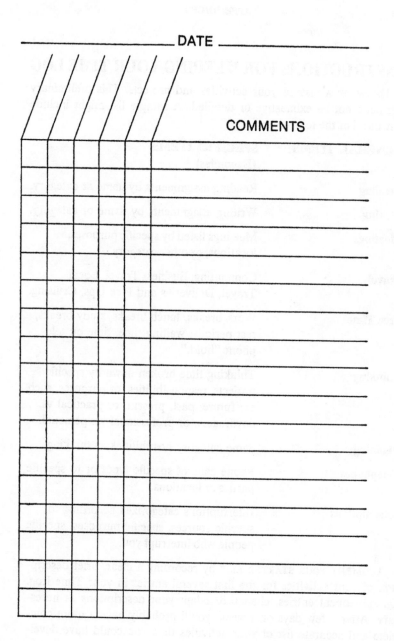

_____ DATE _____

COMMENTS

INSTRUCTIONS FOR KEEPING YOUR TIME LOG

DRAW UP A LIST of your activities and projects. This preliminary list need not be exhaustive or detailed. A sample list might include any or all of the following:

GENERAL ITEMS	SPECIFIC ITEMS (Examples)
Reading	Reading assignments by name or category.
Writing	Writing assignments by name or category.
Meetings	Meetings listed by specific purposes, locations, or other category.
Travel	Commuting, Business Travel, Local Travel, Deliveries and Pick Ups, Cruising.
Free Time	Work breaks, lunch breaks, study breaks, rest periods, waiting time, time on telephone "hold."
Thinking	Thinking time broken down by specific projects, responsibilities, or purposes, such as: future, past, present, or practical vs. daydreams, or professional vs. personal.
Planning	Same category possibilities as thinking.
Telephones	Phone calls of specific types or to specific parties or locations.
Interruptions	Interruptions categorized according to: specific sources, specific purposes, specific people who interrupt you.

AUGMENT YOUR STARTER LIST by recording a clear, brief description of your activities for the first several entries in your Time Log. On subsequent entries, change or adapt your descriptions as necessary. After a few days or a week, you'll probably have a more complete and accurate list of your activities than you could have developed any other way.

CONSOLIDATE YOUR CATEGORIES into eight or fewer descriptions that thoroughly cover your major and minor projects. You may want to create one set of categories for "work," another for "personal" time. Enter these by code number or abbreviation in the column headings across the top of the form.

MAKE ENOUGH COPIES of the Time Log form so you can have a fresh one every day, for as many days as it will take to convince you. Several weeks' worth will probably be enough for a first printing run.

TO MAKE AN ENTRY in your Time Log, simply put a dot, a small x, or any other fast and easy symbol on the chart.

PLACE YOUR MARK HORIZONTALLY opposite the exact time you are marking the Log. For example, at 11:15 A.M. you would make your mark slightly below the line labeled "11."

PLACE THE SAME MARK VERTICALLY under the column heading which best describes what you are busy with at the time.

FILL IN YOUR TIME LOG AS YOU GO through your day. Don't plan on going back later to fix it up. Your memory will play tricks on you and record more about what you *think* you did than what you *actually* worked on.

There tends to be some confusion about how to record your actions: Should you try to mark your Log to reflect everything you did that you remember from the past interval? or to record only one action per interval? the main action? or the action just prior to your Log entry, however humble? You improve or distort the accuracy of your Log according to your interpretation of the procedure. The best way to use the Log is:

a) to make one entry at a time, only at regular intervals
b) to record your main action of the past interval, and
c) to choose your intervals so they best reflect your activities throughout the day.

FIFTEEN-MINUTE INTERVALS are short enough for most people. But if you are in an especially fast-moving situation, you may want to use ten-minute or even shorter intervals. The picture you draw of your behavior patterns becomes more accurate the shorter your intervals. However, shorter intervals double or triple the (very few) minutes your Time Log entries require.

Choosing the interval is like deciding how to sample a truckload of apples. Do you take one, two, or three apples from each bushel basket? Do you sample from every basket, or every fourth? Or perhaps you taste only one apple from the whole truckload? Experience is crucial in making this choice. Here's a method to help you arrive at the best Time Log intervals for you:

1) Start by making entries every 15 minutes.

2) After a full day of logging, if you find that each entry requires a conscious choice of what to record and what to leave out, shorten the interval to 10 minutes.

3) Keep shortening the interval by 25–35 percent until you find that you usually have only one activity to record. This is an appropriate Time Log interval for you and your situation.

NOTE DETAILS OF YOUR ACTIVITIES right on the Log form to facilitate your later recall of your activities. These notes aid in your analysis and also boost the credibility of your Time Log results.

EVALUATE YOUR TIME LOG after a few days to make any changes in your procedure, your recording interval, or your headings that you feel may be necessary. You may want to put your categories in order of frequency, although after a few days you will memorize their locations no matter how you arrange them.

AFTER YOU ARE CONVINCED that your Time Logs are giving you an accurate picture of your daily patterns, begin your analysis.

INSTRUCTIONS FOR ANALYZING YOUR TIME-USE PATTERNS

ANALYZE BY CATEGORY. Add up all the time in each category on your Time Log. What projects take the most? What projects the least? Does this reflect a fair evaluation of what the results of these projects might be worth to you, your organization, and/or your future? Does this account for the entire period you thought you logged? What happened to any time unaccounted for?

ANALYZE BY RESULTS. Compare the time in each category with the results you achieve in that category. Are you getting a fair measure of results per unit of time? Which categories give you the most results per unit? Which categories the least? Are you satisfied with this distribution?

ANALYZE BY VALUE. What activities show up on your Time Log

that you could eliminate from your schedule? What activities on your Time Log deserve a reduced effort? What would be the results, both positive and negative, of eliminating certain items, or reducing your effort by 10 percent, 20 percent, or more? What activities on your Time Log deserve more attention? What results can you expect from a 10 percent, 20 percent or greater increase in your allotment to such an activity?

ANALYZE BY GOAL. What goals do you have that are not reflected in specific actions in your Time Log? Why don't you appear to be working to reach these goals? If you are sure you want to reach these goals, what actions will you add to your schedule to make progress toward them? What actions will you take out of your present schedule to make room for these new projects?

REPEAT AS NEEDED. When you finish the first few weeks of Time Logging, you will have information to help you adjust your efforts and achieve more of what you want. But after a few months, you may well profit from keeping another Time Log. In fact, you can probably gain useful information and motivation from occasional Time Logs over the next several years. The new Logs will reveal improvements you have made, as well as those you still need to make. As you gain experience with this tool, you may be able to reduce the number of weeks in a row you need to obtain full accuracy.

SECOND-STAGE TIME LOG

When you have recorded, analyzed, and improved your behavior patterns with the Time Log, you may want to go a step further to a more advanced methodology. This is the Second-stage Time Log. The procedure is exactly the same as for the regular Time Log, with one difference: use the new Log to record only the times you work on a single project, from start to finish.

Because you are concentrating on a single project, you can keep track of your effort with finely detailed accuracy. Your categories can be much narrower, and your intervals much shorter. The greater accuracy of your Second-stage Time Log will show you many errors, inconsistencies, and poorly directed efforts that you might never have recorded on a regular Time Log. You can safely assume you are making many of these same mistakes on other projects, as well.

APPENDIX B

A Scheduling Work Sheet and Instructions

Sometimes a simple form can help you organize your whole day. The idea for the following scheduling work sheet emerged some twenty-five years ago. Over the years, it has been refined, reworked, and revamped by many people to suit the particular needs of its many users.

I developed the work sheet in this Appendix over the past few years to suit my needs and the needs of many people whom I advise and teach. The form is nicely set up and carefully ruled on the page to be useful, to look well, and to make copying easier. However, before you make too many copies, I advise you to test any changes you feel you want to make in the placement of the various sections, or their relative sizes. Be sure the changes will make the work sheet more useful or easier for you. You may even want to add or delete one or two categories. Once you like the form, make a large number of copies, and use a fresh one for each day.

INSTRUCTIONS FOR USING
THE SCHEDULING FORM

TASKS. This section of the form is the main focus of your scheduling efforts. Here you list all the items you would like to accomplish during the day. Then:

1) Cross off each one as you complete it.

2) Select your next most important task and tackle it.

3) Add new items to the sheet as they come up, and tackle each one when it becomes the "best" action available according to your Basic Choice.

You can fill in these work sheets in advance, and thereby schedule an entire week, or even a month, day by day in detail. You can also use one form for the next calendar month (as in the Daily Prompter file) and distribute the items into specific days as they come closer.

You can simply list each task you want to accomplish. But the work sheet provides room for you to have a more sophisticated list. The "priorities" column gives you a chance to rank all the items on your list, either: a) in numerical order of importance, b) according to any grading scale you find useful, such as the one in Table A, or c) into high-, medium-, and low-priority groupings. The addition of a priority rating for each task helps you make a better Basic Choice of what to work on next from your list.

TABLE A

A Seven-point
Priority-grading Scale

POINT GRADE	DEFINITION
1	Handle immediately—Emergency
2	Next item to work on
3	High priority, finish today
4	High priority, finish within one week
5	Medium priority, delegate for completion by deadline
6	Medium priority, fit into schedule and finish by deadline
7	Low priority, save for free time or slow-work season
8*	Of little value, ignore or throw out

* Note: This is a 7-point priority rating scale. Items that have little or no priority fall off the scale into grade "8" for appropriate inaction.

The "Deadline" column gives you a chance to note any applicable deadlines for each task. If the task has none, you may want to

TO DO TODAY

NAME: _____ DATE: _____

PRIORITY	TASKS	DEADLINE	ESTIMATED TIME	RESULTS & ACTUAL TIME USED	PHONE CALLS (name, purpose)

LETTERS/REPORTS
TO WRITE

LONG RANGE
(task, when due)

PEOPLE TO SEE/DISCUSSION TOPICS

give yourself one on your own initiative. Deadlines are another aid to better Basic Choices from your list.

The "Estimated Time" column serves two important purposes. First, it gives you a chance to indicate approximately how long you expect the task will take. With this information, you can select a task that fits the time available to you. Second, you can later compare the "Estimated Time" with the "Actual Time Used" (in the next column) to improve your future estimates and thus schedule more accurately.

Filling in the "Results" column converts a used-up scheduling work sheet to a permanent record of your daily effectiveness. Your on-the-spot evaluations of the results you obtain from each effort:

1) form one important basis for judgments regarding how well you are making your Basic Choice,

2) help you pinpoint patterns of wasted and well directed energy,

3) promote the feelings of satisfaction you earn with your effort and thus provide motivation for you to do as well or better in the future.

PHONE CALLS. This section of the form gives you a place to note phone calls you want to make later in the day. This allows you to: a) concentrate all your phone calls, and b) consolidate several short calls to one person into a single, solidly useful conversation.

Whenever you reach for the telephone, reach instead for a pencil and jot the name, number, and reason for making that call. Add to the same list any calls you must return, and any calls you refuse to accept so you can avoid an interruption. Then make all your calls during one or two "telephone periods" you establish in your day.

WRITING. Follow the same general principles for your writing assignments, responsibilities, and commitments. Avoid writing individual letters, notes, reports, memos, or whatever—unless you can do them by hand in less than a minute. List the writing you must do in the appropriate section of the form, and do it all at once during special concentrated "writing" periods you designate.

PEOPLE AND MEETINGS. The large white area at the bottom of the work sheet is your place to note both the people you want to talk to during the day, and the items you want to discuss with each one. This helps you avoid running down the hall or around the town repeatedly. Instead, you make notes, then do all your visiting and talking in a concentrated session that you fit into your schedule. You can even save up these items from one day to another and do all your visiting one afternoon a week!

LONG RANGE. This section is the place to jot notes on projects you want to start, work on, or finish in the future. Make a brief note of your idea or plan, then continue with whatever you were working on. The idea remains intact for future action or improvement.

TO DO TODAY

NAME: _____ DATE: _____

PRIORITY	TASKS	DEADLINE	ESTIMATED TIME	RESULTS & ACTUAL TIME USED	PHONE CALLS (name, purpose)

PEOPLE TO SEE/DISCUSSION TOPICS

LETTERS/REPORTS TO WRITE

LONG RANGE (task, when due)

AT THE END OF EACH DAY. Transfer items you have not completed to the next day's form. Try not to transfer items more than once each. Otherwise, your sheet will contain more baggage than action items.

1) Items you continually defer deserve reevalution: a) schedule them for when you will be ready to act on them, b) rework or reorganize them into something you can do, or c) discard them from your daily scheduling forms.

2) Limit the number of items you schedule to what you honestly feel you can complete in a day. Too many items on your schedule only frustrate you. A completed schedule sheet at the end of the day, on the other hand, invigorates you.

Save the work sheets for a permanent record of your past performance. Look back from time to time to spot patterns and notice improvements.

APPENDIX C

Estimating Procedure for Business Executives

Step One:
Estimate By Category

Before you estimate the details of your work patterns, first estimate the total number of hours each month you devote to:

a) your work　　　　　　　_____

b) your personal goals　　_____

c) your career goals
(after working hours)　+_____

Total per month　　　　　=_____

Discounted Effort　　　　−_____

Monthly Responsible Time =_____

The trick here is not to add up the details, but instead to think in broad terms of how many hours you work per month on one of the three categories above. This offers a check on the detailed estimates you will be making in a few minutes.

Step Two:
Discount Unproductive Effort

This figure is your Monthly Total Effort. But some of this effort goes to trivia, socializing on and off the job, and routine or maintenance activities not directly contributing to one of your responsibilities. For many people, these less important chores take up as much as 60–80 percent of their effort. Reduce your Monthly Total Effort by whatever amount you feel you devote to items not on your list of responsibilities. This gives you your Monthly Responsible Time.

Step Three:
Estimate Each Item

Now go through the list and to the right of each item note approximately how many hours you give to that responsibility, on the average, each month. Adjust the figures to keep the total close to your Monthly Responsible Time. You may be surprised to see how much these itemized estimates vary from what you might have guessed. In addition, be alert for a strong tendency to overestimate or to "balance" these figures a little idealistically. Remember that no one is looking over your shoulder at this accounting. Try to make the figures as representative of your true actions as you can.

APPENDIX D

Estimation Procedure for Professionals

Step One:
Set Up Overall Parameters

Before you estimate the details of how you meet your responsibilities, first estimate the total number of hours each month you devote to:

a) your practice   _____
b) your personal goals   _____
c) your career goals   _____
d) other demands on your list +_____

Total per month   =_____
Discounted Effort   −_____
Monthly Responsible Time   =_____

Step Two:
Discount Unproductive Effort

The total you just reached is your Monthly Total Effort. But some of this effort unfortunately goes to trivia, socializing for professional and other reasons, and routine or maintenance activities not directly contributing to one of the responsibilities you listed. For many professional people, these less important hours amount to as much as 50–60 percent of their week. Reduce your Monthly Total Effort by whatever estimated amount you feel you: a) waste doing nothing, b) waste through inefficiency, redundant effort, and mistakes, c) devote to items not on your list of responsibilities. This discounted figure is your Monthly Responsible Time.

Step Three:
Estimate Each Item

Now go through the list and to the right of each item note approximately how many hours you give to that responsibility, on the average, each month. Adjust the figures to keep the total close to your Monthly Responsible Time. You may be surprised to see how much these itemized estimates vary from what you might have guessed. In addition, be alert for a strong tendency to overstate or to "enhance" these figures a little idealistically. Remember that no one is looking over your shoulder at this accounting. Try to make the figures as representative of your true actions as you can.

APPENDIX E

Estimation Procedure for the Busy "Stay at Home" Person

Step One:
Set Up Overall Parameters

Before you estimate the details of how you meet your responsibilities, first estimate the total number of hours you devote each month to:

a) your current activities   _____

b) your personal goals   _____

c) your career goals   _____

d) other demands on your list + _____

Total per month   = _____

Deducted Effort   − _____

Monthly Responsible Time   = _____

The trick here is not to add up the details, but instead to think in broad terms of how many hours you work per month on one of the four categories above. You may estimate times for a week and convert to months by multiplying by 4⅓. This offers a check on the detailed estimates you will be making in a few minutes.

Step Two:
Deduct Unproductive Effort

The total you just reached is your Monthly Total Effort. But some of your effort unfortunately goes to trivia, socializing, and other activities that do not directly contribute to the items on your list. For many "at home" people, these less important hours amount to as much as 30–40 percent of their week. From your Monthly Total Effort, subtract the time you: a) waste doing nothing, b) waste through inefficiency, redundant effort, and mistakes, c) devote to items not on your list of responsibilities. This reduced figure is your Monthly Responsible Time.

Step Three:
Estimate Each Item

Now go through the list and to the right of each item note approximately how many hours you give to it on the average, per month (or per week, multiplied by 4⅓). You may be surprised to see how much these itemized estimates vary from what you might have guessed. In addition, be alert for a strong tendency to overstate or to "enhance" these figures a little idealistically. Remember that no one is looking over your shoulder at this accounting. Try to make the figures as representative of your true actions as you can.

APPENDIX F

A Goal-planning "Workbook"

This Appendix of work sheets contains the most useful goal-planning and goal-awareness exercises currently available, and integrates them into a comprehensive "Goal-planning Workbook." You can use this section three different ways:

1. You can go through it before you read the book to set up a personal series of goals you can believe in, and to help you prepare goals and objectives in advance so you can more readily apply what you learn to your unique situation.

2. You can work through it while you read the book to help clarify your thinking, feeling, and dreaming, and to more readily integrate the techniques, attitudes, and ideas in the book with your special needs and aspirations.

3. You can come back to this Appendix anytime after you finish the book, and work through it as a short "refresher" of the basic goal-oriented ideas. When you do, you will also have the extra benefits of a renewed analysis of your desired goals and an updated look at the best means of achieving them.

LIST OF YOUR DESIRED GOALS

INSTRUCTIONS:

1. Try to make a complete list of everything you would like to do during your lifetime. Include all your hopes, dreams, wishes, and desires. Make sure everything on the list meets the following criterion: If you were offered the opportunity to do it right now, or any reasonable time in the future, you would happily say "Yes!" without hesitation.

2. Count up all your desired goals when the list is done. How many lifetimes would you need to do them all?

People to See	Places to Go	Things to Do
(Sample items:		
David Rockefeller	To live in Paris	Play in an All-Star Game
Francis Ford Coppola	To the moon	Star in a feature film
Stash Karczewski	To Surinam	Earn $1,000,000

You add your own items below:)

_____

_____

_____

_____

_____

_____

_____

CONTEMPLATING YOUR PRESENT FROM THE FUTURE AND THE PAST

INSTRUCTIONS: Use these questions to spark your own investigation of your deepest feelings of accomplishment, ambition, and success. First think ahead to a time when you are ill, unlikely to recover, and feeling near to the end of your life. Then back to an earlier era in your life. From these perspectives, view your life, your goals, and your accomplishments.

1. For what accomplishments would you like to be known after your death?

_____

_____

_____

_____

_____

_____

2. Think of the people whose respect for your accomplishments means the most to you. From your future perspective, which of your achievements most earned you their admiration and appreciation?

_____

_____

_____

_____

_____

_____

3. From your future perspective, which of your achievements make you the happiest? Which ones do you regret the most?

_____

_____

_____

_____

4. Now shift your perspective back in time. Think about where you were, what you were doing five, ten, fifteen years ago. Compare those days to your present situation. Have you made progress? In what direction(s)?

_____

_____

_____

_____

_____

_____

5. From the same perspective, evaluate what you are doing, your current goals. Do you want to continue in the same direction?

_____

_____

_____

_____

_____

6. Back in the present, can you think of other directions that might yield you more satisfaction, pleasure, or personal rewards? Specify.

_____

_____

_____

_____

_____

_____

SELF-EVALUATION WORK SHEET: YOUR LIFE AND CAREER GOALS

INSTRUCTIONS: This is a Self-evaluation Work Sheet. Only your own feelings, beliefs, ideas, and judgments are relevant to the answers you give as you work through it. Incorporate information, ideas, feelings, and goals you developed in the previous two work sheets into this exercise.

1. Make a list of five goals you would like to achieve in your personal life during the next ten years. Each goal should be an achievement, or recognition of an achievement, you would be proud of. Express each goal in specific terms so you (or anyone else) can plainly see when you have achieved it. Examples of personal goals in specific terms:

    a) establish five close friendships with people who truly like you,

    b) travel around the world,

    c) go camping in Brazil, or

    d) learn to play five songs on a guitar.

Your Personal Goals:

1) _____

2) _____

3) _____

4) _____

5) _____

2. Make a list of five goals you would like to achieve in your career during the next ten years. Each goal should describe an achievement, or recognition of an achievement, you would be proud of. Express each goal in specifics so you (or anyone else) can

plainly see when you have achieved it. Examples of Career Goals in specific terms:

a)   win an Academy Award,

b)   earn a promotion or a salary increase to a specific level,

c)   accomplish a specific project or specific amount of work by a certain deadline.

Your Career Goals:

6) _____

7) _____

8) _____

9) _____

10) _____

3. Name two other activities, accomplishments, rewards, or recognitions that would bring you the highest level of satisfaction:

11) _____

12) _____

4. What would you have to give up to have a chance to obtain each of the items you answered for question 3?

for "11)"_____

for "12)"_____

5. What will you have to give up to obtain each of the personal and career goals you specified in questions 1 and 2?

for "1)"_____

for "2)"_____

for "3)"_____

for "4)"_____

for "5)"_____

for "6)"_____

for "7)"_____

for "8)"_____

for "9)"_____

for "10)"_____

6. What preparation would you need to have a chance to obtain each of the items you answered for question 3?

for "11)"_____

for "12)"_____

7. What preparation will you need to obtain each of the personal and career goals you specified in questions 1 and 2?

for "1)"_____

for "2)"_____

for "3)"_____

for "4)"_____

for "5)"_____

for "6)"_____

for "7)"_____

for "8)"_____

for "9)"_____

for "10)"_____

MAKING DREAMS MORE REAL

INSTRUCTIONS: Answer the questions on this work sheet to begin turning one of your goals from fantasy into reality. Use a separate copy of the work sheet for each goal.

1. Review your personal and career goals, contemplated accomplishments, and desired goals. Select one you want to work on starting now. Define this goal as clearly as you can:

   _____

   _____

2. Specify the date by which you feel you can achieve this goal:

   _____

3. Specify enough "objective" criteria so you or anyone can plainly see when you have achieved this goal:

   a. _____

   b. _____

   c. _____

   d. _____

   more? _____

   _____

   _____

   _____

   _____

4. List below all the rewards and benefits you expect to receive and enjoy after you achieve this goal:

a. _____

b. _____

c. _____

d. _____

more? _____

_____

_____

_____

5. Consider the possibility of changing your mind or somehow abandoning this goal before you achieve it. What effect do you think this change might have on you:

_____

_____

_____

6. Consider the possibility of achieving your goal but then not liking the results and the benefits it brings you. What effect do you think this outcome might have on you:

_____

_____

_____

THE MAJOR ACCOMPLISHMENTS REQUIRED TO ACHIEVE YOUR GOAL

INSTRUCTIONS: Use the spaces below to identify and organize the Major Steps required to accomplish the goal you have selected:

CURRENT GOAL:

1. List below the Major Accomplishments required to reach this goal:

a. _____

b. _____

c. _____

d. _____

more? _____

_____

_____

_____

2. Put the Major Accomplishments in chronological order. Make two separate lists: one for accomplishments that must be done in the proper order, and another for accomplishments you can try to do in any order.

Chronological Accomplishments   **Unrelated Accomplishments**

_____   _____

_____   _____

_____   _____

_____   _____

_____   _____

_____   _____

_____   _____

3. Number each accomplishment above, and for each one, specify a
reward you will receive when you achieve it:

_____

_____

_____

_____

_____

_____

_____

ORGANIZING EACH MAJOR ACCOMPLISHMENT

INSTRUCTIONS: Follow the guidelines below to organize one of the Major Accomplishments required for you to achieve the goal you have in mind. Use a separate copy of the work sheet for each Major Accomplishment.

CURRENT GOAL:_____

THIS MAJOR ACCOMPLISHMENT:_____

1. Set a deadline for the achievement of the Major Accomplishment:_____

2. List below the Minor Steps you must take to achieve the Major Accomplishment you have in mind:

a. _____

b. _____

c. _____

d. _____

more? _____

_____

_____

_____

3. Put the Minor Steps above into chronological order. Make two

lists: one for steps you must do in the proper order, and another for steps you can try to do anytime.

Chronological Steps	Unrelated Steps
_____	_____
_____	_____
_____	_____
_____	_____
_____	_____
_____	_____
_____	_____

4. Number the steps above, and for each one, specify a reward you will receive (or give yourself) when you finish it:

_____

_____

_____

_____

_____

_____

_____

ORGANIZING YOUR MINOR STEPS

INSTRUCTIONS: Use the guidelines below to break down each of your Minor Steps into simple tasks you can do quickly. Use a separate copy of the work sheet for each Minor Step.

CURRENT GOAL:_____

MAJOR ACCOMPLISHMENT:_____

MINOR STEP:_____

1. Set a deadline for the achievement of the Minor Step:_____

2. List below the simple tasks you can undertake to achieve the Minor Step you want. Try to break each step down into pieces small enough so you can finish each task in a single day, or better yet, a single hour:

a. _____

b. _____

c. _____

d. _____

more? _____

_____

_____

_____

3. Put the simple tasks above into chronological order. Make two

lists: one for tasks you must do in the proper order, and another
for tasks you can try to do anytime.

Chronological Tasks	**Unrelated Tasks**
_____	_____
_____	_____
_____	_____
_____	_____
_____	_____
_____	_____

4. Number the tasks above, and for each one, specify a reward
   you will receive (or give yourself) from each effort:

_____

_____

_____

_____

_____

_____

_____

CHECKING PLANS AGAINST ACTIVITIES

INSTRUCTIONS: This is a quick way to compare what you "plan" to do with what you "actually" do during a given day. Most of the time, there is a good deal of variance between your "plans" and your "action." The comparison can tell you a great deal about your current achievement problems, unleash more motivational energy, and pinpoint your potential for improvement.

Date:_____

ANSWER THIS QUESTION AT THE BEGINNING OF THE DAY:

1. List everything you plan to accomplish today:

a. _____

b. _____

c. _____

d. _____

more? _____

_____

_____

_____

ANSWER THIS QUESTION AT THE END OF THE DAY:

2. List everything you actually did today:

a. _____

b. _____

c. _____

d. _____

more? _____

_____

_____

3. COMPARE:

    a. How many items in your plans did you actually work on?____

        _____

    b. How many items did you actually work on that were not in your plans?_____

4. a. How much of your time, effort, and attention went toward the most important activities in your daily plan?_____

        _____

    b. How much went toward items you had not planned to work on?_____

5. How would you rate your "effectiveness" today, in terms of:

    a. Progress toward your goals, and separately:

        _____

	Little Progress					**Great Progress**			
1	2	3	4	5	6	7	8	9	10

b. Results you achieved in relation to time and effort you expended.

	Few Results					**Great Results**			
1	2	3	4	5	6	7	8	9	10

INDEX
OF PROBLEMS
AND SOLUTIONS

How to Use this Index:

1. Look up each symptom that seems to describe your situation.
2. Note the page numbers for the references given.
3. Read the text on those pages to identify remedies and techniques you can use to resolve your problems.

SYMPTOM: **LOOK FOR . . .**   **. . . ON PAGES**